HOW TO PUNCH THE SUNDAY JITTERS IN
THE FACE

*Start Living a Proactive Life One
Unstoppable Sunday at a Time*

HOW TO PUNCH THE SUNDAY JITTERS IN
THE FACE

Start Living a Proactive Life One Unstoppable Sunday at a Time

TK KADER

Interior layout and design by Writing Nights.
Book preparation by Chad Robertson.
Cover Design by Ivica Jandrijevic.

For information about permission to reproduce selections from this book, email hello@getunstoppable.com.

Or write:

TK Kader
3111 N. Houston Street, PH1
Dallas, Texas 75219

ISBN: 978-1-7975-7123-2

Printed on acid free paper in the United States of America.

24   23   22   21   20   19   18   17   8   7   6   5   4   3   2   1

Here's to *you*. May you become *Unstoppable*.

belief x discipline makes you Unstoppable

TABLE OF CONTENTS

ACKNOWLEDGMENTS

Thank you to Sabera Kader and Tawfiq Kader, my parents, who have always encouraged me to pursue my dreams and aim for the stars.

For giving me an unbelievable decade of opportunities, growth, life long friendships and for helping me find my own unstoppability through thick and thin, thank you to the ToutApp team and the Marketo team.

For encouraging me even before I believed in it myself that I had a book in me and that I should dedicate my life purpose to helping people become unstoppable, thank you to my brother Shahed Kader, and my dear friends Lin Fox and Adria Hou.

For helping me through countless edits of this book, for encouraging me every step of the way with comments of positivity inside our shared Google document, a special thank you to Ali Mazzotta and Janean Laidlaw.

And most importantly, thank you to the the Unstoppable community across Instagram, Youtube, Facebook and LinkedIn. You inspire me.

INTRODUCTION:
HOW TO GET PROACTIVE ABOUT YOUR LIFE AND BECOME UNSTOPPABLE

I n this book, I will help you escape the Sunday Jitters by showing you how to lead a more proactive life instead of just reacting to things that come at you.

I'll start by helping you punch the Sunday Jitters in the face by teaching you a practice called Unstoppable Sundays, a practice that has unlocked a decade of productivity and unparalleled success in my own life. It'll help you take stock of where you are and get more proactive about the next seven days of your life. Then I'll help you look ahead to the next 365 days and set clear priorities across key areas of your life. Once we've got a good handle on your NOW and immediate future, I'll walk you through setting a vision for yourself for the next five years so that you can start to become the best version of yourself, one Unstoppable Sunday at a time.

I've made this book only as long as it needs to be. I wrote it all myself without the use of a single ghost writer and I've made this book as actionable as possible so that you can get to DOING versus just READING and DREAMING about that proactive life we all deeply desire. And, most importantly, this book is based on the system I have developed for myself: a system that has unlocked nearly a decade of productivity and success for my own personal and professional life.

The truth is, I wasn't always like this. I had Sundays, just like you, where I felt that pit in my stomach. Call it the Sunday Scaries, the Sunday angst, or the Sunday existential "What am I even doing with my life?!" I've been there – and I took the time to read all the books and to research the best ways to break out of it. And I did it.

If I could break down my life into parts, I would describe two distinct phases: the BEFORE and the AFTER.

The BEFORE was when I ran around like a madman, frantic – trying to eke out every single second I could find toward my work. I'd wake up in the morning, and, with my phone in hand, I'd be brushing my teeth, wrangling on my pants, answering email – basically all at once. It wasn't pretty.

And then there's the AFTER. The AFTER is when I wake up slowly. I brush my teeth. I meditate. All before I even think of picking up my phone. I make time for family and friends. I put in a solid set of hours toward my most important goals, and I take breaks. I pause and reflect on Sundays to check in on my goals; and I constantly adapt to take on and conquer bigger challenges in my life.

GUESS which part of my life yielded my best work? The best results? GUESS which part of my life led to the happiest moments, the BIGGEST wins, and the deepest lessons learned?!?

Yeah, obviously. It was the latter part.

I learned (almost too late) in my life that taking a PROACTIVE approach to my days led to a calmer me. A less frantic me.

Why do we become so frantic? It's not because we do our best work when we're frenzied... It's because, deep down, we have no way of checking in and understanding if we're on track. It's because no matter how many hours we work, we don't feel like we're enough and our work was enough.

That all changed when I developed a simple system to check in on myself every Sunday to get rid of the angst I felt every Sunday afternoon, as I thought about Monday. Even today, EVERY Sunday, I still sit down, I open a Word document, and I answer two simple questions:

1) Where am I?

2) What do I do next?

This simple ritual allows me to consistently check in on my goals, check in on my progress, and, MOST IMPORTANTLY, it allows me to course-correct.

This simple ritual became a critical part of a whole system I developed to take control of every day of my life, to be proactive about life, and, most importantly, to eradicate the angst I used to feel in my stomach every Sunday night about the week that was to come.

If you feel like there just isn't enough time in the day for you, your loved ones, and your work... If you're feeling constantly behind... Then this book that I created to help you plan out your life and become PROACTIVE, is for you.

The Japanese embrace a concept called "Kaizen," which I love. The direct English translation is "Continuous Improvement." It's a strategy whereby you work proactively to achieve regular and incremental improvements to a process (in this case: how you live your life). In a sense, Kaizen combines the collective resources at your disposal (your time, your energy, your intellect, your mentors, your friends) to create a powerful engine for improvement in your own life.

This book is not designed to give you a one-and-done "workshop" in figuring out your life's purpose. Figuring out what you want from life and the steps to realize that dream can be a lifelong journey. This book helps you establish an iterative process through which you can switch from being a reactive person to a proactive person, and helps you establish the systems that you can follow for the rest of your life to continue to improve your life.

In this book, I'll walk you through a set of tools, processes, and systems that all work together to allow you to practice the art of Kaizen for your own life's purpose. By following this system, you'll be able to achieve clarity of vision for yourself, set goals for yourself, and create a plan of purposeful and focused action for yourself that you consistently improve upon as you execute your plan. Most importantly, this will help you set an agenda that YOU choose for your life.

I've used this system for nearly a decade and it has unlocked unparalleled levels of productivity and wealth for me, personally. In the little less than a year since I open-sourced this system, thousands of people have downloaded our *Unstoppable Proactive Life Planning Guide*. All of this led to the publishing of the book you are reading right now.

When you think of your life in terms of Kaizen – in terms of a continuous improvement process backed by powerful self-reflection – everything changes. As you learn more by following this book, you'll continue to iterate on your goals and plans. As you make mistakes, you'll course-correct from lessons learned. And as you unlock new levels of success, you'll continue to set new goals that take you to the next level.

In the following chapters, I'll introduce key ideas to help you create a plan for yourself and to continuously improve upon it:

- **In Chapters 1 through 3,** I'll introduce you to the core principles of Dreaming, Belief and Discipline that makes for a proactive life. I'll also dive into what separates the DABBLERS from the DO-ERS and why visualizing the STATUS QUO of your life will help you conceptualize why changing the trajectory of your life is a MUST.
- **In Chapter 4,** I'll introduce you to the concept of a 45-Day challenge. A tool that I've used in my life over and over again to drive focused and purposeful change in my life in an easy way.
- **In Chapter 5,** I introduce you to the idea of practicing Unstoppable Sundays: I'll teach you to reflect on and plan for the next seven days so that you can eradicate the Sunday Scaries and get proactive about the week ahead.
- **In Chapter 6,** I help you zoom out and start to think about your one-year plan by answering a set of very pointed questions that help you to practice gratitude, to assess where you are today, and to then start laying out a plan for your next 365 days.
- **In Chapter 7,** I introduce a new tool that you can use to become proactive about the 365 days you are given every year, so that you

4

can be proactive about how you spend your days and months in a given year, and you will be able to make tough trade-offs on what you spend your time on versus not – ahead of time, instead of two weeks before Thanksgiving.

- **In Chapter 8**, now that you have established an understanding of where you are in your current situation (next seven days; next 365 days), in this chapter I help you really zoom out, think big, and think about the next five years of your life and the vision you want to set for yourself.
- **In Chapter 9**, I walk you through the most significant impediment you face in your life in achieving your goals, and how you can overcome it by making one simple change. (hint: It's all about the law of averages.)
- **In Chapter 10**, the closing chapter, I wrap it all together and walk you through how you can now start to use the tools and follow the systems I gave you and practice the art of being proactive in your life. I teach you the reminders you will need to set on your calendar in order to make sure you continue to iterate on your life plan and become Unstoppable in life.

If you have the **Belief** that what you desire is possible and achievable, and if you have the **Discipline** to pursue that Belief with focused and purposeful action, regardless of the roadblocks that you encounter – you will be Unstoppable.

Let's get started. Let's go create your life plan. Let's go make you Unstoppable.

CHAPTER 1:

WHAT SETS APART THOSE WHO DREAM FROM THOSE WHO ARE SUCCESSFUL?

*"Whether you think you can,
or you think you can't — you're right."*
— Henry Ford

An unbelievable 53% of millennials expect to become millionaires during their lifetime. Before you chuckle and scoff "MILLENNIALS" – it's not just millennials who dream big: 29% of all Americans believe they will become millionaires. Young people dream big about their lives and have high expectations around living the life they desire, but this motivation simply drops off over time.

This dream is not about just becoming financially wealthy. It's about any big and crazy goal that you have – whether it is to graduate college, start your own business, land that dream job, or become a star athlete. What I'm talking about is becoming exceptional by your own definition.

On one hand, you have dreamers; and then, on the other hand, you have those who actually figure out how to make their dreams a reality. What is the difference between these two groups of people? What is the difference between the DREAMERS and the DABBLERS versus the DO-ERS? Regardless of where you are in life, or your age, you have a choice to make as you read this book: Which group will you belong to from this day forward?

When you look at anyone who has achieved massive success in their lives, whether it is the captains of industry or the stealthy next-door millionaires, you will see that they have all learned to master two key principles in their life: Belief and Discipline.

Dreaming is a beautiful thing. It allows us to imagine what is possible in our lives. We dream freely as children, less so in our teenage years, and we seem to stop dreaming when we become adults – instead succumbing to what life has dealt us. Somehow we call this "growing up." Little by little, we get used to accepting crumbs. Dreaming coupled with Belief and Discipline, on the other hand, enables us to take charge when it comes to our goals, so they can become reality.

Somehow, dreaming is easy for us when we are children; yet as we get older, there are fewer of us who dare to dream. And even fewer of us actually accomplish those dreams. This book will give you the tools necessary to dare to dream and turn those dreams into reality.

The formula to accomplish the things we want in our life is simple. You **dream**, you **believe** in that dream, and then you follow through with **discipline** to accomplish that dream. Then, you dream bigger. Rinse and repeat. You revel in the journey and celebrate the wins. In this chapter, I'll walk you through why it is important to adopt all three of those components, particularly Belief and Discipline, so that you can set yourself apart and be one of the few who actually realizes your dreams.

Dreaming is the most idle state of thinking about the life that you want. It's important to understand that it is only the first step to actually achieving the life we want. We dream when we scroll through Instagram and look at a picture of that beautiful kitchen we desire, the fancy sports car we want to drive, that laptop lifestyle traveling the world while we do what we love, or even that big house in the perfect cul-de-sac. It's empty calories. It makes you feel better, it makes you dream "one day..." but it doesn't actually change a thing about your reality.

Believing, on the other hand, is the active state of truly conceptualizing that what you desire is possible and that it can and will happen for you. Believing gets you to commit that you want to make that dream a reality. Furthermore, taking disciplined and purposeful action on that belief turns that belief into actual reality.

You have a decision to make. When I wrote this book, my goal was simple: Give people an actionable framework to help turn their dreams into reality, to turn their lives into the lives they deserve, regardless of their circumstances. But this book won't do it for you; the framework won't do it for you. There is no quick win or fix here. Only you, through applying the actionable framework laid out in the latter chapters of this book, can turn your dreams into reality. And it is done through two simple ideas that you must adopt into your life: Belief and Discipline.

How to Get Belief

The dictionary definition of Belief is simple enough: "an acceptance that a statement is true or that something exists."

What is your dream for your life? You purchased this book because of one simple reason: You know deep down inside that there is more you want out of your life. Your days. Your weeks.

When I was 16, I was an immigrant kid born in Bangladesh and living in Queens, New York in a one-bedroom apartment with six people in all. My father worked seven days a week. My mother supported the family and the business. We all pitched in any way we could in order to achieve the American Dream and make a better life for ourselves in New York. I started working for the family business at age 12, handing out flyers for our business at the corner of 74th Street and 37th Avenue – partly because I just wanted to spend more time with my dad, and partly because I had big dreams even then for myself and my family, and I wanted to do everything that was in my power to have an impact.

I pledged to have a bigger dream as I turned 16. I pledged that I'd grind hard through my 20s so that I could get to a life where I could provide not just for myself, but also for my parents and for my future family. And no, my dream wasn't just about living and providing, but it was to get to a life where I had the wealth to do whatever I wanted with my time, to shape the world and leave it better than I found it. I considered it not only my dream but my duty.

What is the dream for your life? Your dream could be one of these:

> *I am going to have control over my life and spend my time the way I want to.*
> *I am going to spend my days working on what I love.*
> *I am going to provide for my family so that we have more than enough.*

This book is not meant to be a piece of art that sits on your bookshelf or one that just gets forgotten.

So grab a pen, and start writing into this book as you go through these chapters. This book will transform into a roadmap for your life and a physical reminder of your commitment to become Unstoppable in life.

Or perhaps you'd describe it differently. Go ahead write it down here:

How do you get from dreaming to true Belief? Some personal development experts would say you need to get up and scream out your dream and yell out "I BELIEVE!" That may feel energetic and fulfilling for a moment, but will it truly get your whole body to commit and believe? Probably. But will it bring you the lasting change you need to make your dream a reality? It didn't work for me.

The quickest and fastest and most effective way I found to believe in my dreams was to seek out role models who had achieved similar dreams. I didn't have to know them personally; I just needed to know that it's possible.

There's something that shifts within us when we see that something is possible. For me, it always brought forward a feeling of: "Well... if HE can do it... then I surely can pull it off..."

This led me to go through the mental process of actually articulating my dream, what it means to me, and of convincing myself that this doesn't just have to be a dream but that it can be my reality.

When it comes to Belief, the person most known for profoundly turning a dream into reality through a strongly held belief is Roger Bannister. Bannister's legend was born on May 6, 1954, when he became the first man on this planet to run a mile in under four minutes – a feat that scientists of that day simply deemed impossible and perhaps even deadly to the human body.

It had never been done before. And this was 1954 – man was hardly new to running at that time! And yet, within two months of Bannister's accomplishing the first four-minute mile, John Landy and Roger Bannister each ran a four-minute mile again. Just a year later, three runners broke the four-minute barrier again, in just a single race. In 1964, Jim Ryun became the first high-school runner to break the four-minute-mile.

According to the Harvard Business Review, runners had been seriously chasing the four-minute mile record since at least 1886. After Roger Bannister, over the last half-century, more than 1,300 runners have overcome the challenge of running a mile in under four minutes – one that had been considered hopelessly out of reach.

What changed? Did humans all of a sudden evolve quickly to become four-minute-mile runners? No. Did they cheat and use drugs to achieve new heights? No. What changed was the belief that running a four-minute mile is indeed possible. Once the limit was broken by one athlete, others thought much as I did: "Well if ROGER can do it..." They all believed.

Belief helped me grow my career as a computer engineer. Belief helped me start my own company and grow it into a multi-million-dollar business as a startup CEO at 28 years old. Belief helped me become a millionaire and achieve enough financially by my 30s so that I could provide for my family. More importantly, Belief helped me get to a point where I can spend my time on movements like Unstoppable to help people lead more proactive lives, something I am deeply passionate about. That's the dream I had at 16.

If you want to bring lasting change into your life, you have to get serious about your beliefs. And even more importantly, you have to pause and reflect, to understand if there are conflicting beliefs in your life that are stopping you from achieving your dream.

How to Get Discipline

At age 16, I believed I would be 30 by the time I would be able to get to a point where I could do whatever I want. That dream of "Do whatever I want..." was still alive and well for me as age 30 approached, especially for an immigrant kid who had always had a to-do list of things "I must do so that I can..." get to what I wanted to do. I was willing to dream it, believe it. I was willing to take risks to get it. But in fact, I was far from it as 30 approached.

I had a deep belief in what I wanted to accomplish in my life. I had connected with the people who had done it before and had studied them closely. *What am I doing wrong?!* I thought to myself... It wasn't adding up.

I had gotten good at pausing and reflecting. I had gotten great at visualizing the things that I wanted. I even took risks, like quitting my six-figure finance job and starting my own company. I had even had success already, and my software company was just starting to do well with employees, an office and amazing customers.

Truth is, by the time I turned 30, I had developed only half of the Unstoppable Life system that I talk about in this book. The word Unstoppable hadn't even entered my psyche yet. There was a critical component that was still missing in my life: Discipline.

Having Belief, true Belief, in what you want, gets you to start taking real action – as I had in my life. But that is only half of the equation. At age 30, I was working 90-hour weeks. I was burnt out. I was waking up every morning and jumping right at it every single day. But this was still that "BEFORE" in my life. I hadn't yet mastered Discipline.

Before Roger Bannister broke the four-minute-mile record, he failed countless times at achieving that goal. Before he set his sights on that goal, he failed at earning a medal while competing in the Olympics. It is the story since the beginning of time of a person who has experienced "overnight" success: It took years of hard work, mistakes, overcoming obstacles, and life lessons to get to that moment of "success."

At that moment as I tried to figure out *"What am I missing?!"* I realized two critical things that rounded out my beliefs regarding an Unstoppable life:

1) The biggest lie we are ever told in our life is that we get to a point where there are no more problems in our lives. Truth is, there are always going to be good days and bad days, problems and challenges. The key to living an Unstoppable life is embracing this truism, but committing to solve BIGGER problems that have BIGGER rewards, every single day, and determining to grow so much stronger that yesterday's problems seem like an inconvenient speed bump.

2) The road to success is a marathon and not a sprint, and is riddled with setbacks and speed bumps, and only those who take definitive and smart action and who have staying power actually get to realize their dreams. This is where Discipline comes in.

I could've given up at 30. I could've said "This isn't working. Maybe my dream is too big, maybe it isn't achievable." Instead, I doubled down on my Belief and strived to understand what I was missing. I mastered Discipline.

And at age 31, I accomplished one of the early stages of my dream. We grew the company to a critical inflection point which allowed us to raise a large round of investment from a venture capital firm.

If it weren't for Discipline, I wouldn't have gotten there. As I look back, it is truly frightening to realize that I was so close to giving up just moments before accomplishing my dream.

Discipline is:

- Treating life like a marathon that we are running, instead of a sprint where we hold our breath until we get to this mythical finish line where all our problems go away. Treating life like a marathon where we get better and better in all aspects of our life, instead of a sprint where we forsake love, health, and just about everything else, just to reach a point of success that may not taste as sweet as we think.
- Recognizing that in order to win this marathon, we have to learn to have Discipline today so that we will not experience regret tomorrow. It means that we must prioritize the right things while tending to all the important things. It means that we have to master the art of consistency in the daily actions that allow us to run the marathon.
- Most importantly, Discipline is the art of constantly keeping our bigger goals crystal-clear in our mind, taking purposeful action consistently every day, while remembering to enjoy the moment instead of holding our breath only for the reward at the end.

Roger Bannister kept failing. But he mastered the art of Discipline and doubled down on his Belief to finally break the four-minute–mile barrier. Shortly after he did so, many other athletes followed.

There's a famous saying that originated with Persian Sufi Poets and that has been repeated across religions and philosophies, and has even been used by great orators like Abraham Lincoln: THIS TOO SHALL PASS.

This is one of my most favorite mantras in life, particularly in my quest to become Unstoppable, because it reminds me of a simple idea. If I'm having the best day of my life, this too shall pass. If I'm having the worst day of my life, this too shall also pass. It reminds us of the impermanence of the moments in our lives and of the "status" that we seek in our lives. It'll all pass.

So, I choose to smile and constantly practice Discipline through the bad times, even at age 30. In the moments when we are celebrating a win, I smile and revel in the moment, because I know this will pass. In the moments when I'm facing adversity and pain and fear, I still smile, because I appreciate the impermanence of this situation and know that I have the tools in front of me to go punch the adversity in the face.

That mantra led me to rely on another favorite mantra of mine, one I learned when I was working for Ray Dalio at Bridgewater Associates, a famed hedge fund investor and the author of the book PRINCIPLES. Whenever we found ourselves facing a difficult situation or a complex challenge, he'd always remind us: THESE ARE JUST PROBLEMS. PROBLEMS HAVE SOLUTIONS.

Much as we were trained early in life to think we have to work to get to a point where we are "happy" and have zero problems, the same people lied to us and taught us to buckle down and crumble in the face of problems.

Ray always reminded us, "Look, these are *just* problems. Nothing more, nothing less. All problems have solutions. It's up to you, your creativity, your intellect, and your power, to find the solution (usually just one of many) to overcome the problem you are facing. All problems have solutions."

How to Apply Belief x Discipline

In order to become Unstoppable in life, you must realize two things.

First, you must realize what Unstoppable is not. It is not about being perfect or achieving perfection. It is not about having all the answers. It is not about flawless execution of your goals. It is going after big lofty goals that inspire us and motivate us, and about expecting there to be speed bumps, problems, challenges, and obstacles along the way. It is about expecting those things to happen, but having the conviction, mindset and wherewithal to know that no matter what bumps appear in the road, we will find a way to get past them. There will be problems. But all problems have solutions. You are Unstoppable when you find a way to forge ahead with a smile, regardless of the road bumps.

Second, you must become great at practicing Dreaming, Belief and Discipline. Dreaming big and having high expectations of yourself and your life. Belief that what you desire and what you imagine in your head is possible for you, and that one day you will achieve it. Discipline in taking the focused and purposeful action every single day to run the marathon and conquer it.

Belief multiplied by Discipline (Belief x Discipline) became an Unstoppable force in my life. Once I developed this mindset, my life became an Unstoppable screaming freight train from hell that put me on an unrelenting path toward crushing one goal after another. That's what I want for you and your life.

With my simple mantra of Belief x Discipline, I found a way to evolve from being just a dreamer into being a person who actually realizes my dreams. You can too.

Chapter 1,
Questions to Ask Yourself

What is it that you desire from your life that you are afraid of admitting to anyone else?

What are the things "you don't know how to do" that are holding you back from achieving your biggest dream of your life?

Nothing overcomes speed bumps and obstacles better than focused and purposeful action. What kind of daily disciplines, weekly disciplines, even monthly disciplines can you adopt to break through these "Don't KNOWs" in your life?

You're likely in a space right now where you're feeling PUMPED and HOPEFUL about the future. Let's take this moment to practice a quick Unstoppable Sunday (even if right NOW is not a Sunday) together. Just to see how it feels and get you going.

Where am I? What am I feeling?

```


```

What do I do next?

```


```

Chapter 1,
Actions to Take

☐ As you go through your days, start taking stock of the deeply-held beliefs that you constantly reinforce within yourself (good or bad). Write these down on your phone's Notes application if this makes it easy for you to keep track. What're the things you are telling yourself that are stopping you from believing what you can achieve?

☐ In later chapters, we'll start to help you create a new, consistent Discipline for yourself. For now, start to take note of how you spend your days. What do you do when you wake up? What are your routines for the days? How do you like to spend your weekends? As you work through the next few chapters, you'll start to go through exercises that help you pick and choose the Disciplines that help you to get closer to your goals, and to cut out the ones that do not.

CHAPTER 2:

UPPER LIMITING AND FEAR OF SUCCESS

*"Success requires no apologies.
Failure permits no alibis."*

— NAPOLEON HILL

For a major part of my life, I had a fear of success. Early on in life, I wasn't even aware of such a concept. Once I did find out about it, I at first denied having it, and then it took me years to really grapple with and deal with my fear of success. Before I truly dealt with it, I stumbled through small amounts of success through sheer willpower – simply because I wanted it bad enough. Once I dealt with it, I unlocked years upon years of success for myself across my personal and business life.

If one of us were to have a bullet wound in the chest and to be bleeding, people would recognize it right away; we would feel the pain right away; and the entire world around us would come together to help us heal the wound. Immediately.

Unfortunately, we and the world surrounding us are not likewise equipped to deal with deep-rooted issues like fear of success. And although as a society we've grown by leaps and bounds to recognize mental health issues such as depression, the deep programming we have within us around success, money, motivation, and beliefs is nearly impossible to spot unless we ourselves take time to look within.

Back in 2012, my company, ToutApp, was a four-person company. We had raised a little bit of money; we created software that people loved; and it was generating revenue. Much like the early days of a startup, there were glimmers of hope, and early traction, but I was stuck. I knew I wanted more from my business, but I just couldn't get myself to move forward. I felt like someone who was running forward, but there was an invisible hand holding me back no matter how hard I worked and no matter how much harder I pushed forward.

I just told myself... "This is supposed to be hard. I'm supposed to hustle. I just need to put in more hours. More time. More effort. More energy. More, more, more... Nothing huge comes easy."

And yet... as if there was a thermostat set inside of me for my success to be at a four-person company, no matter how much cold air I blew into the room through momentous effort, the internal thermostat kicked in and just neutralized the effort, keeping the company at four people.

I had already adopted the things I teach in this book. I dreamt. I believed in my vision of creating a thriving software company. I paused and reflected every Sunday. I visualized how one day I'd walk into a huge office and it would be packed with people buzzing away at serving our customers and building features I had only dreamed of. And yet... we were stuck at four people.

I knew something was wrong, but I couldn't figure out what. And so I did what I did every time I hit a roadblock. I started reading books on being stuck. I started googling about feeling stuck. Eventually I came across the concept of limiting beliefs, upper limiting, and fear of success.

I then came across an exercise that changed my life. The exercise was simple. It was a set of questions that walked me through to an understanding of my core fear and of what exactly was the limiting belief that was holding me back.

It first asked: *What do you want?*

I want my software company to thrive. I want to have a hundred employees working for me so that we can serve more people, have more customers, make more money, and turn ToutApp into a revenue-generating machine.

It then asked: *What would you have to do to get what you want?*

I knew exactly what I had to do. We had to make our current customers successful. We had to expand our feature set, uplevel our messaging, become more aggressive about getting our word out, and, most importantly, we had to expand our sales capacity so we could sell more.

I knew the answers! What was holding me back, I wondered?

Surely enough, it then asked: *What could go wrong if you did those things?*

I felt a knot in my stomach.

> *The software might not scale.*
>
> *We might hire people who may not be good at what they do.*
>
> *We might have to hire WAY MORE people, and then I'd have to manage all of them!*
>
> *We might run out of money.*
>
> *We might find out that our software is not great and the broader market doesn't want it.*
>
> *We would have to find a way to support all those customers.*

We would have to find a way to educate all these customers on how to use the software, and that might be harder to do for mass adoption versus for the early adopters we have now.

Competitors might start copying us, and then we'd lose our position in the market and get trumped.

I may not be good enough to build a software that so many people would want!

The list went on... Within minutes, I had listed a full page of things that would go horribly wrong if we were to become successful. It was a wake-up call for me. There I was, toiling away, my team was toiling away, and yet all of these things were subconsciously pulling me back from achieving success – because I was afraid of all the things I would have to deal with if we were successful!

The exercise was unrelenting and unapologetic. It then asked: *You're now successful. Those problems that are your demons are now real. How would you overcome those problems, given your newfound success?*

As you might imagine: I had an answer for every single problem I was deeply afraid of.

More customers meant more revenues, meant more dry powder.

More customers, more revenue, meant more employees who could help solve problems.

More growth meant more investment dollars coming in.

More revenues and more investment dollars meant I could hire smarter people to solve problems and help manage more employees.

The exercise then asked: *If you are NOT successful, what would happen?*

Death. I answered. We would die, we would fail, it wouldn't matter anyway.

It then asked: *If you ARE successful, what are the positive things that would happen?*

I would thrive. My employees would thrive. We could deliver MORE for our customers. Our customers would thrive. It would be WIN-WIN-WIN for everyone involved. Our wildest dreams could come true and all our effort would be WORTH IT.

The exercise finished with... *What're you waiting for?*

What was I waiting for?! What was I afraid of?! The worst-case scenario was our failure, which was assured if we didn't do the things necessary to achieve success anyway.

By the middle of 2012, shortly after I completed this exercise, we doubled the number of employees to a whopping eight people on a single day.

By the end of 2012, we sold so much software, we did a pre-emptive Series A round of $3.3m from Jackson Square Ventures to help support and accelerate our growth.

Through 2013, we grew the company 300% in a single year, increased to 40 employees, and raised another $15m from Andreessen Horowitz.

Through 2015, we grew the company again, to nearly 80 people, and through twists and turns (which I'll leave for another time) we sold the company in 2017 to Marketo, a market leader in the space.

The exercise made me realize two important things about living a proactive life:

1. Without doing the basics, such as setting goals, practicing Belief and Discipline, and having a sense of urgency, failure is guaranteed.

2. However, even with doing those things, we may be walking around with subconscious programming in our minds because of our environment or upbringing that may sabotage our own success.

It's unbelievable, isn't it? We could be working tirelessly toward our goals, could wholeheartedly want to be successful, and yet our subconscious programming could be actively working AGAINST us to sabotage our forward momentum. When I felt like I was pushing ahead but there was an imaginary hand pushing back against forward momentum, I wasn't wrong. I *felt* the right thing! The "hand" was my own fear of success, it was my feeling like I didn't deserve success. It was my feeling that I wasn't enough.

What are the limiting beliefs and fears that are holding you back from your path to success?

Was it being taught at an early age that money is evil? Is it a fear of all the bigger problems you'll have to solve tomorrow if you are successful today? Is it the memory of your parents telling you at an early age that you're not *good* enough or doing something wrong? Is it friends or a significant other who is unsupportive of your dreams?

We all have these things in our life. It's just that we're not trained to identify these negative patterns in our lives as they work silently in the background to sabotage our hard work.

Now, I don't mind failing because I got the market trends wrong. Or because I miscalculated a strategic move. Or I made a poor business decision. I can own that. I can learn from that. I can come back stronger than ever from that. But to sabotage myself because of my own fears? That is simply **unacceptable**.

Throughout the rest of this book, I will help you craft a life strategy and a proactive plan. But before we delve into that, I want you to follow the same exercise that I followed, in order to identify the subconscious fears deviously holding you back from the life you deserve.

Chapter 2,
Questions to Ask Yourself

What are you actively working on right now toward achieving in your life?

What would you have to do get what you want?

What could go wrong if you did those things and were successful? How would it complicate your life?

You're now successful. Those problems that are your demons are now real. How would you overcome those problems, given your newfound success?

[blank box]

If you are NOT successful, you maintain the status quo and don't grow, what would happen?

[blank box]

If you ARE successful, what are the positive things that would happen?

[blank box]

What're you waiting for? What are the immediate steps you can take now to move forward?

[blank box]

Chapter 2,
Actions to Take

☐ Go talk to a loved one or a best friend about what you've discovered in this chapter. See if he or she, too, has fears of success and compare notes.

☐ You're doing great. Keep going!

CHAPTER 3:

WHAT DOES THE STATUS QUO LOOK LIKE FOR YOU?

"The riskiest thing we can do is
maintain the status quo"

— Bob Iger

A two-year study by the McKinsey Global Institute found that by 2030, intelligent agents and robots could eliminate as much as 30 percent of the world's human labor. That is an estimated 800 million jobs done better, faster, and more precisely by robots in the place of humans.

The fear that machines will replace human labor has been an existential fear dating back to the Luddites in the early 19th century. Regardless of whether you believe the end of humans in jobs is a groundless fear or is a real threat, there is one undeniable fact: The rate of change in how our world works and how to earn a decent living is rapidly changing and will deeply impact each of us and our families in our lifetime.

This begs the question: If the world is changing, and if you do not change, what does the rest of your lifetime look like for you? If you maintain your status quo, what is the trajectory of your life?

I faced such a question as I was at the supposed peak of my career at age 25, sitting in my own office, at the largest and most successful hedge fund in the world. I looked around for role models, and I asked myself: If I continue on this trajectory, if I live life the same way I am living now, who will I become ten years from now? What will the end of my life look like?

Most 25-year-olds don't think this way. We feel limitless and hopeful at age 25, and we think and dream that anything is possible. However, I had recently come across a quotation that had me thinking about this deeply:

"What is the definition of Hell? On your last day on Earth, the person you *became* will meet the person you could have *become*."

That quotation struck me, not because I felt scared by it. I don't feel scared by the changing world, I don't feel scared by robots, or some existential threat, and I don't bring this up in this chapter to scare you, either.

It struck me because it made me stop, pause, and wonder. It made me wonder: What am I capable of?

What's the absolute BEST version of myself that I can become?

In my wildest dreams, with my most earnest effort, with focus, discipline, and belief, what am I capable of becoming?

What impact am I capable of having on this world?

What would that mean for me and my family?

And, most importantly: Am I living my life and spending my days on a trajectory that sets me up to achieve that greatness?

Greatness is an interesting word. I believe we're all capable of our own definition of greatness, not society's expectation or definition of greatness, but mine.

It made me think: What is my version of greatness?

If I've lived my life, and I look back, what are the things I will have regretted not trying or not doing?

What are the things I am spending time on today that are in conflict with my definition of, vision of, and aspiration toward, greatness?

What are the things *you* are spending your time on today that are in conflict with your definition of greatness?

Greatness to me means that I leave the world better than I found it. Greatness to me means that I become a better version of myself every single day, and that I am able not only to provide for my family and loved ones, but that I am able to reach a plane of success where I can do what matters.

What is your definition of greatness for yourself? What is your vision of your life over a 50-year period? Not tomorrow, not this very minute, but if you take a step back and really close your eyes and imagine what it is you are capable of and what you want to become over a FIFTY-YEAR period... What is that?

As I sat in my office at the largest hedge fund in the world, with all sorts of creature comforts around me, and people even more successful than I running around, I thought to myself: Will this path take me to greatness?

I didn't have the answers to any of this. But in that moment, I had a lot to think about.

Fortunately for me, Bridgewater Associates, at that time, and even today, was a culture and a place that encouraged this type of introspection. We were encouraged to think about and define our core values, our strengths, and our weaknesses – not at a superficial, corporate level, but at a deep, human level. I was reminded of something our leader, Ray Dalio, said at every other meeting: "You can have anything you want. But you cannot have everything. So you better pick."

I sat in my office on a relatively quiet afternoon and started to map out my strengths. I mapped out my weaknesses. I wrote out my beliefs about myself and my worldview. And I started to come to a conclusion that I felt deeply inside but had not been able to articulate previously. I was climbing the wrong mountain. I was on the wrong trajectory. The mountain I was climbing might be someone else's version of greatness, but it wasn't mine. I was good at it, but it wasn't what fueled my soul – and if I were to be on my deathbed, and I were to meet the "person I could have become," I would be meeting someone very different.

I was lucky.

I was lucky to be in a company that encouraged this type of self-reflection. I was in a company that offered me the tools necessary to even think about life in this type of abstract and proactive way. Conversely, my immigrant and middle-class upbringing taught a different way of thinking: Be thankful and grateful for what you have. Keep your head down and do the work. Earn your keep and do the best you can.

And yet, on the other hand, here I was in a company that encouraged me to think bigger, to think conceptually, not just in how we operated the business, but in how we operate our lives.

We're not all that lucky. Part of why I wrote this book and even created Unstoppable was so that I can get others to realize that they can all find just 15 minutes on an idle Sunday afternoon to think about their lives in a proactive way. I wanted to provide people with the framework I developed over a decade of the most productive and successful years of my life so more people on this planet can unlock success and achieve their biggest goals. And most importantly, I wanted to get in front of people and INSPIRE them to take 15 minutes to think more proactively about their lives. It worked for me, and it can work for you.

Here's the question, though. Do you want it?

Sitting for even 15 minutes and envisioning what you can become can be a scary thing to do. Because it can deeply challenge your current situation in your life. It can potentially challenge major life decisions you've made in the past. It can make you think about long-held beliefs and force you to rethink whether they are TRUE.

On one hand, doing this type of work, even for 15 minutes, can get you to look reality in the face and really assess where you are. On the other hand, it is SO much easier to just escape and go back to what we're doing: binge-watch Netflix, or open up a beer and hang out with our buddies. That is SO much easier. And I did that for years upon years. Until. Until I said: Enough is enough.

In the subsequent chapters of this book, I'm going to get into the actionable steps you can take in order to start to pause and reflect on your life, and start to really think about what you want. You can have anything, I truly believed that and still do today. But as Ray said: You cannot have everything, so you better pick.

At age 28, nearly two years after I started to really realize that I needed to change the trajectory of my life, I took the plunge. I quit my six-figure job. I got rid of my fancy BMW. And I took the plunge to start my own business again – something that I felt was core to the trajectory I wanted and needed in my life. Why two years? Because we all have rent, bills, obligations, family, and responsibilities.

When I came to my realization, I took a hard look at reality, and then I said, OK, the trajectory I am on, my status quo, will not get me to the best version of myself and the dream I have for my life. And so I sat down and plotted. I created a vision of whom I want to become, and I spent the next two years carefully navigating my life's trajectory closer and closer to the path that I knew would get me to a point where on my deathbed, I'd be looking at myself in the mirror instead of meeting a stranger.

Achieving a proactive life doesn't mean you make crazy rash changes. It also doesn't mean that you succumb to your limitations and surrender, saying, "That's impossible for me." It means that one week at a time, one year at a time, you move your life to align with the vision you have for yourself. At age 28, I started my business. At age 31, I became financially independent. At age 36, I sold my business, then helped sell the business that bought mine, and then moved even closer to the life's path that I had defined for myself at age 25. I did this by focusing full-time on Unstoppable and projects that I deeply cared about. I dreamt. I believed. I executed with Discipline. And I triumphed. Not overnight. Not without setbacks and roadblocks and failures along the way. But little by little, one Unstoppable Sunday at a time.

What does the status quo of your life look like? If you change nothing, if you keep going down your current path, if you do that for decades? What will your life be? When you meet the BEST VERSION OF YOURSELF will you be staring at a mirror image of yourself at your deathbed, or will you be meeting a stranger?

You have a choice to make. As we get into the next few chapters, where I give you the actionable steps to follow, this Unstoppable Life framework, will you do the work or will you have another beer?

Look, I'm not saying that what you're doing right now is wrong. For me, parts of my life BEFORE I made these major changes were great, and parts were off. But I always felt uncertain about my life and I felt a pit in my stomach every Sunday, wondering "Where am I even going?!" Following the steps help you get clarity on where you are, where you are going, and what you need to do next, and help you to take a more proactive approach to life, so that you don't have to wonder.

So what will your choice be? Assess and evaluate the status quo? Or watch Netflix? You pick.

Chapter 3,
Questions to Ask Yourself

Where will you be in ten years if you maintain the status quo?

What are the great things in your life that exist and that you want to maintain, of the status quo?

What are the things you want to change about the status quo?

What are the big macro worldly trends that may put your life at risk?

```

```

Will you be meeting your mirror image or a complete stranger at your deathbed?

O Complete stranger
O Mirror image
O I honestly don't know, but I sure as heck would love to meet my
    mirror image!

What is the ONE thing you can change today that brings you closer to the best dream version of yourself?

```

```

Chapter 3,
Actions to Take

☐ Building a proactive life for yourself and adopting this framework requires some time every Sunday. Can you commit to even 30 minutes every Sunday to work on this? Will you schedule in time on your calendar to do this?

☐ If you've got a partner, or a family, or even best friends, can you have a conversation with them about how you will commit to spending this time so that you can become a better version of yourself? Would any of them even join you on working on this together?

CHAPTER 4:

EFFECT CHANGE IN YOUR LIFE
WITH A 45-DAY CHALLENGE

*"Change is hard at first, messy in the middle,
and gorgeous at the end."*

— ROBIN S. SHARMA

Making changes in life so that you can reap the rewards you want is hard. I'll be honest. Driving the right kind of change takes focus, it takes discipline, it takes commitment. And in this chapter I'm going to give you a tool that you can use as leverage to drive this change. But let's first talk about why you need to make a change and why it is important to commit up front to it.

Congratulations. You've just hit a critical inflection point in this book. Over the past few chapters, we talked through what separates the DREAMERS from the DABBLERS. We talked about our deep-rooted fears and the limiting beliefs holding us back. And, most importantly, we took a moment to pause and imagine what life would be like for you if you maintained the STATUS QUO in an ever-changing world.

If you're continuing to read my book, it means one thing: You're intent on committing to Belief x Discipline and changing the trajectory of your life. I'm pumped for you.

When I was sitting there at age 25, thinking about the trajectory of my life, I knew I had a lot of things to figure out, and I knew I had some changes to make. From age 25 to age 35, I used the same tools that I am going to present to you over the next few chapters of this book. I used these tools to take stock of everything I had accomplished in my life, to craft a vision for my life true to my own definition of greatness, and to then start to navigate toward that vision, one Sunday at a time.

Why Sunday? Because we as human beings love "fresh starts." That is why we love New Year's Resolutions. It is a new beginning and a new opportunity. Similarly, our bodies recognize the fresh start and tighten up on a Sunday. It's a new beginning, and our body is subtly asking us: "What's the plan?"

The subsequent chapters of this book are going to introduce you to actionable ideas that you can adopt in order to bring change to your life. These practices will help you go from just reacting to life to taking control and becoming more proactive in life.

Those changes that I made in my life unlocked nearly a decade of success and productivity for me. The methods, tools, and ideas I used to make those changes came from hundreds of hours of reading, researching, going to conferences, and talking to mentors. Ironically, none of the things that I learned were taught in schools; they weren't taught by my teachers; they weren't taught by my parents; they weren't even taught in the world-class corporations like GE and Bridgewater Associates where I worked. And yet, it is all knowledge that has been available for us to access for thousands of years.

Part of my motivation to write this book was exactly that. I thought it was silly that I wasn't handed a basic, actionable, and simple handbook on how to plan out what I want from life right at the sixth grade. While I was proud of what I had accomplished at age 25, can you imagine just how much farther along I would've been had I learned how to set a vision for my life and how to set goals and how to manage my time and prioritize –- instead of learning how to compute derivatives in Calculus class?!

Before you can start to take action and adopt the mindset that the subsequent chapters of this book will present to you, you'll have to make a decision and make a commitment to **change your status quo and the current trajectory of your life**, so that you can become Unstoppable.

There are certain changes in life that are easy to adopt. It just so happens that they're often not good for us, but we adopt them anyway – because those easily-adoptable type of changes tend to give us an immediate reward.

On one hand, if you have a drink of Scotch or eat an amazing steak, you almost immediately get the reward and gratification from it, even though in the long term it may be bad for you. Convincing yourself to have steak and Scotch every day is very easy!

On the other hand, if you work out at the gym just once, you feel okay, but it may take 45 days straight of workouts before your body starts to tighten up and you start to feel amazing both physically and mentally. Convincing yourself to go to the gym three times a week in order to reap the long-term rewards can be very hard!

The going-to-the-gym reward is delayed, even though the net positive impact on your life is far greater than is the impact of the Scotch-and-steak meal. But in order to get to that reward, you'll have to make the change in your life to work out for 45 days to reap the long-term, positive rewards of that change. Therein lies the conundrum.

We optimize our lives and build habits that give us immediate gratification, and yet we yearn for the results and success that come from things that require discipline and delayed gratification. In life, whether we realize it or not, we're constantly faced with the choice between discipline now versus regret later.

So the question becomes... How do you start doing the things that provide delayed gratification (thus avoiding that later regret) when doing so means that you are giving up rewards RIGHT NOW? The greatest treasures in life come from delayed gratification and focused and purposeful work through discipline. How do you build Discipline? How do you get unstuck and start taking action on the things that you know are good for you long-term?

You need to start by building momentum. Once you are done working through this book, and once you create the habits to drive change in your life, you will become an Unstoppable freight train.

However, much like any locomotive, you first have to get the momentum going. Which brings me to the key focus of this chapter. How do you get that initial change going? How do you take that first sustainable change? How do you create that Discipline? Especially when you might not feel the rewards right away?

First, the key to getting started is to *actually* start. This is why I've structured the steps you need to take in this book by prioritizing the things that give you shorter-term rewards. We'll start with practicing Unstoppable Sundays, where you can start to take stock of just the immediate seven days of your life and where you are now, just so you can positively impact the next seven days in your life. Simple, right? Then, as you start to get that momentum, you'll start to think about the next 365 days. And then we'll get to the deeper and meatier aspects of your life plan by starting to look at the next five years of your life, looking at your circles of influence, and looking at taking on bigger challenges that shift the direction of your life.

Second, I've learned over the past decade that there is a distinct art to bringing change into your life. If you start too fast, try to get too big, and move too fast, then you'll fall apart before you even get going. You'll give up. That's why I hate 50% of the lose-weight-fast, change-your-life fast, and become-a-millionaire-easily-tomorrow books. They cause more disillusionment than success because they set expectations too high and people give up before they can reap any rewards; thus, the readers of those books only go back to their old habits. "I tried it... It didn't work. I must not be meant for more." Incorrect. You didn't approach it with a long-term-enough view.

I've learned that in order to bring long-term and sustained success to life, you have to approach change in multiple phases and with a long-term view. You also have to approach it with commitment, discipline, and purposeful and focused action. If what I just said sounds contradictory, well, it might be – but that is why long-term sustained change is art and not science. It's two opposing and seemingly diverging forces coming together as one.

This is why, as you set out to bring about change, you have to start in the right way. This means that you're not going to feel THAT different tomorrow as you start. Nor will you feel THAT different a week from now. But as you sustain your actions and work at change for a specific period of time, you'll start to build momentum and you'll start to see small rewards. As you work at it for a year, your following year will be even better. Much like the locomotive that starts out slow and sluggish at the station and then picks up speed and becomes Unstoppable, as you continue on your journey toward Unstoppability, you will become Unstoppable, like that locomotive.

So the question is, how do you start? How do you start the RIGHT way? It took me years to master all the core principles around how to do this right. But there is one tool that I now use regularly and that makes it easy for even beginnings to start the right way. It's what I call the 45-day Unstoppable Beast Mode Challenge. Let me explain.

A 45-Day Unstoppable Beast Mode Challenge
CONSISTS OF THE FOLLOWING:

- **Dream and Establish Belief:** You set a clear intention and goal that you will work to accomplish over the next 45 days.
- **Commitment:** You identify what accomplishing this goal will mean for your life; what it will mean for your life if you DO NOT accomplish

it; and then, most importantly, you make a promise to yourself about how you will reward yourself when you do accomplish the goal.

- **Discipline:** You establish a schedule for when you will work on this goal, and you create an action plan for how you will accomplish this goal. You also define the key metrics by which you will measure the progress on your goal.
- **Pause and Reflect:** You will check in every Sunday on how this goal is progressing. You will course-correct your action plan. And you will tweak your approach to ensure success toward your goal.
- **Win and Build Momentum:** At the end of the 45-day period, you will take stock of what you've accomplished, and then you will define your next 45-day Beast Mode Challenge, based on what you've learned from the previous 45 days.

A 45-day Beast Mode Challenge is something I've used countless times in my life when I wanted to start something new, when I wanted to build a new habit that I knew would be good for me, and when I felt like I was stuck on a project and needed to unlock massive productivity.

While it seems simple to say "Just do a 45-day Challenge!" the mechanics of doing a Challenge tap into all the core principles needed to bring change into our lives. Let me walk you through the mechanics of WHY this works.

DREAM AND ESTABLISH BELIEF

We talked about this in an earlier chapter. In order to bring change and be successful in our lives, we must dream big and establish Belief that what we dream is possible. But so often, dreams can be daunting and Belief can be just a tad bit beyond our reach.

By looking at a 45-day window of time, you allow yourself to ask... "OK... What is a *small and meaningful win* that I can accomplish within this short period of time?" It also forces you to think... "If I have to worry about just this ONE thing and I wholeheartedly pursue it, could I do it?"

By shrinking the problem space and going after a small step toward a larger goal in your life, by time-boxing it to just 45 days, something magical happens. Belief becomes just a tad bit closer to the span of your reach, just close enough for you to actually grab it.

Commitment

Nothing happens in our lives unless we commit to it. When we commit, we pledge to put in the time toward it, we pledge to overcome the obstacles that stand in our way, and, most importantly, when we commit, we decide to focus on it.

The thing is that commitment doesn't come for free. Commitment comes when we decide that our goal is a MUST instead of a NICE TO HAVE. This is why as part of a 45-day Challenge, we help you visualize and understand what accomplishing this goal would mean to you, how it would change your life. We also have you visualize what it would mean if you DIDN'T do it. How would you be negatively impacted by it? How would you fall behind in your longer-term life goals if you didn't do this one important thing today and over the next 45 days?

By thinking through the repercussions on your life both in the short term and the long term, we help you conceptualize why this goal and this challenge is a MUST DO for your life, and thereby we help you drive commitment to your 45-day Challenge and goal.

Discipline

Accomplishing and winning in life is EASY. That's right, I said it! The formula for winning is easy. Most of us, the DABBLERS, just don't want to do it. My most favorite saying in the world is: "Discipline now versus Regret later." Discipline is having the sustained routines established that allow us to continuously work toward our goals no matter what.

And so, as part of the 45-day Challenge, we have you open up your calendar and establish work blocks where you will continuously work on your 45-day Challenge. No. Matter. What. That's Discipline. That's Unstoppability. No matter the road blocks, no matter the competing priorities. We commit and establish the Discipline that we MUST work on this challenge and accomplish our goal.

PAUSE AND REFLECT

Very rarely in life do things go according to plan. In fact, for every great endeavor that I take on, I *expect* to hit roadblocks; I *expect* to learn about flaws in my plan and my approach. And because of these expectations, I always set aside time to pause and reflect.

When we're deep in the thick of things, we get so enamored in the details and knee-deep in the details, that we stop being able to see the forest for the trees. And because I *expect* this, I explicitly set aside time on Sunday afternoons to NOT DO WORK, and to instead just pause and reflect.

- How are things going?
- What am I doing that is working?
- What am I doing that is NOT working?
- What's stopping me that I need to fix?

We'll talk in greater detail about the practice of Unstoppable Sundays, where we pause and reflect, in a subsequent chapter. But I want you to flag this in your mind right now. As part of your 45-day Challenge, you will set aside time on Sundays to pause and reflect and just that. So that you can course-correct along the way.

You see. Here's the thing. Being UNSTOPPABLE doesn't get you to perfection. It's that you get to a state of mind where, regardless of the roadblocks that you face, you find a way to overcome them and continue toward your goal. Pausing and reflecting helps you do exactly that.

Win and Build Momentum

You are going to accomplish your 45-day goal. I know it. Deep down inside, if you commit, practice Discipline, pause and reflect, and execute, you, too, know that you will.

Have you ever noticed how the rich get richer? How the winners just keep winning more? There is one simple reason for it: MOMENTUM.

When you get a small win, you go after another win, and then another, and then another, and much like that Unstoppable freight train from hell screeching along the tracks at full speed, you gain so much momentum that you keep winning more and more.

That's why these 45-day Challenges work. Each one allows you to take a small step. A successful Challenge helps you FEEL what winning is like, and then your subsequent Challenges, one after another, start to build more and more momentum and you keep winning.

Throughout the last decade, I've often finished one 45-day Challenge only to kick off another, bigger one. It's an amazing feeling when you win. It is addicting. It is contagious. And these 45-day Challenges help you get unstuck from the patterns in your life that stop you from winning and help you build momentum to create one win after another.

Can you imagine where you'll be five years from now, if you practice Belief x Discipline? I've done it for the past decade and this practice has brought me great fortune, great success, and, most importantly, fulfillment and the ability and freedom and wealth to do whatever I want and to effect the change I want to see in this world.

The Next 45 Days of Your Life

Starting with the next chapter, I'm going to begin teaching you the core tools I have used over the past decade, and continue to use today, to live an Unstoppable and proactive life.

These tools will help you realize the promise of this book: to live a proactive life and go GET the life that you deserve. The life that your family deserves. The life that your loved ones deserve. So that at your deathbed, you are not meeting a complete stranger, but you are meeting a mirror image of you, the absolute BEST VERSION of you.

Here's the thing, though: You will not succeed in adopting these tools, you will not succeed in adopting these new habits, and you will not succeed in changing the trajectory of your life, if you do not commit.

How do you commit?

We'll kick off a 45-day Challenge, of course.

I want you to kick off a 45-day Challenge starting today – to adopt the ideas I am going to present to you in the subsequent chapters of this book.

I want you to kick off a 45-day Challenge starting today – to commit to making a change in your life.

I want you to kick off a 45-day Challenge in which you will schedule in time to WORK on this.

I want you to kick off a 45-day Challenge in which you will spend every Sunday afternoon to pause and reflect by practicing Unstoppable Sundays.

I want you to kick off a 45-day Challenge in which you will map out your next seven days, then your next 365 days, and then your five-year vision for your life.

Over the next 45 days, you will turn this book – which has just my words and empty boxes – into a concrete, proactive plan for your life. This book will become your book. Your roadmap. Your path to the life that you deserve.

Are you ready?

Chapter 4,
Questions to Ask Yourself

Are you willing to commit to a 45-day Challenge to create a life plan for yourself?

○ Yes

○ No, I'm good with the status quo, give me my money back

What is my ONE measurable 45-day goal?

To wholeheartedly adopt the tools presented in the subsequent chapters in this book.

At the end of this 45-day Challenge, I will have:

- Practiced Unstoppable Sundays every Sunday to pause and reflect.
- Created a 365-day proactive life plan for myself.
- Created a 365-day proactive life calendar for myself.
- Created a five-year vision for myself.
- Created a support network of like-minded and growth-oriented people around me who will support me in my life goal and plan.

What would life look like after I've accomplished my 45-day goal?

What will happen to my life if I do not do this now?

What does the status quo of my life look like?

How would I dramatically move forward my agenda in my life if I succeed?

How will I celebrate and reward myself when I accomplish this goal?

What will successfully completing this challenge mean for my loved ones?

What bigger things can I pursue after I lock in this WIN and build MOMENTUM in my life?

Who else can I convince to do this 45-day Challenge along with me? (optional)

Chapter 4,
Actions to Take

☐ Open up your calendar and let's schedule in time for you work on this 45-day Challenge. Here are the things you need to schedule in:

- Every Sunday afternoon, "Practice Unstoppable Sundays" for 30 minutes.
- At least twice a week, instead of watching Netflix, "Work on my Unstoppable Life Plan" for an hour and a half.
- At least once a week, instead of going out every night, "Work on my action plans on my 365-day goals." (Don't worry. In a later chapter, we'll walk you through clarifying your goals. But let's schedule in the time right now to work explicitly on these goals.)

☐ Grab your phone. Take a picture of your commitment to this 45-day Challenge from the worksheet you just completed. Make it your wallpaper or set it as a favorite picture so that you can often go back to this picture and remind yourself of the commitment you just made.

☐ One last thing: You might be an overachiever (like I am) and you may be able to create your life plan, and to complete this book and the worksheets well before the 45-day deadline. There is NO SPEED LIMIT to life. If you finish ahead of time, you can always declare victory early and kick off a NEW 45-day Unstoppable Beast Mode Challenge centered around one or more of your 365-day goals. Consider this a challenge. ;)

☐ Onwards!

CHAPTER 5:

GET RID OF THE SUNDAY SCARIES: PRACTICE UNSTOPPABLE SUNDAYS

"A sunday well spent brings a week of content."

— PROVERB

W e've all been there. It's Sunday, and that feeling *deep* down in our gut starts to creep in. It's the pre-Monday, "Oh-God-why-isn't-this-a-four-day-weekend?" dreary feeling. It's the "What am I even doing with my life?" feeling. It's the "I love my job. I love my job. I love my job... If I keep saying it, it'll come true..." feeling. It's the feeling that lingers through Monday and into Wednesday, as you count down to the weekend, feeling — and it's the "hamster-wheel-of-life" feeling, because you've been on it for nearly a decade and you're not quite sure whether it's worth it all.

Where am I even going?

At 27, I felt like I had it all. As an immigrant kid from Bangladesh who had spent the first ten years of his life there, then moved to grow up in Flushing, Queens in a one-bedroom apartment where six people lived together — now, my townhouse, my sports car with the red leather seats, my double degree in Computer Science and Management from a prestigious institution, my office — all of it showed that I had MADE IT. And yet, I dreaded every Monday. I was deep in my finance job at one of the most successful hedge funds in the world and I experienced that feeling. I kept asking myself –- there's supposed to be a K'ABoom! Where's the K'ABoom?!

I knew I couldn't make dramatic changes on a whim — I had far too much to lose and I didn't exactly have a trust fund to fall back on. So, I started to take it a day at a time to start to figure out: *Where am I?... and What do I do next?*

Between the years 2010 and 2018, I started to set aside 30 minutes every Sunday to answer those two simple questions. Much as you might spend your Sunday doing chores to keep your house running and in order, I started to spend a portion of every Sunday thinking about and writing down where I am and what I wanted next out of my life.

For some reason, when I first started to practice this simple exercise, it just made me feel better. It instantly helped me stop feeling restless and I immediately started to feel like I was in the driver's seat for a change.

Through that nine-year period, the simple exercise of pausing and reflecting unlocked unparalleled productivity and growth for me as a person. I went from being a Product Manager at a hedge fund to quitting my job to starting my own company. I went on to scale my company from 0 to 70 people and went from $0 in revenue to millions in annual recurring revenue. I went from being CEO of that successful venture to selling it to a market leader and joining their executive team as the youngest Senior Vice President in the company's history. It doesn't stop there: We then went on to sell that company to one of the largest technology companies in the world.

Throughout that ten-year period, I went from living paycheck-to-paycheck to being financially independent. Throughout that ten-year period, I went from being reactive to my life and just doing what was expected of me, to taking control of a vision for my life and executing on it.

As Step 1 of this Unstoppable Life system, I want you to start practicing this simple exercise, because it will be your first step in assessing your current situation and starting to become more proactive about your life, just one week at a time.

Most importantly, this will be your first step in eradicating the Sunday Scaries, the Sunday angst, the Sunday "What am I even doing with my life?!" existential crisis.

This ten-year period of productivity and success resulted in large part from this simple exercise I call Unstoppable Sundays. Every Sunday, I sit down, I open up my document (which is now 200+ pages), and **I answer the two questions:** *Where am I? And... What do I do next?*

The most important thing to do is to start carving out just 30 minutes every Sunday, and start to take your time reflecting on these two questions and recording the answers in this document.

Because I've been using the same document over the years, I'm able to scroll back years at a time to review how I was feeling and what I was tackling on any given Sunday. Because I write down my thoughts, I'm able to really think through and conceptualize my deepest subconscious feelings.

Your ability to write well, your ability to write something that may sound wrong, or your likelihood to "get it wrong" – NONE of these things matters. This document is for you, by you, and so you have to treat is as an extension of your inner thoughts. All this does is to get your thoughts out of your head and onto paper, which then allows you to take a step back and really understand what is going on.

I also like starting with a seven-day view, because so many personal development books tell you to think big, dream big, and you'll accomplish it all. That's just plain unrealistic. I get it; I've been there. There are existing commitments, real constraints, bills to pay, and things to finish. So, I always like to prompt you to start by reflecting on where you are and getting your week in order. Over time, you can start to get even more proactive about your next month, then your next year. And as you start to appreciate how you will operate within your current situation just that much better, we can start to think bigger and figure out what walls to knock down to remodel the house and make it your dream house (and life)!

It's important not to overcomplicate this. All you need to do is open up a Word document on a Sunday, write down the date, and start to answer these two questions. Easy! And from my experience and what I've heard from our community practicing Unstoppable Sundays, you'll quickly start to feel at ease about the week ahead instead of trying to escape from the Sunday Scaries.

The simple practice of doing this every Sunday does a few things for me. First, it eliminates my Sunday anxieties. It provides an immediate outlet for all the feelings that might otherwise rush through my head about Monday. Second, it allows me to stay tethered to a stream of consciousness. I am easily able to look back at where I was last Sunday and what I had committed to doing and how I was feeling, and thus I'm able to compare to see whether this Sunday I'm doing better or worse. And, third, it allows me to be proactive about my situation instead of trying to escape it; I do this by laying out an action plan for the next seven days.

These two questions of *Where am I?* and *What do I do next?* are seemingly simple. Here's how to think about answering them and why they are just so powerful.

WHERE AM I?

This question is designed to help you take stock of where you are right now in your life.

- How would I describe my current situation?
- What am I feeling? Anger? Frustration? Happiness? Anxiousness? Worry?
- What are my current sources of anxiety? What am I worried about?

- What's going on in my inner monologue? You know... that pesky voice inside our heads...
- Not only is it incredibly cathartic to get it all out of my head and onto paper, but this process of writing and articulating what is going on in my head and my subconscious also allows me to gain a deeper understanding around exactly what I am feeling, and it'll do the same for you.

WHAT DO I DO NEXT?

- One of the core principles of Unstoppable is purposeful and focused ACTION. Raise hell and be badass, I say. *Go punch that obstacle in the face!* reads my iPhone wallpaper.
- If all I did on Sundays was spend 30 minutes pontificating about my thoughts, I would not have experienced the decade of productivity that I just did.
- In this part of the exercise, I look at "Where I am..." and then create a bulleted list of the action steps I need to take in the coming week in order to start moving forward in terms of my goals for the year.
- Mind you, this isn't meant to be a to-do list; you keep that elsewhere. THIS is more of your inner voice syncing with YOU on... "All right... Given everything that is going on, here's what I'm going to do to move forward."
- I capture these items in bullet points, a few paragraphs, and, honestly, it varies from long ramblings to succinct bullet points. It doesn't matter how you capture it; what does matter is that you take the time to pause and reflect on where you are and then to define/refine and write down your action plan to move forward.
- Note that your action plan may not vary wildly from week to week. That's OK. Sometimes, I'll look at my action plan from the prior week and just copy-paste the same. Sometimes, I'll realize that last

week's plan just doesn't make sense, or that it isn't realistic, and I'll chart a new approach. Either way, what matters is that you do have a plan, that you are proactive, and that you write down your plan and commit to it so that you can keep yourself honest.

To make it even easier for you to begin the practice of Unstoppable Sundays, we've created a simple template that you can use to get started quickly. Just go to: https://getunstoppable.com/templates/sunday

Something magical will begin to happen as you start to practice Unstoppable Sundays. First, you'll find that you're going into each week with a plan. That alone should put your mind at ease as you execute on your week. But, more importantly, as you start the ball rolling on Unstoppable Sundays, and as this becomes a habit week after week, you'll start to ask yourself: Well.... Here's where I am... Here's what I'm going to do in the coming week... But where am I going?

The first hurdle to overcome as you create a life strategy and plan you can tether yourself to, is to establish the practice of pausing and reflecting on a weekly basis. In the next chapter, we'll help you think through how to start reflecting on your life through a broader, 365-day aperture, so that you can tether these weekly sessions to a broader plan for your life.

Lastly, do remember that you're not in this alone. There's a whole community of people who practice Unstoppable Sundays. In addition to that, I personally publish a brand-new episode on our YouTube channel EVERY SUNDAY to give you some food for thought for your own reflections.

Subscribe to our YouTube channel (https://getunstoppable.com/youtube) to be notified every time I drop a Sunday episode. The links to the different parts of our community of tens of thousands of people can be found here: https://getunstoppable.com/community

If you learn something new every Sunday (from our community) and spend 30 minutes every Sunday to become proactive about your life – can you even begin to imagine what you're going to accomplish over the coming decade? Onwards!

Now here's the thing: You can just read this book, make a bunch of mental notes, and just move on with your life. That is not going to be what brings about transformative change in your life. The only way you will change the trajectory of your life and get to a proactive lifestyle is if you actually start practicing now. So for this chapter and onwards, there will be a worksheet for you to follow <u>right now</u> as you read so that you can start taking focused and purposeful action right now in changing your life.

Let's start making a change in your life right now. Let's practice Unstoppable Sundays together, right now.

Chapter 5,
Questions to Ask Yourself

How do you typically feel on a Sunday afternoon as you start to think about Monday and the week ahead?

What are the things you typically "escape" to so that you do not have to think about the week ahead? What do you do to ignore or "feel better but not solve" the angst and the pit in your stomach on a Sunday afternoon or evening?

What are the non-negotiable commitments that you have on a Sunday afternoon that you must do and cannot get out of? These are okay to have, let's just acknowledge those things here.

When on a Sunday could you schedule in 15 to 30 minutes on your calendar, or an alarm on your phone, so that you are reminded to pause and reflect? What small "escapism" on a Sunday could you delay or give up so that you can start to get proactive about your life and your coming week?

Let's try our first Unstoppable Sunday (even if right NOW is not a Sunday) together. Just to see how it feels and get you going.

Where am I?

What do I do next?

Chapter 5,
Actions to Take

☐ Schedule a time into your calendar or set an alarm on your phone for every Sunday for your 15 to 30 minutes of Pausing and Reflection time; for practicing Unstoppable Sundays.

☐ Pick a spot where you can have some peace and quiet so you can practice Unstoppable Sundays.

☐ Download our Unstoppable Sundays template and set it up: https://www.getunstoppable.com/templates/sunday

☐ Practice your first Unstoppable Sunday in this book and then start practicing it every Sunday.

☐ Onwards!

CHAPTER 6:

GET PROACTIVE ABOUT THE NEXT
365 DAYS OF YOUR LIFE

*"Tomorrow, is the first blank page of a 365 page book.
Write a good one."*

— Brad Paisley

In order to be successful in life, you need an Unstoppable strategy, and a plan to implement that strategy through purposeful and focused ACTION.

Strategy can be a complicated word; it can even seem fru-fru when you think of it in the context of your own life. But it doesn't have to be. In fact, it shouldn't be.

Great strategy is the efficient organization of resources. Your resources. Your most precious resources, such as your time, your money, your conscious attention, and, most importantly, the inner monologue of your mind.

When you think of strategy in simple terms like that, all of a sudden it sounds absolutely crazy that so many of us go through life without having thought through a strategy (an efficient organization of our resources) that we can tether ourselves to and improve over time as we learn.

For all of us, regardless of how much money we have in the bank, the most scarce resource we have is time. How you spend your time, what you burn your calories on in a given 24-hour period, is the most critical strategic decision you have to make in your life. And, yet, we spend our days working at jobs we don't love; we spend our evenings cruising Netflix to de-stress from the perils of the day; and we spend our weekends getting drunk with people who won't help us grow, but who will help us pass our time so we can go back to Monday and count down to the next weekend – only to do it all over again. I call this the Hamster Wheel of Life.

As you start to move into the discipline of practicing Unstoppable Sundays, as you start to hone in on "Where am I" and "What do I do next" – something magical will happen. You'll stop reacting to every day of your life and you'll start to be proactive about how you take on each day. And as you shift your consciousness from being reactive to being proactive, from having a fixed mindset to having a growth mindset, you'll naturally start to ask yourself some seriously strategic questions about your life: What's the big plan? What do I want to accomplish over the next 12 months of my life? Where do I want to be five years from now?

Now that I've shown you how to become proactive about the next seven days of your life, it's time to start zooming out a bit and thinking about the next 365 days of your life and time to start laying out a strategy and plan: Think of this as if you were plotting a bank heist.

Before I show you the Unstoppable way of planning the next 356 days of your life, let's just talk through the BEFORE of how I used to try to plan life, and how most people still do that today.

BEFORE I developed this system, I didn't think of yearly planning as an active sport. It was a passive activity that happened unofficially between Christmas and New Year's. Nothing was written down; there was no reviewing of last year's goal; it was all in my head during brief moments of time.

BEFORE I developed this system, my goals really consisted of a wish list of common New Year's Resolutions around losing weight, making more money, and finally quitting my job to start that dream business. I also really wanted to learn another language... Yeah, that'd be great, too.

BEFORE I developed this system, even if I set some resolutions or goals, I'd pretty quickly forget about them – or, even worse, become uninspired by them and kind of just go back to the grind by the time February rolled around. In fact, 80 percent of people break their New Year's Resolutions by the time the second week of February arrives. Sound familiar?

Truth is, you can go to the most prestigious schools and universities, yet never will you actually find a class on how to create a strategy and plan for your life.

This whole system of goal-setting is flawed due to three reasons:

1. First, we completely overestimate how much we can actually accomplish in the 365 days of the year. First, 365 days, or a year, feels like a long time. But when you really break it down, out of the 365 days, there are only 261 working days, and after you take away vacation days, you're down to 247 working days, and after you subtract sick days, down time, and family commitments, you're left with a mere 220 days, or roughly seven-and-a-half months out of every year to really take action on your goals.

2. Second, we don't set up a system to be proactive about our yearly goals as we work through the year. So, we become uninspired about our goals, we forget them, and we return to just reacting to the day-to-day. Finally, the next year rolls around, and we ask ourselves: "Where did the time go?!" only to adopt the same defunct goals all over again – sound familiar?

3. Last, while we may fail at achieving the goals that we overestimated our ability to accomplish, we also, at the same time, fail to acknowledge and give gratitude for whatever DID go well during the past 365 days, whatever DID work out, that DID move us maybe 20 percent closer to meeting a greater challenge, even if we're not 100 percent there, as we had hoped or anticipated.

Now, let's talk about the AFTER. The Unstoppable Proactive Life Planning system didn't come together all at once for me. It is based on all sorts of different tools that I learned from friends, read about, and developed over the course of a decade. These all came together to unlock a period of unparalleled productivity for me. This system is all rooted in the idea of proactively planning for my life instead of just reacting to it.

AFTER I started to treat my planning process as an active sport, I started to take my goals a lot more seriously.

AFTER I started to check in on my goals on a regular basis, and to pause and reflect on a weekly basis on how I'm doing, I started to execute on my goals a lot more aggressively.

AFTER I started to express gratitude for even the small wins, I started to accomplish greater challenges that took multiple years to execute on – but I didn't give up along the way.

So for this next step in developing your Unstoppable Proactive Life Plan, we're going to walk you through creating the first version of your strategy and plan for the next 365 days. Why the first version? Because, remember: Kaizen, combining the collective resources at your disposal (your time, your energy, your intellect, your mentors, your friends) to create a powerful engine for improvement in your own life.

This yearly planning process is similar to Unstoppable Sundays, where you answer two questions in a Word document; you'll do the same for this part of the process in a Word document, except that there will be a few more questions.

These very simple questions, to which you will write the answers, will help you pause and reflect about the past 365 days, and then to start to organize around the next 365 days. By taking an hour (or more) to do this, you will accomplish the following:

- Instead of haphazardly setting the same New Year's Resolutions over and over, you will have actively thought through what you want to accomplish over the coming year.

- By answering a couple of simple questions about how your past year went, you will have an opportunity to learn from what went well and what didn't go well over the past year.
- By writing down your goals in a structured way, you will make it easier for yourself to refer back to these goals throughout the course of the year, and then, most importantly, to see, a year from now, how they turned out.

You know what's the best feeling? My favorite, most absolutely, BEST feeling is when I'm at the end of the year, and I'm looking at the list of goals I wrote down at the beginning of the year, and I am able to cross them off one at a time — because I crushed them! I want you to enjoy that feeling. I want you to experience that feeling of success, of triumph, of winning. So let's get started...

To start, you'll first answer a set of questions that helps you to reflect and learn from the prior year:

1. What are the things I am grateful for?
2. What are the things I am stressed about?
3. What are my key accomplishments over the past year?
4. Looking back, what did I say I would accomplish in the past year? How did this go?
5. Looking back, what is the ONE weakness of mine that held me back the most during the past year?

Again, just as with the Unstoppable Sundays exercise, don't overthink it. All that is important is that you put your thoughts on paper (or screen), so that they're not just percolating in your head.

Once you've gone through the first set of questions, here's how you will be feeling:

- You'll have a renewed sense of the events and circumstances that happened during the past year and that you are thankful for. Our memories are incredibly flawed, and we often have recency bias. Thinking back through the past year and identifying ALL the lucky breaks that went my way and for which I am grateful really helps me hone in on the happenstances that are going well.

- You'll take account of the things that are stressors in your life right now, both in the conscious and the subconscious mind. Dig deep here. Think about the things that are stressing you out and be specific about it all, out on paper. I find this to be incredibly cathartic, and it also helps me start to frame some of the smaller goals I want for the year to address the things in my life that are stressing me out and stopping me from accomplishing bigger things. Even during my BEST years, when I have absolutely crushed it, there were still circumstances, needs, disappointments, personalities, and so on that stressed me out. It's okay. It's life. Describe it all on paper (or screen).

- You'll come away with a succinct list of what you have accomplished during the past year, regardless of what your original goals were. Life throws all kinds of twists and turns, fraught with problems and opportunities. That's normal. And answering the question about your key accomplishments (regardless of what your goals were) again helps you hone in on what went well.

- You'll also go back to the set of goals that you set for yourself a year ago, and you'll check in on how they went. If this is your first time at this and you hadn't set goals a year ago, that's okay — but just imagine how awesome it's going to be once you write down your goals now, check in on them throughout the year, and then check them all off as "accomplished" at the end of the year!

74

- And, finally, as you reflect on your wins, your losses, and your stressors, you'll dig deep inside and identify the ONE BIG WEAKNESS that has held you back over the past year. Everyone has one: What's yours? Find it.

After this first set of questions, your mind will probably be racing. You will probably feel invigorated, and you'll feel excited by the prospects that lie ahead in the next 365 days. You might also feel a bit of angst about how you'll ever achieve the objectives you want to in the coming year, given your natural stressors or the circumstances in your life!

Good or bad, excited or scared, the important thing is that you're taking time now to create a plan, instead of relying on *hope* as your life strategy. Even for the problems that exist in your life, no matter how bad they are, solutions do exist. And know that problems can be opportunities for growth in your life.

Now, as the next-to-last step, you'll start to write down your FIVE key goals for the next 365 days. You've got 365 days ahead of you. How do you want to go and pull off those 365 days like a bank heist, and what treasures would you like in the end? How do you want to overcome your stressors and the problems in your life?

You'll want to answer and capture these questions by writing a set of FIVE clear and easy-to-measure goals. Why five? Because for some reason, anything more just becomes unmanageable. Why measurable? Because a year from now, when you're looking back at these goals, you must be able to answer, without a doubt, whether or not you succeeded in hitting your goals.

You may also want to capture five goals across specific aspects of your life. I usually break these down into core categories. Here are some specific and measurable goals you can set, spanning across the key categories of your life:

1. **Health:** Weight ___ lbs.
2. **Wealth:** Earn $____ after taxes.

3. **Relationships:** Make five new friends that I'm on a texting basis with, who are growth-oriented.
4. **Giving Back:** Spend 14 days of the year on volunteering my time to give back to my community or extended family.
5. **Self-Improvement:** Read one book every month.

Given where you are in your life and what your priorities are, these key aspects of your life may vary. Honestly speaking, there were years when I was working on coming out of debt and I just didn't have the ability to prioritize giving back. That's okay. We're all on our own journeys. What is important is that you clearly define what works best for you as you plan where you want to go in life.

Finally, even the world's best strategies are useless unless you follow up with purposeful and focused action. As the final step, I want you to make a bulleted list of the action plan that will help you mobilize these goals.

Use our template to work through this easily: To make it even easier to begin the practice of your 365-day strategy and plan, we've created a simple template that you can use to get started quickly: https://www.getunstoppable.com/templates/365-day-goals

Even if you're spending just one hour to proactively reflect on your past year and to write down specific goals for your coming year, you'll be significantly ahead of the average person out there. By reviewing these goals on a monthly basis, you'll have significantly increased your chances of success.

This process can be daunting. I'm ten years into following this (as the system has evolved over time), and even I can feel overwhelmed at times. Take your time and remember: There is no perfect answer, and you can always tweak the plan as you learn more throughout the year. What matters the most is that you're taking the steps now to craft a strategy, tether yourself to it, and become proactive about your life.

Now remember! This book is not meant to be a piece of art that sits on your bookshelf or one that just gets forgotten. So grab a pen, and let's work through what you've processed through this chapter.

Chapter 6,
Questions to Ask Yourself

Do you typically set New Year's Resolutions? Do you write down goals for yourself every year? What usually happens to them?

How often do you review and check in on your goals throughout the course of a year? If you did it more regularly, would you have been more likely to pursue the right goals and crush them?

What would happen if you sat down, wrote down your goals, and checked in on them every three months to course-correct?

Chapter 6,
Actions to Take

☐ Schedule a time into your calendar or set an alarm on your phone for every 45 days to write down, review, and iterate on your goals.

☐ Pick a spot where you can have some peace and quiet so you can practice goal setting for your life.

☐ Download our 365-day goal setting template, set it up, and start to commit to creating a 365-day proactive plan for yourself: https://www.getunstoppable.com/templates/365-day-goals

☐ Onwards!

Chapter 6,
Bonus Materials

- Watch my episode on *How to Go from Having a Fixed Mindset to Having a Growth Mindset,*
https://www.getunstoppable.com/3-ways-to-invest-in-yourself/

- Watch my episode on *Getting Off the Hamster Wheel of Life,*
https://www.getunstoppable.com/the-hamster-wheel-of-life/

- Watch my episode on *How to Be Proactive in Life by Creating a Life Plan,*
https://www.getunstoppable.com/how-to-be-proactive-in-life/

CHAPTER 7:

GET PROACTIVE ABOUT HOW YOU ALLOCATE YOUR TIME OVER THE NEXT 365 DAYS

There's a famous saying:
*"Show me your calendar, and I'll show
you your priorities."*

N ow that you've gotten into the practice of Unstoppable Sundays, and have started to think through your attack strategy for the next 365 days, there's ONE EVIL THING IN YOUR LIFE that you've got to eradicate – and that's your calendar as it stands right now.

Whether we realize it or not, much of our lives is spent according to priorities set by others, who decide what they want us to be doing. Whether it is meetings at work, family commitments on weekends, or those work trips that we're endlessly on – we spend all those hours and days constantly REACTING.

Regardless of what we put on our to-do lists, despite our New Year's Resolutions, and notwithstanding the intentions we set at the beginning of the day – ultimately it is what is on our calendars that dictates how we spend our time.

So the question then becomes: What is on your calendar? Who is setting the agenda for how you set your time on your calendar? And, if you haven't spent 30 minutes each week to map out the week ahead, and at least a couple hours to map out your next 365 days, do you think you're making the most of your time ahead?

Let me ask you another set of questions. Where will you be spending Thanksgiving? Fourth of July? Christmas? Do you have your two weeks of vacation planned out through the year? How about Spring Break? Have you thought about strategically taking a few long weekends throughout the course of the year to pause, restore yourself, and make sure you're on the right track?

In the BEFORE part of my life, I didn't use my calendar as a proactive tool. And I wouldn't have been able to answer most of the questions I posed above. I was working hard, but not working smart. I was burning through the hours, but only to burn myself out. And worst of all, as the major holidays approached, anticipation of these dates only increased my anxiety level, because I didn't think to properly plan ahead and make the most of them.

In the AFTER part of my life, I became more purposeful about the goals I wanted to accomplish for the year; I started to pause and reflect on a weekly basis. But, most importantly, I began to set up my calendar to cater to my goals instead of others' goals. In the AFTER part of my life, I started to answer these strategic questions about my life and developed the habit of mapping it out ahead of time for the next 365 days:

1. Where, with whom, and how will I spend the major holidays? Here in the United States, these holidays include Memorial Day, Independence Day, Labor Day, Columbus Day, Thanksgiving Day, Christmas, and New Year's.

2. When will I be taking my one major vacation (even if it is a staycation) of the year? Where will I go? Whom will I spend it with?

3. How can I take time away every six to eight weeks, either because of a holiday or as a day off, so that I can pause, reflect, and course-correct on my plan for the year?

4. What are the necessities of life I need to take care of every four to six weeks to ensure I'm running in peak condition? Doctors' appointments? Haircuts? Massage?

5. What major conferences, networking events, and charity functions will I be attending throughout the next 365 days to broaden my network and increase my net worth?

6. What family-and-friends commitments do I have over the next 365 days? These include weddings, birthdays, reunions, etc. Will I prioritize them or decline with regret, based on my other priorities for the year?

7. Given what I've prioritized over the next 365 days, as well as my time commitments, will I be able to accomplish the goals I've set for myself?

You may first notice, as you read the set of questions above, that they're not your average "Do I go to my Monday morning team meeting?" type of calendar questions. These are broader, more strategic questions to answer about how you will spend the next 365 days of your life. These are questions that are designed such that, if you spend 30 to 60 minutes addressing them up front, in a proactive way, your answers will not only help you run the rest of your year smoothly, but your responses will also help you to be proactive and to prioritize the right things in your life.

You'll also notice that most calendar applications (like Microsoft Outlook or iCalendar on the Mac) aren't really designed to map out your year in this way. In fact, most calendar applications are designed for the exact opposite purpose: They're there for others to easily send you calendar invitations to events THEY think are important and to fill up your days.

So, to help you map out and become proactive about the next 365 days of your life, we've created a spreadsheet that helps you map out your whole year. This spreadsheet gives you a MACRO view of your 365 days, instead of being zoomed in to just this week – or, even worse, just today – which is how we often approach our calendars.

Using this spreadsheet, you'll be able to take a step back and ask yourself some important questions:

1. How many days of the next 365 are already committed? (hint: More than you think.)
2. How many of those commitments are actually important?
3. How many days have I set aside and committed to accomplishing my life goals?
4. How do I plan out the next 8, 12, even 24 weeks of my life so that I know to prioritize and be PROACTIVE about the most important things?

Once you've completed this exercise, you'll have realized and sorted through a few key things:

1. First, 365 days, or a year, feels like a long time. But when you really break it down, out of the 365 days, there are only 261 working days when you can actively work toward your goals both personal and professional. When you take away vacation days, you're down to 247 working days. And when you subtract sick days, down time, and family commitments, you're left with a mere 220 days, or roughly seven-and-a-half months out of every year to really take action on your goals.
2. Second, when we don't take a proactive approach to the 365 days, many decisions are made for us. We find ourselves signed up for a ton of commitments that take away even more of those 220 golden working days. It's no wonder we ask ourselves after a year of not hitting our goals: "Where did all the time go?!" Truth is there wasn't

a lot of time to begin with, and after that, others took the remaining time away from us, to be spent on activities that weren't necessarily aligned to our own goals.

3. Most important, you'll start to feel a sense of calm and control from having been able to hit head-on some of the tough questions about how you want to spend your year. I always share this spreadsheet with my loved ones so that we can have a discussion about how we want to collectively take on the year. Negotiations on "which parent's house" we need to spend Thanksgiving in become easier; having vacations planned ahead of time gives us something to count down to as we're grinding through the days to work on our goals; and, most importantly, we're able to keep ourselves honest regarding whether we are taking on and prioritizing the right goals for the year.

I open up my 365-day proactive calendar every week during Unstoppable Sundays, to review what's ahead and course-correct as I learn more. Most importantly, it always gives my family and me a sense of calm, because there is a real plan that everyone can rally around and look forward to. No one ever freaks out when there is a plan in place!

Now remember what we said about this book! This book is not meant to be a piece of art that sits on your bookshelf or one that just gets forgotten. So grab a pen, and let's work through what you've processed through this chapter.

Chapter 7,
Questions to Ask Yourself

Have you taken stock of all the time commitments you have through the course of the year? Where will you spend Thanksgiving? Long weekends? Are there critical trips that you have for this year that you still need to plan and account for?

If you could, what are the three key things you'd proactively schedule for yourself throughout the course of the year? Vacations? Long Weekends? A half-day to check in on your goals? A girls' or guys' trip?

What would happen if you mapped out your time commitments and also time for yourself ahead of time in a proactive way instead of having to tend to it last minute?

Chapter 7,
Actions to Take

☐ Make a list of all of your big time commitments for the next 365 days.

☐ Make a list of the trips, activities, and time you'd like to schedule FOR YOURSELF for the next 365 days.

☐ Download our 365-day calendar template, set it up, and start to commit to creating a proactive 365-day schedule for yourself: https://www.getunstoppable.com/templates/365-day-calendar

☐ Onwards!

Chapter 7,
Bonus Materials

- Watch my episode on *How to Avoid Burnout,*
  https://www.getunstoppable.com/burnout

- Watch my episode on *My New Years Resolution and Goals for 2019,*
  https://www.getunstoppable.com/my-new-years-resolutions-for-2019/

CHAPTER 8:

GET A CLEAR AND PROACTIVE VISION OF "YOU" FIVE YEARS FROM NOW

"Most people overestimate what they can do in one year and underestimate what they can do in ten years."

— BILL GATES

I agree. This is why it is super important that you start to take a longer view on life and what you want to accomplish. But before we get into that, let's just take a moment and recognize how far we've come in your journey toward thinking about living a more proactive life.

- **In Chapter 5,** we introduced you to the idea of practicing Unstoppable Sundays, as we taught you to reflect on and plan for your upcoming seven days.
- **In Chapter 6,** we helped you zoom out and start to think about your one-year plan by answering a set of very pointed questions that help you practice gratitude, assess where you are today, and then start to lay out a plan for the next 365 days.

- **In Chapter 7,** we introduced a new tool that you can use to become proactive about the 365 days you're given every year, so that you can be proactive about how you spend your days and months in a given year and can make tough trade-offs on what you spend your time on versus not.

Listen, before I set out to write this book, and before I set out to create an online course on living a more proactive life, I first became aware of the statistics:

- Only 15 percent of people who purchase a course or book about making a change in their lives actually complete it.
- 92 percent of people who set goals never actually achieve them, according to a research study conducted at the University of Scranton.

The reality is that the world has a lot more DABBLERS than DO-ERs. A very small percentage of the population is actually ambitious. The reality is that all the statistics show that you'll have downloaded this book, will have read parts of it, and yet you won't make a single change in your life.

Nevertheless, here are some statistics that are even more daunting, and the reason why I still thought it was worth a shot to write this book and inspire at least 1,000 people to be more proactive in their lives:

- 40 million people today are suffering from anxiety,
- 14.8 million people are suffering from depression,
- and 7.7 million people are suffering from post-traumatic stress disorder.
- In 2016 alone, the U.S. spent 446 billion dollars on medications – almost half of the global market.

The reality is that people are hurting: They're feeling anxiety and depression, and they're struggling to find true meaning in their lives. And yet they struggle to take the decisive action necessary to break free. More than half of the battle, I believe, is that people aren't given a practical framework for taking action and making changes in their lives. (That is where this book comes in.) And the other half of the battle is that your friends and your family won't let you. (More on this in the next chapter.)

Why say all of this now? Well, if you've reached this chapter, or if you've skimmed this far ahead, that means you've got a chance. You've got a chance to be one of the select few on this planet who can break free, take decisive action, and make necessary and critical changes in your life.

And so that's why I'm here checking in with you. Have you started to practice Unstoppable Sundays? Have you started to think about the next seven days? Have you answered some of the tough questions about what you've accomplished, and started to lay out goals for the next 365 days?

It's easy to read a book. It's easy to dabble. It's harder to actually DO what's necessary to make the changes and go punch your goals in the face.

But you know what's harder? Lack. Not having enough. Or even worse, poverty.

You know what's harder? Regret.

You know what's even harder? Not being able to live the life that you know you deserve.

All of those things are harder. Much harder, than actually facing your reality and taking essential action to go chase down your goals.

You now have a choice to make. You have to choose between being a DABBLER and a DO-er. Will you just continue skimming through this book? Or are you going to begin work? Are you going to start taking the steps that will change your life?

The next step in your journey of becoming Unstoppable is to develop a longer view of your life. When it comes to developing a long-term, proactive view of your life, you must look at life through three lenses (zoom levels, as I like to refer to them):

- How am I going to proactively spend the next week of my life? This is what Unstoppable Sundays are all about (Chapter 5).

- How am I going to spend the next 365 days of my life? I go through a very specific yearly planning process to define this (Chapters 6 and 7).
- And, finally: What do I want my life to look five years from now? This is your macro view. This one is super-important, because we tend to OVERESTIMATE what we can accomplish in a year, and we tend to grossly UNDERESTIMATE what we can accomplish in five to ten years.

There's a trick here. We first have you grab hold of your current situation by looking at seven days, and then at 365 days. Then, we'll have you start to think about the next five years. The longer view helps you break out of the current constraints in your life and start to think about the necessary transformations you can bring over the next half-decade to full decade. As you think through this, you'll then be able to go back to your seven-day and 365-day plans and start to tweak things. Don't stress about making this happen all at once; just focus on the act of thinking about these three different time horizons, and as you practice Kaizen and continue to improve on your plan, it'll start to come together beautifully. I promise.

To start to think through the next five years, you'll first answer a set of questions that helps you to reflect and learn from the five-year (similar to the one-year) exercise:

1. What are the things I am grateful for?
2. What are the things I am stressed about?
3. What are my key accomplishments over the past five years?
4. Looking back, what did I say I would accomplish in the past five years? How did this go? Are these goals still relevant?
5. Looking back, what are my strengths and secret powers? You've worked on quite a bit over the past five years: Identify the key skills and capabilities you've developed to a point of mastery.

Again, just as with the Unstoppable Sundays and 365-day exercises, don't overthink it. All that is important is that you articulate your thoughts on paper (or screen), so that they're not just percolating in your head.

Once you've completed these questions, you'll have (again) gotten a great handle on just how far you've come from five years ago. You'll have identified your significant accomplishments, the skills you've developed, and what you love spending time on versus what you'd like to do less of. Most importantly, you'll hopefully start to realize just how much you can accomplish over the course of a five-year span.

As the final step, you'll sit down and write out in story form (or letter form) a vision of yourself as you will be five years from now. I want you to sit and close your eyes. You today are grabbing coffee with a stranger. This stranger was introduced to you as a potential mentor who is wildly successful. A mutual friend thought the two of you should meet because you have similar values, goals, and aspirations, and she is much farther ahead and can help you.

So as you're grabbing coffee, the stranger starts to tell you her story. How does she spend her time? What does she do? What excites her? What are the goals that she is working toward? How does she look physically?

This stranger is actually you, five years from now – after having practiced nearly half a decade of **Belief x Discipline**. After nearly half a decade of Unstoppable Sundays, of planning out her years, and taking focused action in accomplishing her goals.

Write down the story of this person. Go into as much detail as possible and don't hold back. Don't let yourself be limited by what is possible versus what is not (because, remember, we tend to underestimate what we can accomplish in five to ten years). And keep writing until you feel an overwhelming emotion. That's when you'll know you've hit your true north about who you want to become.

As you round out your five-year vision for yourself, here are a few additional questions to ask yourself:

1. Does this feel true? Is there a part of this that Teenage You aspired to?
2. Zooming back into your one-year plan, and your next seven days, are you doing the things today that get you toward becoming this person?
3. What're the circumstances in your current situation that you'd need to eradicate or change in order to become a better version of yourself and closer to this vision of yourself?
4. What would you change about the priorities you've set for yourself for the next seven days to get closer to this vision? How about the next 365 days?

Use our template to work through this easily: To make it even easier to begin the practice of your five-year vision and strategy, we've created a simple template that you can use to get started quickly. You can download it here: https://www.getunstoppable.com/templates/five-year-vision

Much in the spirit of being proactive, you'll use this five-year North Star to guide your decisions going forward. How will you spend your next seven days differently? How about your next 365 days? If you continue to pause and reflect on your next seven days, tweak your plan for your next 365 days, and then enrich your vision for yourself over the next 1,825 days (five years), you can not only start to develop a personal strategy for your life, but you'll also be able to stay tethered to it and to improve it over time. Most importantly, you'll stop being a DABBLER and you'll become a DO-er.

Now remember what we said about this book! This book is not meant to be a piece of art that sits on your bookshelf or one that just gets forgotten. So grab a pen, and let's work through what you've processed through this chapter.

Chapter 8,
Questions to Ask Yourself

What was the last emergency that came up in your life where you had to completely reorder your schedule to tend to the matter at hand?

What did you do to recover from having to take time away for the emergency? How bad did it get? Were you able to get back on track and on schedule?

Creating a vision for ourselves and a plan for our lives never makes it to the top of our priority lists. And yet doing so can have such a profound impact on our lives, on our ability to provide for ourselves and our loved ones and our family.

What would happen if you treated creating this life plan for yourself like an emergency? What activities could you pause briefly to tend to this matter at hand?

Chapter 8,
Actions to Take

☐ Identify time on your calendar where you can take a half-day: perhaps it is time gained by skipping a party, or not watching a movie, or even by playing hooky from work... So that you can take some time, create some space, and tend to this urgent matter of creating a five-year vision for your life.

☐ Download our Five-year Life Plan template, set it up, and start to commit to creating a proactive five-year vision for yourself: https://www.getunstoppable.com/templates/five-year-vision

☐ Onwards!

Chapter 8,
Bonus Materials

- Watch my episode on *Visualize You 5 Years from Now*, https://www.getunstoppable.com/your-five-year-self/

- Watch my episode on *Jobs and Career in your 20s and 30s*, https://www.getunstoppable.com/career

- Watch my episode on *3 Ways to Invest in Yourself*, https://www.getunstoppable.com/3-ways-to-invest-in-yourself/

CHAPTER 9:

GET PROACTIVE ABOUT THE FIVE PEOPLE YOU SPEND THE MOST TIME WITH

"You are the average of the five people you spend the most time with."

— JIM ROHN

I n this final step, as you're hopefully deep into doing Unstoppable Sundays and executing on your life goals, I want to talk to you about your community of friends and family.

Who are the five people you spend the most time with? Are they as growth-minded as you? Are they taking a proactive approach to life? Truth is, unless you support yourself with other growth-minded people, you will not grow. The inertia is just too much.

In an earlier chapter, I mentioned that there are TWO key reasons why people can't switch from being DABBLERS to DO-ers. There are TWO key reasons why people can't switch from hoping and dreaming to actually achieving. These are the same TWO key reasons that account for the BEFORE in my life and the AFTER in my life:

1. The Dabblers don't have the right actionable framework to go make change happen.
2. The Dabblers don't have the people in their lives who push or inspire them to do it.

You need people around you who are constantly pushing you to do more and be more. I'm not talking about hiring an accountability coach, nor do I mean a best friend or partner who nags at you all day. I'm talking about people who are already performing at the level that you want to be at. They're the ones who are already living the life you want to be living – and just simply won't hang out with you unless you step up – because otherwise you'd just be slowing them down.

I'm not saying that this means you need to get rid of your best friends and family. I'm not. However, what I am saying is that if you want to be performing at a different level, you need to start spending more time with the people who are already performing at that level.

Which is why, as the final step of the book, I'm extending you a personal invitation to join our Unstoppable Sundays Facebook group at https://getunstoppable.com/facebook-group.

There's a reason why I bring this up only at the end. It's for people who are truly committed to becoming the best version of themselves and who are starting out on that journey – just like you.

Our community on Instagram of tens of thousands of people, over 4,000+ people who have gone through our guides, and my closest friends and I have joined and are committed to this group so that we can check in with each other every Sunday and check in on our progress.

In order for you to succeed in becoming Unstoppable, you must take stock of the people in your life and start to level up.

Now remember what we said about this book! This book is not meant to be a piece of art that sits on your bookshelf or one that just gets forgotten. So grab a pen, and let's work through what we've talked about in this chapter.

Chapter 9,
Questions to Ask Yourself

Who are the five people you spend the most of your work and leisure time with? A good trick to figuring this out is looking at your phone and seeing the five people you text the most often.

If you were to print out your wildest goals over the next five years and show it to each of them, how would they react? Would they laugh? Would they be skeptical? Would they think you're crazy? Who in the group would say, "Yeah... Let me show you my goals..."

If you were to look beyond your big five, and think about everyone you know, who is pushing him or herself and going after the same type of goals as you? Who is the person who is chasing down their dreams with the level of energy, belief, and discipline that is needed to actually achieve those goals?

Chapter 9,
Actions to Take

☐ Who are the people in your life who are holding you back from achieving your goals?

☐ Who are the people in your life who inspire you and are pushing as hard as you should be pushing to achieve the life they want for themselves?

☐ How can you respectfully and with love – spend less time with the people who are holding you back?

☐ How can you spend more time with the people who will propel you forward?

☐ What new communities, conferences, meetups, and/or online groups can you join with more like-minded people?

☐ Join our community and connect with others following the Unstoppable life: https://getunstoppable.com/community

☐ Onwards!

CHAPTER 10:

IN CONCLUSION, AND CONTINUING YOUR JOURNEY TO BECOME UNSTOPPABLE

I learned (almost too late) in my life that developing a PROACTIVE approach to my days led to a calmer me. A less frantic me.

I spent a significant part of my youth as a person who constantly wanted to do "what's right." I wanted to please others, especially my elders and my parents. I grew up inclined to think about optics and how things look, and I prioritized things that I thought would bring me happiness – but that ultimately failed to do so. I became incredibly great at setting and crushing goals, but they consistently turned out to be the wrong goals.

Through my 20s, I constantly did things based on what I thought society expected of me – or what I thought you were *supposed* to do. This desire to please others led to me marrying a wonderful person at the young age of 25 – which led to a divorce. It led me to pursue a job in finance that produced career success, but left me wholly unfulfilled. Ultimately, I discovered that I had created a life that was careening along at 90 mph on curvy roads, but at the end of the day, I found myself asking: *Is this it?*

Through this experience, I learned that while you can have anything you want, you can't have everything. So you better get proactive and pick what you want.

And so I made a change. I decided to become more proactive about my life. I decided to focus more on what was important to me and on my dreams, and I focused on substance instead of optics. Most importantly, instead of letting others or society as a whole set the agenda for my life, I started to be more proactive about my life. I made the changes necessary to follow a life path that was true to myself, one Unstoppable Sunday at a time.

As I crushed goals, moved the goalpost to bigger challenges, in my late 20s, and as I entered my 30s, I started to come to terms with a few realizations:

- If you set a goal and define a purpose, you can achieve anything that you want.
- You will never be perfect, you'll never nail the goal perfectly, but even allowing for the speed bumps along the way, with resilience you can accomplish anything and be Unstoppable.
- Not everyone will believe in you in the beginning, but you will never have to explain your success in the end; they'll come around.
- No matter your circumstances, socioeconomic status, level of wealth... Ultimately knowledge is power and with enough knowledge and grit you can accomplish anything. Fortunately for us, knowledge is widely accessible today.
- Given the above, you can indeed be Unstoppable in life, but you have to pay careful attention to what it is you choose to be Unstoppable in.

Through my 20s and 30s, I've worked at the world's largest hedge fund; I started a company from scratch and built it into a multi-million-dollar business while partnering with one of the world's best venture capital firms;

and I then sold that company (twice over) while working with the world's best enterprise software private equity firm. I finally started to unlock levels of success that felt right and true to my own path – all because I decided to become more proactive about life.

During this journey, and through my trials and tribulations, I picked up a specific set of skills and insights into what it takes to pick the right goals in your life, go after them, and win. I learned that it's not enough to know how to crush goals; it's equally important to pick the right goals – those that are true to yourself and your purpose on this planet. Most importantly, I learned that with anything worthwhile, there will always be bumps in the road, and that those who can build resilience and persevere will become Unstoppable in this life.

All of this wraps around the simple idea of being more PROACTIVE in your life through Belief and Discipline. Shockingly, none of this knowledge needed to be learned from experience. None of this knowledge is taught at schools. And yet it was plainly available in age-old books that were readily available – sadly, it isn't in plain sight to the average person.

Unstoppable is the movement I created to share everything that I've learned. It's the idea that with **Belief x Discipline**, you can be more proactive in life and achieve your wildest dreams. It's the idea that if we can take this common knowledge around designing and living a more proactive life, and if we persuade even 1,000 people to be ten percent more proactive, we will forever tilt the axis of the planet.

Unstoppable, today, is a movement spanning the globe – with thousands of people in our community at the time of printing – across Facebook, Instagram, YouTube, and our Website at (https://getunstoppable.com/community). Our globally distributed team hails from San Francisco, Dallas, India, Serbia, Philippines, and more – and we all come together every day to help inspire and teach people to live more proactive lives.

This life planning book is our first real educational system covering some of our most basic principles on how to design and live a proactive life – and we expect to do more. Thank you for being part of our movement, and I hope the core ideas we present in this book help you go on to practice Belief and Discipline every day, and go on to do incredible things for our planet.

If there is one core concept I want you to walk away with from this book, it is this: You can either let life happen to you, or you can take control of your life. Somewhere in the middle of that is a beautiful equilibrium where universal forces collude with your innermost desires to help you manifest the beautiful life you deserve. This equilibrium point is the perfect balance of being proactive and refusing what is not right for you, while opening up to what the universe is guiding you to.

In the beginning of this book, I made a simple promise to you: I'd teach you the tools I utilize regularly to live a more proactive life. These tools and processes unlocked over a decade of productivity and success for me, my career, and my family:

- **In Chapter 5,** I introduced you to the idea of practicing Unstoppable Sundays, where we taught you to reflect on and plan for your next seven days.
- **In Chapter 6,** I helped you zoom out and start to think about your one-year plan by answering a set of very pointed questions that help you practice gratitude, assess where you are today, and then start to lay out a plan for the next 365 days.
- **In Chapter 7,** I introduced a new tool that you can use to become proactive about the 365 days you're given every year, so that you can be proactive about how you spend your days and months in a given year, and make tough trade-offs on what you spend your time on versus not.
- **In Chapter 8,** I helped you really zoom out, take a long-term unconstrained view, and think about the next five years of your life and the vision you want to set for yourself.
- **In Chapter 9,** I walked you through the most significant impediment in your life relative to achieving your goals (the five people you spend the most time with).

Through every exercise, through every chapter, I stressed one thing: It doesn't have to be perfect.

The majority of the people on planet Earth do not bother to sit down to pause and reflect, and even fewer set goals and check in on them on a regular basis.

Even by starting to do this and by developing the discipline of practicing Kaizen on your personal life strategy, even by tethering yourself to a strategy and plan – you're putting yourself into the top of the planet's population.

So, it doesn't have to be perfect. What you DO have to do is the following:

1. Stop DABBLING and switch to becoming a DO-er.
2. Keep practicing Unstoppable Sundays and pause and reflect on your next seven days.
3. Check in on your 365-day goals every month and course-correct as necessary.
4. Keep honing in on your five-year vision for yourself and navigate toward that North Star.

I kept rinsing and repeating on these four key steps over and over and over for nearly a decade and accomplished and achieved the life that I always wanted. I want you to live that way, too.

And, most importantly, your journey doesn't have to be lonely. The Unstoppable Community is here to grow with you. Unstoppable, today, is a movement spanning the globe, with tens of thousands of people in our Community across Facebook, Instagram, YouTube, and our Website.

You can join the different parts of our community easily by going here: https://getunstoppable.com/community.

Our globally distributed team hails from San Francisco, Dallas, Serbia, Philippines, and more – and we all come together every day to help inspire and teach people to live more proactive lives. Follow us, join the conversation, and let's go tilt the axis of the planet.

Chapter 10,
Actions to Take

☐ Kick off another 45-day challenge to dramatically move forward a specific 365-day goal you've set for yourself. You can join our exclusive online 45-day beast mode course that helps you do exactly this: https://getunstoppable.com/beast-mode.

Belief x Discipline makes you Unstoppable

About the Author

TK Kader is a business builder, a life and business strategist, and an eternal optimist. He believes that you can achieve anything through belief, discipline and an Unstoppable strategy. Previous to leading the Unstoppable movement, TK worked at Bridgewater Associates (one of the best hedge funds in the world), then founded ToutApp (backed by Andreessen Horowitz and Jackson Square, two of the best venture capital firms in the world), sold it to Marketo (then owned by Vista Equity Partners, one of the best private equity firms in the world) and was part of the executive team at Marketo that helped drive its transformation and eventual $4.75bn sale to Adobe.

We're at the end, Dear Reader. I'm so incredibly excited for you.
Here's what you can do next.

SHARE THIS BOOK

Please write a review on Amazon and tell others who you think will enjoy this book. Spreading the word helps to reach new readers, grow this movement and the continued production of similar content.

START A 45-DAY UNSTOPPABLE
BEAST MODE CHALLENGE

You can also join our exclusive online 45-day Beast Mode Course that helps you dramatically move forward with a specific goal you've set for yourself as part of your life plan.

https://getunstoppable.com/beast-mode

PAY IT FORWARD

I wrote this book because I wanted to pay forward the blessings I received in my life and help others from my experiences. You don't necessarily need to write a book (although I hope that you do someday), but you can also pay it forward today by telling five friends about this book.

https://getunstoppable.com/pay-it-forward

SUED FOR PEACE

The Kurtherian Gambit 11

MICHAEL ANDERLE

COPYRIGHT

Sued for Peace (this book) is a work of fiction.

All of the characters, organizations, and events portrayed in this novel are either products of the author's imagination or are used fictitiously. Sometimes both.

DEDICATION

To Family, Friends and
Those Who Love
To Read.
May We All Enjoy Grace
To Live The Life We Are
Called.

Sued for Peace - The Kurtherian Gambit 11
Street Team

Beta Editor/Readers

Bree Buras (Aussie Awesomeness)
Tom Dickerson (The man)
Dorene Johnson (DD)
Dorothy Lloyd (Teach you to ask…Teacher!)
T S (Scott) Paul (Author)
Diane Velasquez (DD)

JIT Beta Readers

Heath Felps
Andrew Haynes
Kelli Orr
Leo Roars
Hari Rothsteni
Björn Schmidt

Editors

Stephen Russell
Kat Lind

Kurtherian Gambit Special Call-Outs

Troy Shafer (Thank you for sharing your family (How was U.T.?))
Joseph Anderle (Stop Slowing Down the Process!)
Jacob Anderle (Stop making the kitchen smell so good I want to
stop writing!)

**Thank you to the following Special Consultants
for RELEASE THE DOGS OF WAR**

Jeff Morris - Asst Professor Cyber-Warfare, Nuclear Munitions
(Thank God!)
Stephen Russell - Ideas & Suggestions
Heath Felps - USN
Dorene Johnson - USN (Retired)

DEDICATION

To Family, Friends and
Those Who Love
To Read.
May We All Enjoy Grace
To Live The Life We Are
Called.

Sued for Peace - The Kurtherian Gambit 11
Street Team

Beta Editor/Readers

Bree Buras (Aussie Awesomeness)
Tom Dickerson (The man)
Dorene Johnson (DD)
Dorothy Lloyd (Teach you to ask…Teacher!)
T S (Scott) Paul (Author)
Diane Velasquez (DD)

JIT Beta Readers

Heath Felps
Andrew Haynes
Kelli Orr
Leo Roars
Hari Rothsteni
Björn Schmidt

Editors

Stephen Russell
Kat Lind

Kurtherian Gambit Special Call-Outs

Troy Shafer (Thank you for sharing your family (How was U.T.?))
Joseph Anderle (Stop Slowing Down the Process!)
Jacob Anderle (Stop making the kitchen smell so good I want to stop writing!)

**Thank you to the following Special Consultants
for RELEASE THE DOGS OF WAR**

Jeff Morris - Asst Professor Cyber-Warfare, Nuclear Munitions (Thank God!)
Stephen Russell - Ideas & Suggestions
Heath Felps - USN
Dorene Johnson - USN (Retired)

FUTURE

The historian Ahrgri-vactix of the Ristorian Sept looked over the latest entry in his history of the Human Military Power, Queen Bethany Anne. She was a favorite of his. Not only was she still alive, but alive long enough that she had made history far back in his past, as well as his present.

He was writing a story and keeping as much of the truth of the story as he could. Part of his challenge was finding source material to recreate what must have happened on her planet, so many solar turns ago.

He reread his most recent entry and decided he liked it.

One of these days, he would have to ask his contact, Adam, how he knew so much of her history.

He started reading it one more time, and his satisfaction and pride grew as he read.

SUED FOR PEACE

PLA GENERAL STAFF HEADQUARTERS, BEIJING

The Chinese general walked into his conference room on his way through the door into his private office. He grasped the handle to open the door when he suddenly stopped. His right hand remained on the knob as he slowly turned his head back towards the table.

The table was black, polished to a high shine, and had the symbol for power inlaid in the center in gleaming brass. The table had room for ten, with another eight chairs set up around the walls for support personnel.

In the middle of his own room, in this well-protected PLA base, was a letter. A letter that hadn't been there when he left just two hours before.

Certainly not with a sharp knife impaling it into the wood between the brass lines of the symbol. He let go of the doorknob and took the four steps to approach the table. He leaned over to grab the knife.

It wouldn't budge.

The general used his left hand for leverage and pushed and pulled the knife back and forth several times before he could finally wiggle it free. He yanked it out and pulled the paper closer so he could read it.

His lips compressed as he read the words.

"There are two ways to stop my vengeance. You can kill me, or you can sue for peace. But you had better decide soon, or there will be nothing left of your military except machines blackened by fire and people praying for the souls of your dead."

CHAPTER ONE

EARTH ORBIT

Bethany Anne gazed at the beautiful blue globe beneath her. It was one of the few calming influences that helped her ground her emotions.

And TOM, of course.

Bethany Anne, I'm not blocking any emotions. You are handling the residual pain from Michael's... absence... on your own.

Thank you, TOM. I recognize the aching void, but I can deal with it.

Bethany Anne put her foot up on the little step made for her, cupped her chin in her hand, and rested her elbow on her leg.

I miss him, TOM, she admitted. *Not being able to kill those son of a-bitches who desperately needed it was a lot tougher than I thought.*

What about Johann?

TOM, what is the first rule of Johann?

That we don't speak about Johann? TOM replied immediately.

That's right. We don't speak about Johann's particular manner of death. To anyone. That was one individual that wasn't going to be allowed a painless death.

Is that what Joshua had?

Well, Barnabas took care of that ass. My emotional hands are clean of that one. I didn't realize Barnabas could trap a human in his own nightmare before I tossed him into the Etheric. If I had, I would have had Barnabas do it to a lot more of those self-serving cretins.

Johann?

No, I would have kept him for myself. I just needed to get cleaned up before anyone saw the blood on me.

You ruined another set of clothes.

Worth it.

Bethany Anne and TOM settled into a comfortable silence together before she spoke again.

You know, I understand why Michael put in the strictures. At least with those, you knew the penalties in advance. It also explained why no one wanted to be around him.

TOM gave a mental grunt in reply.

>>Bethany Anne, I have an incoming message from Dan Bosse.<<

Switch it to the speaker, please.

"Bethany Anne?" Dan's voice came over the Pod's speaker. "Are you sitting down?"

"I'm in space, Dan. Damned difficult to stand up in a Pod. It's not like we have a standing version," she said.

"Yeah, well, you can in the ones we put in the Space Station. But that isn't why I called."

"How bad is it?"

"Have you been told?" he asked.

"No, but you started with whether I was sitting or not. So, who is it, what are they trying to do, and what do you want to do about it?"

"We don't know who yet, but we have fourteen companies in five different countries that have been attacked, physically broken into by armed intruders. We have four casualties including three security guards and a woman in India."

Bethany Anne's eyes started shimmering red. "Is this the Black Cabal?"

"No, I doubt it. It's possible, but I think we have someone bigger."

"How the hell do you get bigger than those fucks?" she asked, her voice grating in anger.

There was a pause. "Bethany Anne, I think we're being threatened by a nation-state this time."

Bethany Anne switched into vampiric speed, thinking through the many permutations.

ADAM, find out which companies. Run through their surveillance video, try to track down the assailants' weapons and their operations for anything, including team member count, tactical weapons and gear, and what time they went in. Get back to me when you have that information. Also, check to see if there's any commonality between the companies.

Dan continued, not realizing Bethany Anne was already issuing orders to ADAM. "Frank walked in a few minutes ago, he wants to add some stuff. Here he is."

Bethany Anne could hear Frank clear his throat. "Hey boss, sorry to hear about the problems. We have a few more things to consider. I'm getting wind that some of the outsourcing companies we're using for materials and manufacturing are getting harassed. I've got some threatened in South America, Africa and one in Las Vegas, Nevada."

"What are they doing?" she asked him.

"I don't have full details, but at the moment it seems like local crime is trying a protection racket scheme. This time it seems they want both money and the prints for anything they're manufacturing."

Bethany Anne heard Dan's voice. "Another vote for the nation-state, BA." Then she heard a woman say that the company's lawyer was on the line for Dan, who said he would take the call.

Frank continued, "Well, it would make sense. So, they're probably funding local assets in-country. They pay them to focus their protection on our resources, and give them a spiff for acquiring technical prints."

"We need to know who this might be, Frank. Get with Dan and ADAM, I want to know as quickly as we can. Give me the names of those we lost and get with Ecaterina and Cheryl Lynn to provide support to their families."

Frank replied, "On it. Dan's back, here he is."

"Okay, just got off the phone with Jakob Yadav. He has a couple of close friends in the U.N., and it seems that some countries are getting pressure from their business interests. Specifically, governments are being pressured to refuse to work with us unless we share the technology, 'with the world, for the world.'"

"Any idea who's putting them up to this?" she asked. "And I don't believe it's for the world at all. Someone is doing a full court press. Could it be the U.S.?"

Dan replied, "I doubt it, the countries that are making the requests are either unaligned or have seen a significant amount of investment in the last two to five years from China."

Bethany Anne paused a second before continuing, "I'm not going to back down. If we are getting attacked by a country, I'll fight back at the same level. It won't be my preference, but if I have to go to war to deliver peace, it will be done."

Dan said, "Bethany Anne, I'm with you. From a small tarmac in Florida to distant galaxies, you got my back, I got yours."

A tear escaped Bethany Anne's eye. "I need the addresses where we lost people, also send Ashur, and Gabrielle's team, Dan." She paused for a moment to look at the beautiful blue ball hanging before her in silence.

"I'm coming down."

―――――

PLA OFFICES

"We have successful results from the raids, save one." General Sun Zedong turned towards his assistant and raised an eyebrow for him to continue. "There was an unexpected researcher who tripped an alarm before she could be silenced."

He nodded his understanding. "Any casualties?"

"No, sir. None of ours. Three guards and the research scientist for them."

Zedong asked, "Do we have the next targets?"

"Yes, sir," his assistant agreed. "The first teams are all safely out of the strike zones and are moving to secondary locations to regroup. The hit teams are in position for the two targets in D.C."

"Please make sure the council has been updated with this

and pass the acquired information to our R&D review team." General Sun nodded, pleased with their efforts so far.

General Sun had been brought in to deal with TQB. The Committee had given support and, more importantly for a Chinese general, introduced him to others who would be able to assist him as he went even higher in the PLA. With the Navy's failure to track and retaliate appropriately after the sub incident, he had been called to a very private meeting with those at the top of the Party CMC in control of the People's Liberation Army. He had been contacted by three senior generals who, he was led to believe, had been speaking with the chairman on this subject.

There were four areas of concentration, a common model among countries, which included diplomacy, intelligence, military, and economics. He was responsible for intelligence and military while others had responsibility for diplomacy and economics.

Zedong was aware that while he was powerful enough, he was also pretty damned expendable. This operation was going to be a pass-fail test for movement up the power ladder. Zedong knew enough to make sure his exit strategy was in place. He would use the new authority granted him to both implement his plan, and engage in a significant amount of relationship building and solidifying.

One way or another, Sun Zedong would be coming out of this a more powerful man.

———

HOSPET, KARNATAKA, INDIA

Nikhil Patel stood to one side, watching as the paramedics took the body of one of his researchers out on a stretcher, a white cloth draped over her.

In shock, he saw her beautiful, dead eyes staring out at the floor of her lab early this morning. Rushing out to the offices when he got word that the alarms had been tripped, he was struck dumb with horror and grief.

The alarm had been tripped internally, by Anjali herself, apparently.

Nikhil tried to hold back tears. She was the devoted wife of his close friend. Nikhil had been amazed his friend Talan had been able to keep the interest of a woman with her intellect and beauty. Nikhil had asked her about Talan once when the three of them were out for drinks. She told him that he could make her laugh no matter how bad her day had been.

Now, Nikhil doubted he would be able to stop Talan's tears.

Ever.

The police were inside the building, and Nikhil was outside trying to understand the purpose of this when he saw someone pointing up to the sky.

He turned to look up, shading his eyes from the morning sun, when he saw small black dots surrounded by the blue coming down towards them. In a few seconds, he could tell that they were slowing down.

And still coming right at them.

A few people standing in the parking lot started moving quickly towards the building as the objects paused their descent about a hundred feet up and then began to descend again, slower this time. The mysterious shapes moved carefully onto the parking lot where those people had been standing just moments before.

Nikhil's eyes opened wider when he finally recognized the shapes. These were the famous Pods, the gravitic transportation of Bethany Anne, the CEO of his company's parent company.

The top boss had arrived.

Nikhil unconsciously straightened his jacket as he walked towards the Pods. The first door opened, and a raven-haired beauty and a large white dog got out. She was dressed in black leathers with a jacket that barely concealed her pistols.

The woman stepped away from the Pod and looked around, as all but one of the Pods opened. Nikhil watched as many men and another woman stepped out.

Finally, the last Pod opened, and Nikhil gawked as the biggest man he had ever been near stood up. He was dressed all in black and many weapons were strapped on his body.

None of them were concealed. That man looked around before turning and offering a hand to the woman still inside. She pulled on his arm to step out and straightened up.

Nikhil swallowed. Here was the ultimate owner.

He noticed that her people spread out looking for threats when he found himself inside a circle that included him and his CEO, who was walking straight towards him.

She was wearing a modified suit. The pants were leather, her top some type of black spandex. Covering it up was a nicely tailored dark red jacket.

She held her hand out to him. "Mr. Patel, I'm Bethany Anne." Nikhil shook her hand, and she turned towards the ambulance. "Is Ms. Anjali inside the building or in the ambulance?"

"The ambulance, but I'm afraid she was killed," he said.

"I know, I'm going to pay my respects," she replied. He walked with her as she moved determinedly towards the ambulance.

One of the paramedics was about to close the door when he saw the people coming right at him. He looked around to see if they were walking to another destination but realized that the ambulance was their goal when a big black man separated himself and approached. Since they seemed focused on the ambulance's occupant, he stepped back. After all, there was no living patient to protect in that quiet enclosure.

The big black guard opened the door for Bethany Anne to step in. Nikhil was allowed to step inside with her before her guards blocked anyone else from getting closer.

He watched as she reached down to hold the corpse's hand through the sheet and pulled the top of the sheet down just enough to see Anjali's face. A lone tear tricked its way down her face.

Not thinking, Nikhil said, "She was pregnant, going to tell her husband Talan the good news tomorrow when both of their parents arrived." He sniffed once and wiped a tear from his eye. "She loved to read the old stories from other countries, from centuries in the past. If the baby was a boy, she wanted to name him Alexander." Bethany Anne turned to face him as he finished. "If it was a girl, she would name her Alexandra."

Nikhil saw something he would swear was true for the rest of his life.

His boss' eyes turned red.

She turned back towards Anjali's body and put her left hand on the dead woman's forehead, her voice deadly. "I swear to you, the sea will run red before I fail to avenge you and your unborn child's death. You have the Queen Bitch's promise."

After a few moments, when she looked at Nikhil again,

her eyes were normal in appearance. "Whatever Anjali's salary was, Mr. Patel, triple it and create a fund to help children learn to read the classics or whatever they want. Name it the Princess Alexandra fund in her unborn daughter's honor. Then, create another fund and make it ten times her salary and make monthly payments to her husband."

She stood up, and Nikhil asked, "Excuse me, but from where do you want me to pull the funds to make this happen?"

She turned towards him, vengeance clear in her eyes. "For now, from this company. But I will reimburse it from the accounts of those who stole her life. One way or another. They will pay it all." With that, she turned away and stepped back out of the ambulance.

"She was pregnant, John." Bethany Anne said into the silence inside the Pod. "They fucking killed an unborn child."

Inside with John, where no one in the world could see her unmasked, he popped the locks on his harness and turned to open his arms as Bethany Anne laid her head against his chest. "A child, John. She never got to tell her husband. For what?"

He felt her shoulders shake as she cried almost silently, the two of them flying towards destiny.

Ten minutes later, the team was gone. It wasn't until after they left that Nikhil wondered how his boss was so sure it was a daughter. Two weeks later, he was comforting Talan when his friend happened to mention the autopsy report said his wife had been carrying a little girl.

Nikhil felt cold chills run through his body.

CHAPTER TWO

SEVEN DAYS EARLIER, WASHINGTON, D.C. USA

It was half an hour past midnight when the President and two of his secret service agents walked the distance from the residential wing to the Deep Underground Command Center (DUCC) located adjacent to the West Wing. As they arrived next to a conference room, two of his security staff stepped out.

"David, is the other side secured?" the President asked the ranking agent who had just come through the door.

"Yes, I've locked the door from the inside and confirmed that both agents on the other door are there for the next six hours. There are no personnel authorized to come down from the other entrance," he confirmed.

"I only need an hour, probably less," the President said.

David smiled. "Sir, I doubt you'll need more than fifteen minutes. There isn't anyone who's going to make it through the other doorway, and between Rod and myself here, we swept everything from the other side to this door for anything, organic or electronic. There is no way, no how anyone is going to meet you in there."

The President smiled. "I'll tell you what, I'll bet you a dinner I'll have a meeting."

David regarded the President for a moment. "Okay, but I want the nicest, best-aged filet mignon and a baked potato soaked in butter." David looked around to make sure the three other secret service agents were listening.

"Agreed," the President said as he stepped to the door and turned to look at his men before closing it. "Remember, no one enters this door, either, gentlemen." With that, the President closed the door. Three seconds later, the door opened, and a hand stuck out. Secret Service Agent Mark Tims smiled and put the sports section from the newspaper into the waiting hand. Both the hand and the sports section disappeared and the door shut with a click.

David looked over at Mark. "I give him ten minutes, fifteen on the outside before he admits I'm right."

Mark looked back momentarily before turning to face towards the room and got into position. "Do you have any idea who he expects to meet?"

"Nope," David admitted. "Not that it matters. There isn't any way that someone is going to turn invisible, sneak through the entrance on the other side without our temperature and movement detectors alerting us, and bust the lock to get inside that room. Hell will freeze over first."

Mark shrugged. "You're probably right. Unless he was meeting the CEO of TQB Enterprises. They probably have some scary techno-shit."

David snorted. "Like she'd want to show up here in the States."

SUED FOR PEACE

———

The President sat down in the same chair he had the last time he met this person. That time, like this evening, was off the books, off the record and frankly, would never be admitted to at all.

He opened the sports to the second page to see the latest scores. He made it to page three when he sensed, rather than heard, someone in the room with him. He looked up to see her eyeing him, a little smile on her face. She was wearing a pair of dark jeans, a red camisole and a black jacket. She didn't have on any jewelry, but then, she didn't need any.

The President smiled. "Well, looks like I won the bet."

"Oh? What bet would that be?" she asked him as she walked over to sit facing him.

"Whether I would have a meeting in here or not," he said. "Although I'm going to have to play like I lost the bet. At some point, I should throw a fit over how you keep standing me up." He grinned. "But since these meetings aren't on the record, how would that work?" The President closed the sports section before asking, "Just curious, how did you get in here?"

Bethany Anne raised an eyebrow. "While it isn't at the level of a national secret, I do have a few important ones." She smiled and continued, "Maybe someday I'll take you on a walk that will change your life."

The President laughed and shook his head. "I'm not sure my wife would like me to take any walk that could change my life. She's told me at least three times every week since I came into office if I decide to run again, she'll castrate me, or I'll be sleeping on the couch for the duration of my time in office."

He sobered. "But if there's a way to get in here that others can use, I'd be incredibly appreciative if you explained it."

Bethany Anne shook her head. "There is no way for another living person to enter using the means I do. Should that change, I'll give you a warning device of some sort to help."

He shrugged. "Best I'm going to get?" She nodded her answer. "Okay. How about the next item on the agenda? What's this about a real Illuminati?"

Bethany Anne leaned forward. "There's an offshoot of the original Illuminati group, a splinter if you will, which was responsible for the attack on our facilities in Colorado and the backpack nuke. They're also behind many different plots against TQB, trying both legal and illegal means to acquire our technology."

"You know that's true for damn near any major company in the world and most of the minor countries, right?" he asked her, wondering how she would answer.

"I'm entirely aware of their desires, Mr. President." Bethany Anne considered how much to share before continuing, "I'm mindful of most attacks and plans, most secondary plans and their follow ups. I'm not trying to upset the world. That's the reason for not using our technology to disrupt the world's economies in the first place. However, I won't simply stand by and allow my people to be threatened. That's not in my nature."

"A lot of think-tank scientists are trying to figure out what your nature is, exactly."

"In what way?" she asked.

He paused a moment. "Well, are you human?"

Bethany Anne started chuckling. "I was born on this planet with two human parents. If that doesn't make me human, I'm not sure what would clarify it further."

"Well, parental names?" he pressed.

She put up a finger. "Mr. President, I do this as a favor to you, not as an opportunity for you to play twenty questions."

He shrugged. "You can forgive me for trying. I do have the responsibility of four hundred million people to look after."

Bethany Anne's face sobered. "Mr. President, I'm concerned with the seven and a half billion on Earth, and those coming after us. My parents' names aren't going to accomplish much except to give some annoying researcher more useless information to try and analyze me. If you want my thoughts on something, you can ask." She pulled a USB flash drive out of her jacket. The President didn't fail to notice the small pistol and holster she was wearing.

He wasn't accustomed to having anyone with weapons around him but Secret Service agents. If any of the guys on the other side of the door knew he was talking with an armed woman just a few feet away, they would be trying to break down the door to protect him. He smiled.

"This is..." she started before her eyebrows drew together in confusion. "Why are you smiling?"

"I'm just thinking how my protective detail," he jerked a thumb over his shoulder, "would react if they knew I had an armed person sitting in here with me. It amused me to imagine them trying to bust down the door in frustration." He smiled at her and said, "Sometimes, it's the little things I think about that bring a smile to my face." He pointed to his hair. "I take my enjoyment where I can get it, I wasn't expecting to go gray quite so fast."

Bethany Anne put the USB flash drive on the table. "Talk to me when you get out of office if I'm still around, and I'll help you with that." She slid the USB to him. "On here are the names of the members in the United States and all of your territories. There are thousands in total, although there are probably no more than a hundred and twenty-five that I would rate as the highest priority to review. Those are tagged."

>>**A hundred and twenty-seven.**>>

I know that, ADAM. What have we talked about when being exact with humans?

>>**That to always be precise points to you not being human.**<<

If an AI could sound miffed, ADAM was accomplishing the feat pretty well, she thought. *Yes, so while you're an Entity, and you're working to accomplish the most incredible feats ever for me, I need you to understand that if you grease the wheels, it will help reduce trouble. Make sure you update the EVE project for me with that understanding.* She thought quickly, *Except in battle, you don't fudge anything during battles.*

>>**I understand and will make the adjustments.**<<

The President eyed the USB drive. "I'm not going to like what's on that, am I?" He reached to take it. "Pandora's box?"

"Some, not all of it. Some of the people on that drive are just family, people who can be used to blackmail other people to get them to do what the Black Cabal wants them to do." When he raised his eyes to her, she explained further, "My name for them."

He nodded his understanding. "What should I do about General George Thourbourah?"

"Well, his boss is out of the equation. Don't ask about him if you want plausible deniability. George believes I was seriously hurt, but that will go by the wayside the next time I'm photographed."

"Oh, earlier than that," he assured her. He shrugged at

her raised eyebrow. "We have assets that track all important people. That could mean important for any number of reasons: you just happen to trip a few of them including financial, technological and security."

ADAM.

>>Yes?<<

Find out how many countries are tracking me, and start planting information that shows me everywhere so that they can never tell what's the right answer.

>>When do you want this to occur?<<

Can you make it happen retroactively so that the information seems like it happened before this conversation?

>>Not easily, no. Countries will have a paper trail.<<

Damn. Okay, figure out the countries' data feed and start adding additional false positives if you can. I suppose changing their data would alert them that you're in the system.

>>Not to mention it might be too risky, unless you believe this must occur?<<

No, it isn't that big of a deal. I just didn't realize I'm on various countries' morning reports, and it bugs the shit out of me.

TOM?

Yes?

What are you working on at the moment?

Still on the gravitic issues with Marcus.

Please add a request to your queue about considering what it would take to change someone to look like me.

I can answer that question already. The Pod-doc can't do it. It works on the person's DNA, so it isn't going to change another person to look like you.

But I thought since you can change the structure of the

materials in a body, this might be possible?

That was changing the design, not how you look. The Pod Doc hasn't been set up to change a person.

Wait a minute, TOM—you paused! I sense you thinking about something, 'fess up.

Well, if a patient is considerably damaged physically or their DNA has been corrupted, the Pod-doc can use a super-set of DNA to try and fix them. Doing it that way would certainly change the person as they heal.

So, it's feasible?

Yes, but not very recommended.

Okay, I'll push that idea off to the side.

Are we good?

Yes, sorry. I don't like being a target, and I figured if there were copies, it would be hard to confirm which version is me.

It would be the version with four large guards walking around her, he quipped.

Did you just zing me... again? she asked, amused.

Yes and here's your sign, he added in a Southern drawl.

You ass!

She heard his version of a chuckle as he withdrew from their conversation.

That's another one I owe you, she thought privately.

Bethany Anne returned to the President's conversation. Her conversations with ADAM and TOM were over so quickly he didn't register the pause. "When you find a suitably safe computer to review the contents of the USB drive, you'll find incriminating evidence on a lot of powerful and influential people. I have also included general information on critical people in your allies' governments and significant industries. You can distribute it as you think best."

The President looked down at the USB drive he was holding. "Truly Pandora's box, then. I can't say I'm happy with the present you've delivered."

Bethany Anne shrugged. "Well, you could destroy it and go on your merry way."

"No," he sighed. "I can't. I have a duty and however distasteful it is, I'll see it done." He looked at her. "How do you handle stuff like this?" he asked as he lifted the USB drive and waved it a little.

"I have people responsible for tracking down the truth and bringing those guilty to justice," she admitted, wondering what the President would say.

"What about juries, judges, and the rest?"

Her grim face told him the answer. "Mr. President, in the harshness of space, you don't allow stupidity." She wasn't about to fess up regarding Barnabas and Tabitha. "So we have a strict policy. While we aren't a hundred percent effective, almost all of the people with us are focused on a bigger goal than just working for their own ends. So, there's a significant amount of self-policing. Those that we miss?" She paused. "They're warned, and they are adults. We treat them as such."

"You don't have a positive opinion about our court system?"

"Do you?" she countered.

"Well, I think it's the best thing we have going at the moment."

"Let me ask you a question. What are the two things that drive people?"

"Fear and greed, usually," he answered.

"So, take that to the logical conclusion. At a certain age, an adult will be driven by fear, greed, or a challenge—something bigger than themselves. Fear of repercussions for actions they have taken is a strong motivator for not committing punishable offenses. If the system for punishment is broken, then the power of fear diminishes, and you have more and more people shrugging off the threats and acting anyway. But people learn quickly. Greed can be considered in a positive light. I'm not talking about wanting more money or power, I'm talking about being greedy or desiring something good in your life that benefits yourself and others. What about the person who's greedy about wanting to be in space? They have to prove themselves deserving that position, of protecting not only themselves but others. Everyone depends on what a person is willing to do to save everyone else."

"That works when you take the best of society that wants to get ahead," the President stated.

"No, it works when you stop supporting those who do nothing."

"That isn't a very Christian attitude."

She smiled at him, like a cat looking at a mouse. "Christian? I'll give you a few things to ponder, Mr. President. Look them up when you have time. '*The appetite of the laborers works for them; their hunger drives them on.*'" She continued, "And the best yet. A quote by the Apostle Paul, who said to those in Thessalonica, '*We were not idle when we were with you, nor did we eat anyone's food without paying for it. On the contrary, we worked night and day, laboring and toiling so that we would not be a burden to any of you... For even when we were with you, we gave you this rule: The one who is unwilling to work shall not eat.*'"

She leaned back in her chair. "Do you have some idle hands? Then dream bigger for your country. Give them something to use their minds, their strengths, their abilities and stretch your people. Make them earn their keep, and then they'll have pride in themselves. If some don't? Well, be a man and strap a pair on—if you need a pair you can borrow my ovaries. Your infrastructure needs fixing! You have the ability to create work centers by the thousands. You need to fucking dream bigger. We are human beings. Every one of us has worth, talents and skills. Fucking put them to use! Stop taking the easy way out and punting the problem to the next generation. Don't support a nation of people sitting on their asses and taking money from those who work without trying to make it better. Make a change, even if it's just starting the change before you step out of office."

The President had nothing to say in response. While he didn't doubt she knew the difficulties of making this happen, she also wouldn't care that it was a challenge. He pursed his lips and nodded his head sharply.

She stood up and faced him, both hands held up as if in supplication. "Don't give up, don't accept mediocrity, don't accept the status quo. You're the most powerful man on this planet. Now, fucking act like it." She stepped backward and disappeared right in front of his eyes.

It took the President a few moments to come to grips with someone disappearing like that. He pondered her comments, her challenge. Standing up, he turned towards the door. Stopping briefly, he looked over his shoulder and whispered, "I may be the most powerful man on earth, but you are certainly the most powerful woman."

With that, the President turned back to open the door. Once he stepped outside, he sighed dramatically before admitting to David that he owed him a steak dinner.

WASHINGTON D.C. USA

"Congressman Richards!" Mark Billingsly called out. The tall man with shocking blond hair turned to see who had called him on the street outside of his office building.

A man smiled at him. Terry Richards thought he looked familiar and the two women behind him, one with a camera, were certainly attractive enough. Congressman Richards decided to stop and turn around to speak with them. Maybe he had seen the Hispanic-looking reporter before? They certainly weren't here on the Hill very often.

The cute short woman lifted a camera up, first pointed away from him, and he acknowledged the camera. When he did that, she turned it back around towards him. That was an unexpected courtesy, and he was pleased by the consideration.

Terry turned on his million dollar smile. Well, at least it should be a million dollars, as he had well over fifty thousand dollars of dental work to make it pretty damned perfect. The male reporter stepped closer to him and looked a little towards the camera, so Terry stepped slightly sideways and joined the reporter looking into the camera.

"Hello! My name is Mark Billingsly, and I have with me Congressman Terry Richards from the great state of New York." Terry smiled at the audience and wondered if this was going to be a conversation about his solar energy initiative, or the cleanup they were accomplishing around New York City water pollution.

Mark turned just slightly in towards Terry. "Congressman Richards, I appreciate you taking time out of your busy schedule to answer just two questions for us. The first, of course, is a question about the use of solar energy and the advancement of the funds to implement such a system in to-day's climate."

"Certainly, Mark," Terry aimed his mouth a little towards the microphone on the camera, but kept his eyes on Mark except for a couple of glances to the camera. "Right now is the time we all have to focus on expanding our renewable energy usage. With oil such a highly volatile product and the use of oil in manufacturing harmful to the environment, we need renewables such as solar energy to become a viable alternative. As long as we have the sun above us, we will be able to depend on solar power to help us achieve ongoing energy independence." Terry waited for the softball follow-up question, and the reporter asked it.

"So… everyone agrees that solar energy is pretty inefficient right now. Yet you believe that we as a country, and specifically New York, should fund the development and manufacturing of solar installations as a way to create energy independence from foreign countries?"

Well, this wasn't the softball question Terry expected, but he could handle it easily enough. "Certainly. When you only depend on the sun, which is up above your own nation, not oil drilled out of the ground thousands and thousands of miles away, you have options. The option to continue to depend on the sun above us. Or the political and military expedients that continue to infect the machinations of countries that are oil rich. They're constantly trying to involve the U.S. in their problems, as we are so heavily dependent on their oil. Right now, I'm fighting for a future of energy independence. This requires an investment by the government. It may take twenty years to recoup the investment, but I believe we need to focus on the long view. A long view that is sorely lacking in the House and only slightly better in the Senate."

Damn, he was on a roll! He was going to ask for a copy of this interview.

"Right now, Congressman Richards, of the top solar component manufacturers, five are Chinese, two are Korean, two are here in the U.S. using parts from what country—we don't know, and one is Canadian. I'm curious, Congressman Richards, if the use of so many manufactured panels from a foreign country concerns you in any way?"

Terry smiled, not sure where the reporter was heading, but who cared? "Certainly not, Mark, when the solar panels are accumulating the sun," Terry pointed up and winked at the camera, "above our own heads, I'm not sure I worry about a foreign country turning off the lights, so to speak, in our part of the world."

Mark nodded sagely at everything Terry said. When the congressman finished, he asked, "So, the fact that the foreign-made components inside the majority of solar energy products could have a kill switch in them, easily controlled by a foreign country, and possibly rendering them useless as an energy provider doesn't bother you?" Mark took the surprised look on the congressman's face as an opportunity to nail him. "And in this future," Mark mimicked the man's previous gesture by pointing up. "Where we only have to depend on the sun above us, we should trust that no kill switches were put in place by any of the solar component manufacturers. Even when these organizations include those from governments that have not demonstrated any concern for our country's well being?"

The congressman's smile seemed a little strained. "Well, I don't think we need to look behind every bush and find an evil plan to take over America, Mark," Terry answered, in an effort to defuse the conversation.

SUED FOR PEACE

"But Congressman Richards," Mark set him up. "When you personally take over $232,532 in donations from lobbyists who have themselves been hired by these same Chinese solar component manufacturers, does it not cause a conflict of interest? Many of your donations were received the very same day you had meetings with those lobbyists, interestingly enough. You don't believe that these companies, these solar manufacturing companies, have ulterior motives?"

"Of course not!" Terry exclaimed, smiling with everything he had. "The use of donations to facilitate an independent energy effort should be applauded." Terry turned towards the camera. "I want to thank you both for such an excellent opportunity to continue the discussion of how solar power will support the energy independence of the American people. Good day!" With that, he waved and continued down the street, making his escape.

Mark turned towards the camera. "We appreciate the good Congressman Richards, himself a recipient of almost a quarter of a million dollars of lobbyists' money, giving his views on the switch to solar energy. Money focused on the continued use of solar panels and components manufactured in China. That in itself is not a bad thing, but when almost all of the core infrastructure that makes this country work can have concealed kill commands inside them, it puts America at risk. These back doors could fry the component circuitry in an internet attack, instantly destroying all energy acquisition and distribution without the option of physical replacement. Well, it seems a little worrying that no one is considering the ability of a foreign country to wreak havoc with our needed and necessary infrastructure without one bomb being dropped."

Mark turned to look off camera in the direction the

Congressman continued to walk. "And let's not even begin to discuss the significant and unique electrical pieces that require manufacture in China itself." Mark looked back towards the camera. "Pieces that once destroyed, will keep your city dark for months or significantly longer if we should be at war."

Two blocks away, Terry Richards pulled out his cell phone and punched in a number. This phone number was memorized and was restricted to a single use. Halfway around the world, after seven different forwards to hide the eventual destination, a woman picked up the phone. "Hello?"

"This is T.R., I've been questioned and had my connections and exact funding delivered to me in detail by a reporter. You told me this wasn't possible!" he fumed.

"Was the group headed by a male reporter?" the woman asked.

"Yes! Mark Billingsly and two women," he answered while looking for cars before crossing the road.

The woman responded in a calm tone, "You are the third concerned citizen to ask about this situation. You know what they say in America about three strikes?"

Terry said, "Yes."

"Well, don't expect to receive another request for an interview," she replied.

"Fine, that works for me. What about the video?"

"We'll work on it. Give us time is all I can say to that question."

"Understood, goodbye," Terry said as he hung up and closed the phone.

In a foreign country, a colonel hung up the phone and turned in her seat. She was part of the approximately seven and a half percent of the PLA that were responsible for long-term foreign investment. She picked up the phone and made another call. "I need the approval to send out a cleanup squad."

CHAPTER THREE

QBS POLARUS, PACIFIC OCEAN
HEADING TOWARDS CHINA

John Grimes walked into the shared space where he and his guys had their rooms. Darryl gave him a nod from the couch. Scott and Eric were getting set up to arm-wrestle. "Eric, why are you doing this to yourself?" John asked. "We both know Scott's going to eat your lunch."

Eric grunted as Darryl said, "Go," and the contest was on. Eric's biceps were massive, easily dwarfing most men's. But he wasn't budging Scott, who was steady, holding Eric's other hand under the arch of their two arms clasped in a titanic struggle of strength.

"You know," Scott told Eric, smiling. "We can stop now, and you can walk away with your manhood intact."

"Huh," Eric grunted, trying to get Scott to lose focus so he could drive his arm down in a sudden burst.

He barely moved Scott's hand a half-inch.

"I'll take that as a 'no,'" Scott grinned. "Ready to give me twenty pushups?"

Eric ground out, "I'll give you twenty pushups when you stop being such a weak-ass bitch."

Darryl warned him, "Don't let Bethany Anne hear you use that lame-ass name."

All of the men turned towards the door when they heard Bethany Anne's voice arrive right before she turned the corner into their room. "I did hear that lame-ass name, and after Eric gives Scott twenty, he can do another twenty-five while I stand on his back."

Eric's eyes opened slightly before they darted back to his grip with Scott, who was still paying attention to Bethany Anne over his shoulder. Eric drove his shoulder into the challenge and caught Scott off-guard. Scott barely stopped the sudden drive halfway down to the table, his knuckles mere inches from touching the wood.

"You..." Scott started speaking through clenched teeth as he tried to offset Eric's better leverage and damned impressive effort to drive his hand down. "Are... a... bloated...." Scott's arm started rising, an inch for every word. "Semen... packing... animal... fondling... fuckfaced... cockthistle... cockroach... ass... bandit!" With the final word, Scott slammed Eric's hand down on the table, making sure he would feel that pain for a while.

Eric pulled his hand back and started massaging his knuckles. "Shit, you pig, that fucking hurt."

"Not as bad as these heels on your back," Bethany Anne said. The two men looked around the side of the table.

She had on three-inch heels.

Scott looked over at Eric's face, his jaw dropping in surprise. Scott grinned as he said, "Damn dude, those are going to hurt."

Eric looked back up to Bethany Anne's face. "Isn't that going to be a bit much?"

"No, a bit much might be me lifting something while I'm standing on your back to increase the weight."

Darryl spoke up from the couch, "I'll volunteer, you can lift me!"

Eric flipped Darryl off, his hand carefully blocked from Bethany Anne's view by the table.

She turned towards Darryl and said, "I said something, not someone." She walked over to the couch and sat down. "Before you do your pushups, Eric, I have a request of you guys." The four men joined her. John sat next to Bethany Anne, Eric beside Darryl, while Scott took the chair. Akio was out at the moment.

"The ladies have come up with a way to potentially help us in the PR department, make money for a charity, and apparently, have a good time. Well, at least the ladies will have a good time."

"Why do I sense a 'but' arriving soon?" John asked, looking sideways at Bethany Anne.

She opened her mouth, then closed it again. Finally, she opened it again and said, "Because I didn't expect this and I've got to say I'm sorry in advance. So, I'm sorry." She turned to John. "But you guys are going to get thrown under the bus on this one."

"You want us to do it, regardless?" John asked. "I'm assuming that since it's for charity, I'm not being shot, so I'm in. What do you want us to do?"

The guys all looked towards Bethany Anne, who was obviously having a hard time with this request. Coming from the lady who chewed up and spit out Forsaken for breakfast, their curiosity was in overdrive. Scott glanced towards Darryl and Eric before Darryl minutely shrugged his shoulders.

Bethany Anne put her hands on her knees and took a deep breath. "Okay, I'm just going to say it. The girls want you guys to do a pinup calendar." She exhaled noisily and looked around at her team.

John pointed to Scott, then Darryl, Eric and finally himself. "You want us four to pose for a pinup calendar?" he asked, the question clear on his face.

"Yes," she admitted, her voice a little higher than normal. "Oh God, fine!" she blurted out. "They want you to do a beefcake calendar!" She threw her hands up. "No shirts, tiny underwear, baby oil and in like, four countries in twenty-four hours." She put her hands over her face. "I've created a set of monsters." She mumbled through her hands, "It started with Jean Dukes."

"Jean?" Darryl said. Bethany Anne nodded.

"What did Jean have to do with this?" John asked.

"What didn't she have to do with this?" Bethany Anne retorted. "She came up with the idea and rallied the other women to get behind it. Then Cheryl Lynn got involved, and Patricia was asking questions." Bethany Anne pulled her hands from her face to look at John. "Did you guys know you have fan clubs?"

John's blush told her everything she needed to know. She pointed at him, then the other three. "You guys know you have fan clubs?"

They all tried to keep their faces from showing anything, but finally, Darryl gave up and just smiled broadly. His grin was contagious, and soon they were all laughing. "Bethany Anne," Darryl said. "We're the Queen's Bitches, of course, we're going to have fan clubs!" Eric turned and high-fived Darryl. Scott just laughed.

John spoke while pointing at Eric and Darryl. "Those two asswipes have been making bets on who can get more fans. But someone leaked pictures of Scott without a shirt on, and he got something like three thousand in twenty-four hours."

"Unbelievable," Bethany Anne murmured looking at them. "So, you guys don't have a problem with this?"

"Well, are we going to have to get rid of the chest hair?" Eric asked. "Because, I'm a hunk of burning love, but I'm not sure I can handle having a wax job. Scott and I watched the *Forty-Year-Old Virgin* Tuesday night. I'm pretty sure I'm going to be just as big a baby as that guy was." He rubbed his chest in a circular motion. "I don't think anyone can Photoshop a bad wax job off all this!"

"Hell, just have a woman running her hands through that chest hair, a few girls will get jealous and perk up!" Scott tossed out.

"Hell yeah!" Eric's eyes lit up, and he turned to Bethany Anne. "What's our budget for this? Can I hire a model or two to pose with me?"

Bethany Anne stared at the man, dumbstruck. "You want models in your beefcake pictures?" She turned to them. "You do realize this is a calendar for women, right?"

"Well, The Fire Department of New York is doing one. Guys on one side, girls on the other." John said before realizing he might have given too much information away. He got a surreptitious glare from Scott.

"What?" Bethany Anne turned towards John as John watched Scott put up his fingers to his head and act like he was shooting himself as he rolled his eyes behind Bethany Anne.

"Well," John ad-libbed, "I was looking into New York after our little episode there a few months ago, and I ended up on a website that was talking about the new addition of women from the Fire Department doing a calendar. And… Uh…" John faltered, trying his best for slightly embarrassed. "Well, for research purposes I went to go see what the women's pictures might look like." He shrugged as the guys all smiled at his discomfort.

Knowing full well if they didn't pull this off, there would be hell to pay later.

"I'll tell you what, how about you guys agree to the beefcake, but I'll say there's a condition that the women have to do a few poses for a personal calendar that can only go to you guys. That way, they can put up or shut up."

Scott grinned. "Hell yeah!" Then he asked, "Do we get to choose?"

"Choose?" Bethany Anne turned to him. "And who would be on your list, Mr. English?"

Scott's face went red, "Uh… who's in the group again?"

"Uh huh…" she smiled. "Okay guys, I want you to think of who you would like in the calendar!" She clapped her hands twice, loudly. "Come on! You know who it is!"

The guys all looked at each other when she started laughing and stood up. "Oh my God. This is priceless!" She walked towards the door, "Don't forget your pushups, Mr. Escabar. I'll have Scott stand on your back in my place. He doesn't have heels!" She waved over her shoulder to them and exited their rooms.

Once she was gone, the guys turned to each other, confusion on their faces.

"Does she know we bugged the last meeting?" Eric asked.

John turned back to look at the door and his missing boss and admitted, "I don't think so, this is much worse."

"Worse?" Darryl asked. "How the hell could it be worse?"

John said while still watching the door, "I think she just got the names of every woman we like."

"Oh shit," Darryl said.

———

"They want WHAT!" Cheryl Lynn gasped, her look of shock complete as her eyes darted around the three other women in Bethany Anne's suite.

"Wait a fucking second," Jean said. "This was about getting those guys to bare their bodies, not for us to expose ours!"

"Why are you worried?" Cheryl Lynn turned to Jean. "You have a gorgeous body. I've pushed two kids out, and if the girls aren't a little less perky, I don't know what is!"

Bethany Anne had told the ladies the request, modified for her personal reasons, and sat back to watch the fur fly.

Damn, she wished she had thought to pop some popcorn.

"And who's going to ask Natalia to join this?" Cheryl Lynn continued. "She didn't even start this project, and someone is going to have to ask her to pose in a bathing suit? She's the XO on the Ad Aeternitatem for Pete's sake!"

"Hey, you guys are asking them to go shirtless with really tiny skivvies, all they want is a one-piece," Patricia reminded them.

"That's easy for you to say, your name didn't get drawn out of the hat!" Cheryl Lynn hit back.

"Why are you having such a hissy fit?" Jean asked Cheryl Lynn. "You've got a body to die for, if I had the extra three inches in height you have, I'd be dancing a pole somewhere."

Cheryl Lynn turned back to Jean and pointed at her.

"This is your fault, you hussy!" Cheryl Lynn kept going, even as Jean started laughing. "What the hell am I going to say to my kids?"

"Momma's got back?" Patricia suggested.

Bethany Anne couldn't stop the short laugh escaping from her lips. She quickly put her hand over her mouth as the arguing women turned towards her. She got out a 'sorry' before Cheryl Lynn continued the conversation, looking at her, "Who's going to ask Gabrielle?"

"Oh hell, that's easy," Patricia said and pulled out a phone. She hit a couple of numbers. "Hey, Gabby baby, it's Patricia. You know that favor you owe me? Yeah, that one. Hey, it's time to pay me back for a good cause. What? No, you don't have to off someone for me." She paused for a moment then laughed. "No, I can take care of him all by myself."

Now, all three of the ladies were engrossed in Patricia's side of the conversation. Jean looked over at Bethany Anne and mouthed 'your dad?' Bethany Anne shrugged as they continued to listen.

"No, I want you to wear a hot bathing suit and get pictures taken with Jean, Cheryl Lynn and Natalia just for the guys. No, they didn't ask," Patricia glanced over at Bethany Anne, who returned her look with an innocent smile. "I guess someone ratted them out. No, I don't know who asked for you. I could speculate, but so can you. Who knows, maybe it was John."

"Oh, he can ask for Gabrielle when I yank his pecker off," Jean muttered. Bethany Anne could hear Gabrielle's laughing as she heard Jean.

"That's harsh, don't you think?" Cheryl Lynn asked Jean.

Jean turned to Cheryl Lynn. "Okay, so how about it was Scott that asked for Gabrielle?"

Cheryl Lynn's lips pressed together before answering, "Well, I would have to accept that he was interested in someone else. Not every person is going to return my interest."

"Trust me, if you have their pecker, they will be focused on you, and you alone." Jean told her. "I mean... it doesn't have to be in a bad way, a careful pull, then another careful pull, and you..."

"Enough!" Cheryl Lynn put up her hand, shaking her head. "How can you go from yanking their pecker off, to jerking it off in two seconds?"

"That's not jerking it off, that's called a 'come along' gesture," Jean informed the other woman, winking saucily at her as she used her hands to make as if she was pulling a rope. "Guaranteed to get their attention."

"And a clean up on aisle twelve," Patricia added, holding the phone away from her ear to reduce the pain as Gabrielle laughed hard and loud on the other side of the line.

"Only if you're really, really good." Jean agreed.

"Or, it's been a while, so don't get too full of yourself," Cheryl Lynn retorted.

"Baby, when I get done with John, the only name he better remember is mine. If there's another name, I'll just have to try harder." She paused for a second. "Or get Gabrielle to off the other bitch."

"I'm not even going there," Cheryl Lynn said. "That would be too easy for you."

"With what part?" Jean asked.

"Harder."

"Oh, let's talk about the..." Jean started before Bethany Anne put up a hand to stop her in mid-sentence.

"Would you ladies mind continuing this another time? We're on a schedule. Patricia can ask Natalia, and if she agrees, then Operation Beefcake is a go."

Patricia pointed to her phone and nodded that Gabrielle was fine with doing the photo shoot.

Bethany Anne wasn't worried about the five hundred year old woman. A slinky bathing suit wouldn't offend her at all. Hell, she would pretend to care, but Bethany Anne doubted full nudity would bug her either. As you age, you tend to lose your inhibitions and five hundred years is a lot of time in which to lose them.

"Okay, next step is the photographer, who's going to take the pictures?" Bethany Anne asked.

"Why not get the same guy that did the shots of your cars?" Jean asked.

"What was his name?" Cheryl Lynn asked. "I can look it up if you don't know it."

"Mark Koeff, from California. I think he goes by another name as well for some of his work." Bethany Anne said. "I'll call him and ask. If he'll do it, I'll get a Pod over to pick him up later so he can work with the guys."

"Do you think they'll have problems in front of the camera?" Jean asked.

Bethany Anne eyed the shorter woman. "I think if I let you rub John down with the baby oil, he won't be able to get in front of the camera.

Jean smiled mischievously, "Sure he would… eventually."

CHAPTER FOUR

RANCHO SANTA MARGARITA, CALIFORNIA, USA

Mark Koeff had been surprised to get a phone call from Bethany Anne earlier that day. It took him about three seconds to say 'yes.'

He grabbed two bags of camera equipment to hand to the man who had landed a black Pod in his backyard. It was a good thing the vehicle could fly straight up and down, his yard was pretty small. Orange County had a lot of positive things going for it, but large lots weren't one of them.

Tanner, the guy helping him, grabbed the two heavy bags that contained the lighting equipment and walked out of Mark's kitchen into the backyard. Mark watched him for a second as it sunk in that Tanner wasn't struggling with the weight at all.

Kari, Mark's wife, came and kissed him goodbye. He stepped over to the twenty-seven inch iMac he used for business and shut it down. Mark had rescheduled some headshot work to do this gig, but only one person complained. He offered to do his pictures for free, just a week late, which seemed to please everyone.

"Come back safe, sweetheart," Kari said. They kissed again, and they walked out to see Tanner standing in front of the Pod.

"Ready?" he asked Mark.

Mark turned to Kari. "I'll be safe. I'm going to be shooting pictures of heavy-duty guards. I'll just hide behind them if anything happens." He smiled as he sat down in the Pod and Tanner helped him strap in with the five-point harness.

Kari watched as the black Pod lifted into the darkness before disappearing from view. She turned to go inside, hoping she didn't hear about her husband on the news.

Mark was amused to be teaching four of the most famous guys in the protection business the ins and outs of his profession to calm their fears. While he often had to reduce anxiety for those he photographed, doing that for these four, who probably walked through walls rather than bothering to find the door, was funny.

As long as he didn't let them know he was laughing on the inside, he should be fine.

Mark had made it to the Pacific to land on the QBS Polarus with the famed Ad Aeternitatem a couple of hundred yards away, heading west at a slow pace.

His stuff was offloaded as he was shown to the conference room on the huge ship. It was in here that he found the four guards waiting for him. Mark had kept a few things with him to help with the discussion. He shook everyone's hand and exchanged names before opening his bags. Placing the contents on a table at the front of the room, he looked up to see that the four men had taken seats in the front row.

Mark held up a camera body. "This is a Canon 5D Mark III. I have the Mark IV pre-release version Canon gave me to review before release, but for this shoot, I'm going with my tried and true tools." He looked at his attentive audience. "I'm sure you have preferred tools you use." He got some nods.

Mark set the camera down and picked up a long cylinder. "This is a Canon 70-200 zoom lens, which gives me the flexibility to go slightly wider if I need to, but primarily to take advantage of its 2.8 aperture at a 200% compression factor to get dappled, indistinct backgrounds. I also love the way it flattens the nose and brings out the eyes, making a deeper spiritual connection with the viewer. This lets the viewer catch a glimpse into the soul, which is eminently more appealing."

He put down the lens and picked up the next piece of equipment. "For lighting, I'll use the on-camera flash as a fill. It's called that because it fills in shadows caused by the main lights. It also triggers slaved kicker strobes, which I'll put on each side to rim light your torso and your face. This will also create more detail, texture, and dimensionality, showing your muscles better."

Mark put down the flash and leaned back against the table to speak to the guys. "Regardless of the site, I'll want the positioning or pose not only to reflect the natural activity of the location but to possibly tell a story. That will create a feeling of catching you in action, unaware of being photographed."

Scott put up a hand, and Mark paused. "Can you give us an example?"

Mark nodded. "Sure, for instance, suppose we choose to shoot at an animal shelter demonstrating your compassionate nature and love of animals. I'd have one of you comforting a small dog, wrapped in your shirt. Should we to go to a beach location, you might be standing in line for lunch at a quaint bistro in the noonday sun, no shirt, or walking away with your hands full with a small plate, sandwich, and drink. Should Cheryl Lynn's goal be to capture you in work-related activity, like guarding, I'd have to consult with you and ask you what sort of scenario would either stop you from wearing a shirt or cause you to disrobe and then we'd recreate that scene. The idea is to create images that make women viewers feel a bit of the voyeur, catching you involved in real activities. This allows the ladies' imaginations to run wild, engendering emotional connection and a sexier image." He smiled at the guys who were all nodding their understanding.

Mark took a second to make sure they were all looking at him again before continuing. "Look, trust the process and know that I will not allow you to do anything that would make you look anything less than powerful. If I don't like how things are developing, we'll simply start again and take a new approach. If you don't feel comfortable with any direction or requested action, stop and tell me. It's integral to the process that you OWN the story and feel it. Our goal is to create an image that is *illustrative*, which means capturing believable situations or stories with honest emotions. Together we can make it happen. But we will only be successful when you trust me. Don't *try* to be or do anything... just be and do as you would if you were all by yourselves with no one watching."

Mark paused for a moment and continued, "Okay, here's an example scenario. Just as you stepped out of your brownstone to pick up your paper early one morning, wearing only towel or boxer shorts and coffee cup in hand, your front door suddenly slams behind you and you don't have your key."

"That's Eric," John commented and got a punch on his shoulder from Eric.

Eric smiled. "Mark, I'd have to use the towel, beach size, of course, assets must be hidden, and beach size is the only size appropriate."

"Stop lying," Darryl shot back, laughing. "I'll get you a washcloth, which will be sufficient to hide anything. Hell, you don't need a fig leaf, just pull a blade of grass, and you'll be just fine."

"I'm sorry, but there hasn't been a piece of grass that can hide my anatomy since the Jurassic period," Eric retorted.

Scott leaned forward to look past Darryl and ask John, "How the hell does Eric know the word Jurassic?"

John smiled. "He saw the movie."

"Right, good point." Scott leaned back. "I thought my view of reality was being called into question here."

"Look, you ass!" Eric started.

Mark was watching the men fire jibes back and forth, his head going from one to the other and then back again. He interrupted to try and get the conversation back on track. "Hey guys?" He felt almost a click of a laser sight as all four snapped their eyes back to him immediately. "May I continue?"

"Sure, sorry." Eric said. "Just have to make sure I protest this obvious effort to spin a falsehood about my manhood here."

Mark nodded. "I got it, beach towel. So, moving on. Once a storyline is established, we will then set it in motion... My

words will focus you, much like a movie director's, remind-
ing you of the scene, and interjecting surprises. You just re-
called you have a meeting in thirty minutes, or you suddenly
see your girlfriend pulling up and she's doesn't know your
mistress is inside or…"

"Hold!" John said, putting up a hand. "Can we skip the
mistress idea? If you aren't aware, the ladies we work with
will take that shit pretty fucking seriously, and it would hurt
like hell to heal from their anger."

"Imagine if Cheryl Lynn," Darryl started before Scott interrupted.

"Or Jean, huh, John?" Scott laughed.

"Oh, hell no!" John grinned as he pretended to shake. "I
can imagine waking up with a howitzer aimed at my privates.
It would totally ruin my morning."

Darryl whooped. "You would be hogtied and sweating!"
He put his arms by his side and acted out being tied up. "Jean,
we can talk about this. I'm not sure who that woman is, but I
assure you…" Then, Darryl switched to a higher voice, "Oh,
I'm sure there will be some assurance here, Mr. Grimes. Like,
I assure you that I will cause untold pain if you ever mess
around on me."

"Love at the end of a one fifty-five… one fifty-five…" Eric
started singing.

"That shit isn't funny," John said, grinning. "You might
think you got it easier, Scott. But Eric here is going to be up
shit creek if…"

"Ho, ho, ho, hold on!" Eric interrupted. "Let's not get
ahead of anyone here. I'll admit John might have some plans
for the delectable and delicate Ms. Dukes."

"Delicate?" Darryl laughed. "Are we talking about the
same lady?"

"Hey, I'm trying not to scare John away before he makes a move on the woman!" Eric said.

John said slowly, "I don't know, the idea of that one fifty-five howitzer staring at me when I wake up is a little worrisome."

"Shit, John," Scott said. "You don't worry about a howitzer. That thing is too big to fit in your bedroom."

"That's true." John agreed.

"Nope," Scott continued. "What you worry about is what new gravitic tool she would concoct to smash your balls twenty times before you got the first scream out of your mouth!" He started laughing so hard that he almost fell off of his chair.

At this, everyone laughed.

John just shook his head. "That's not the kind of support I need right now, Scott."

Scott acted like he was wiping away tears. "Don't worry about it. The truth hurts, but Jean Dukes will elevate it to a new level of pain if there is a mistress involved."

"Hey, I didn't say anything about a mistress," John said, then pointed at Mark. "He started this mess."

Mark realized that joking with four tough guys maybe wasn't the best way to get out of this unscathed.

Mark grinned and put a finger into his shirt's collar. "Is it getting hot in here or is it just me?" He looked at John. "Wow, tough crowd. Let's keep going shall we?" He rubbed his jaw. "Okay, this step is going to be tough to do because your training is going to make this difficult."

"Our training?" John asked.

"Yes. You see, I would normally do something or have someone off screen to distract you and try to get you to lose your awareness of the process so you're more comfortable and natural. Since you guys are trained not to be off guard, I can't do that. So, suggestions?"

"Not a one," John admitted.

Mark considered the problem and shrugged. "I'll just have to improvise."

MANUFACTURING FACILITY 01, ASTEROID FIELDS

Gott Verdammt, but she was beautiful.

Captain Paul Jameson was going around the ship, his ship, for the fifth time. It had taken him only twenty-four hours to send a message to Bethany Anne that he accepted the role of piloting this badass motherfucker in front of him.

He went under the ship, noticing the massive guns under her belly and on her wings. He wiped a tear away from his eye. "Aww damn, Justin. I wish you could see this son of a bitch," he said softly into the silence of his Pod. "I promise you, buddy, I'll do my best to make you proud."

Paul thought back to the night before his friend died in a non-engagement-engagement. Rules stopping both his friend and himself from doing what they felt was right. Rules that ended up costing his friend his life. It had been years ago, and yet the pain was still as fresh as if it was last week.

"She's the right one. She's the one I can follow and whether I die of old age, or I come see you soon, we are going into battle behind one badass leader. I wish you could be here to enjoy this with me." Now tears were falling down Paul's face.

He just let them flow... it was past time he had this conversation.

"I've just been piloting, Justin. I've just been waiting, I thought. But I was taught how to trust, how to serve again. How to follow one more time into the breach." Paul flew the Pod around over the side and then the top to view the long guns running down the flanks. "And now, she has trusted her life, her future and the future of the world with me at the helm of the baddest, biggest, and meanest ship man has ever built. I'm going to be her pilot, the man who is going to point this beast wherever the fuck she tells me to aim it."

He stopped the Pod and looked down at the men and women still swarming on the ship's exterior, trying to finish the modifications to the gravitic sensors and armament changes that Bobcat and Marcus came up with after Paul started flying the ship.

Paul saw three cargo containers floating into the section behind the biggest guns and grinned mirthlessly.

Paul said aloud, to his friend—wherever he might be. "If Bethany Anne points towards Hell itself? Well, I'll just see you sooner, my friend, because I'll storm Hell itself for her."

———

William walked into the commander's office, the one Bobcat was working out of until Bethany Anne and her team could arrive.

"I got the news from Dan via Samantha," Bobcat told his friend before he could speak. "Take a seat. We need to talk."

William sat at the large wooden table, set his tablet in front of him and said, "A metric shitload."

"Enough to take out a country?" Bobcat asked, looking over at his friend. "Say one the size of China?"

"Enough to put the world into another Ice Age if we

needed to. I know Bethany Anne isn't going to do that, but we can pound the shit out of everything down there, and they can't touch us." William shrugged. "And that's just with rocks."

"Can this ship withstand a nuclear bomb?" Bobcat asked.

"I've talked with Marcus and the other eggheads. By the way, did you know he brought that chick scientist up here?"

"Of course, I know, since it had to be approved by me," Bobcat replied.

"Oh. Just curious. I thought maybe he would still go after Gabrielle."

"I think their date did a world of good for his ego. I didn't realize how messed up he was after his two divorces. I understand Gabrielle told him a few things after she gave him *the* kiss."

"So, we know for sure he got kissed?" William asked, smiling.

"Yes, I asked Gabrielle," Bobcat said.

"What, she'll kiss and tell?"

"She said she is no gentleman, nor a lady. Something about giving up being a lady back in the 1700s or something. Then, she grumbled something else about paying back Richard and Samuel again. Whatever the hell that means. So, long story short, she admitted she tried to make his short and curlies stand straight out."

"Fucking lucky bastard..." William whispered.

"I know, and you know what?" Bobcat asked as William raised an eyebrow. "We only have ourselves to blame for his luck."

The two men fist bumped each other and said in unison, "One for all, and all for one!" They laughed together for a moment before William continued, "Yeah, we can take a nuke. The EMP bullshit won't get through the gravitic shield. Apparently, this stuff doesn't work on the same principle as our normal electronics, which is good. Otherwise, we'd throw nuclear devices at each other out here in space to take down shields all the time."

"Do they know nukes can't get through shields back on Earth?" Bobcat wondered.

"Yes. I confirmed with Marcus that Lance has a shield going up and over the Australian base right now. Anyone tries that bullshit again like they did in Colorado and they're in for a surprise."

"Probably right before Australia sends something up the attacker's ass. The Aussies don't mess the fuck around."

"Messed up the accent, though," William commented.

"Not with the women. Sounds awesome with the women."

"That's because everything a woman says or wears is awesome. Put a man's dress shirt on a woman and now it becomes a sexual tease."

"Word." Bobcat agreed.

"Do you think she'll do it?" William asked.

"Which part?" Bobcat asked, "Bomb them back to the stone age or... what?"

"I don't know. Bethany Anne was kind of restrained after Colorado, and she's been relatively calm about taking out the Cabal. I'm wondering if she's settling down."

Bobcat looked into the distance, thinking of the many miles and galaxies they had in their future from his talks with Bethany Anne over the last few years.

"Not a fucking chance." Bobcat told his friend. "China has no idea who they just pissed off." He smiled at William.

"I'd admit to feeling sorry for the poor bastards, but that would just be lying."

"Now," Bobcat said, pulling his tablet up and hitting a button on the screen. "Let's talk about what's left before we can move this son of a bitch."

CHAPTER FIVE

CLAN TEMPLE NEAR SHENNONGJIA PEAK, HUBEI

The pain seemed like it lasted forever and yet had never been. Stephanie Lee's eyes opened, and she took in the medical device she was laying in. She reached out to touch a small button, and the top cracked open.

She looked around and saw the robe she had been wearing was gone. It had been taken away while she was asleep.

How long was I out? she wondered.

Fourteen days and three hours, Yin said.

Stephanie Lee considered the familiarity of the voice and remembered the pain, the mental fight to retain control. *You tried to take over my body!* She accused, furious. *You thought to push me out of control, why should I believe anything from you?*

Yang replied, *We do as we have been told. We were told that we would be able to command your body. But we are in fact the controlled. We are trapped in here!*

SUED FOR PEACE

What? Stephanie Lee asked. She looked down at her body, no hair anywhere. She was completely without hair except on her head. She seemed slightly taller than she was before and even a small birthmark on the left side of her stomach was no longer in evidence.

Yin answered, *The process is supposed to allow us the opportunity to inhabit a body instead of being primarily connected in the Etheric. It is a rare situation. Our consciousnesses were tied to this spacecraft. Apparently, our connection to the spacecraft and the Etheric are severed. We were supposed to have been given this vessel, your body, to take our next steps. Now, you are in control.*

Yang spoke next. *Don't believe we are without options. We can make your life continuously painful. I know how to stop the pain from affecting you, I also know how to cause it. But this can be a harmonious relationship.*

Stephanie answered, *Let me suggest that you starting this relationship by expecting to take over my body is not the beginning of anything harmonious between us.*

Yang's mind speech changed to one aggravated. *Listen, you are a sub-optimal being! Our intelligence and wisdom dictate we do not submit to one such as you.*

Then why, Stephanie asked, *did you want this body in the first place?*

The Leopard Empress is our avatar, Yin answered, exasperated. *Do you not remember anything taught to you as a child here?*

Those fairytales? Stephanie Lee replied. *The ones about gods and goddesses, changing to our animal spirits and... oh... my... god.* She stopped for a moment, thinking. *You have been planning this how long?*

Centuries, Yang said.

Why me?

Because you are genetically perfect. Your children will be able to procreate and carry the gene to the next generation. Within just a few generations, we can infect the world, Yin answered.

Stephanie asked, *What is the rush, again?*

Yin answered, *There is an avatar for one of the five here on Earth. The technology we hear rumors about, and what we could learn from your memories suggests it is of a particular clan.*

One we thought destroyed centuries ago, Yang added.

They might be destroyed, Yin said. *They could be from centuries before.*

So, you guys have technology that is better than TQB's?

Perhaps, Yin qualified. *But, we are leaders, not technologists. It might have been a different role that landed here. We are not familiar with the systems. Our specialties include the manipulation of genetics for the effective growth and most enhanced abilities from our stock.*

You mean humans? Stephanie Lee asked.

Yes, Yang answered, we mean humans. *Remember, your species is advanced, but you are still significant levels of advancement beneath the weakest of our race. Of Kurtherians.*

Why do you want humans, anyway?

Space is large. There are many races and species that fight whether another race cares to fight or not. Our clan, the Tre'learth, is responsible for advancing a race more quickly to prepare themselves for the onslaught of another.

How are we supposed to know when this will occur? Stephanie Lee asked.

When we warn you, of course, Yin replied.

Stephanie Lee bit her lip, considered what she had learned, and what she had not. If anything, her time with the Illuminati was a doctorate course in lying by omission.

SUED FOR PEACE

<u>WASHINGTON D.C. USA</u>

The President walked down to the meeting, leaving both of his agents outside the door as he stepped in. He nodded to a man who was bald and wearing the typical Washington power suit and a dark blue and red tie.

The man, the Secretary of State's behind the scenes power broker, sat ready to inform the President of what had been going on. Well, what had been happening behind the scenes once the President dropped the data in their hands and ordered them to disperse it to the relevant countries.

The President sat down. "Okay, give me the highlights, Jimmy."

"We have a shitstorm," he began before realizing what he said exactly. "Oh, sorry."

The President waved it away. "In here, tell me straight. Bad language offends me less than kissing my ass."

Relieved, Jimmy continued, "Well, the French are demanding to know how we know this. Germany is asking if we have more that we haven't given them, and England is asking the same thing. Except, they asked it as whether they should expect another axe to fall?" Jimmy looked at the President to answer the question.

"Frankly, Jimmy," the President responded. "I don't know." The President almost wanted to laugh at the face Jimmy made. "This information was provided in a unique fashion, and I can't demand more just show up because I want it. I suspect from what I was told that these are the major players that each country should worry about. If there's anyone bigger, well my feeling is they're already a target and won't be a problem in the near future. If they're smaller, then they will lose their ability to act once the big fish are taken care of, or they will be dealt with in some other form or fashion. Or, they aren't really a significant problem."

Jimmy tried to frame his next question. "What about all of their requests that we explain how we know this?"

"Well, we could tell them the truth," the President said. He started laughing when Jimmy's mouth opened and shut a few times.

Finally, Jimmy answered, "Mr. President, isn't the truth we received it from a concerned party, and we don't know what they know?" The President nodded in agreement. "I'm not sure that's going to work too well." Jimmy allowed. "My experience over the last decade suggests they would prefer to be sold a lie than told the truth, sir."

"Mine too, Jimmy," the President said. "But in this case I'm going to have to give them the truth. If we sell a lie, and the provider of the information gets wind of it, we could be in pretty hot water. I'm too damned concerned it would happen, so we need to think about that now."

"Us?" Jimmy asked, perplexed.

"Yes, us. As in, if we aren't ethical with the information and the truth, or non-truth, of how we acquired the information. Say nothing if you can't tell the truth." The President tapped his fingers against the table for a minute, and Jimmy stayed silent. He was accustomed to waiting for those in power to think through a solution. "Tell you what. If they want to know more, then the only person who I will discuss this with is their head of state. I will need to speak with him or her directly to know they will accept my conditions."

"What are those conditions?" Jimmy asked.

"The leader comes alone. Transportation will be provided.

When I know who is potentially coming, I'll negotiate with the owner of the information. Should that person agree, we'll make this happen and share the information at this meeting. Those that join are not to share the information to those that do not show."

"How would we possibly enforce that agreement?"

"Well, I believe those who do come will be persuaded as I was persuaded," the President answered mysteriously. He stood up. "That's all Jimmy. Tell the Secretary of State and you guys get moving." He turned and stepped back out of the room and continued to his next scheduled appointment.

CHAPTER SIX

QBS BATTLESHIP, MANUFACTURING FACILITY 01, ASTEROID FIELDS

Marcus walked into the room on the spaceship and his two friends, with solemn faces, turned to look at him. Both were sitting at the end of the table with Bobcat at the head and William to his left. This room, he noticed, was carpeted in a deep red and the table was made of wood. He sure hoped nothing made it this far into the ship or all of this wood would become tiny little shards of death for anyone in here when it exploded.

The chair to Bobcat's right was pushed back, inviting him to sit. Marcus pulled the chair back and sat down tiredly.

"You look like shit, buddy," Bobcat told him.

"Have you looked in a mirror lately?" Marcus shot back.

Bobcat turned to William, "See?"

William nodded sagely. "Him too, huh?"

Bobcat nodded and turned back to the rocket scientist and said, "You're working too hard."

"Do you know of any other gravitic experts around?" Marcus asked. "No, of course not. I'm it, and I'm not teaching at the moment. I'm doing."

"This wasn't a course on how to train up someone to take over your position to move forward," Bobcat explained. "It's more about two friends looking after the well being of friend number three."

Marcus smiled. "You know, I've been with you guys for a while, and I still have problems getting used to you."

"That's because we're an acquired taste," William said. "One my mom used to say should be washed out with soap."

"Yeah, you remember that one weekend we were supposed to show up for dinner on Saturday?" Bobcat asked while William grinned.

"I don't," Marcus interrupted.

"Well, it started like this," Bobcat leaned back in his chair. "Sir Can't-hold-his-liquor here—"

William jumped in, "Hey, that was early in my drinking career."

"A career you never did very well in, either," Bobcat assured him. "Lest you make me talk about the great bar fiasco of '02?"

"Um, no." William said quickly. "And the less you mention '02, the better."

Marcus was slightly surprised to see red on William's cheeks. He decided he would need to follow that little tidbit at another time.

"All right then," Bobcat continued. "See, William here invited me over to his parents' house for a Saturday afternoon lunch. We were supposed to show up about two in the afternoon, seeing how his mom knew that William liked to sleep." Bobcat looked down at the floor to his left as he spoke and grunted before sitting forward in his chair and grabbing something.

A second later, he pulled a cold six pack, sides still icy, and plopped it on the table. William turned to the chair next to him and tossed him a blue towel. Bobcat set the six-pack on the towel.

"Don't want to get water rings on Bethany Anne's new table," William said.

"Word." Bobcat agreed. He pulled a beer off of the six-pack and handed one to Marcus. Marcus was surprised to see Bobcat pull another and give it to William. He hadn't seen William drinking very often up here.

"So," Bobcat continued after everyone popped their beers open. "We show up. Now, we think we're pretty damned good because we get there at one forty-five. The problem was, William starts looking around the yard as we park and muttering about there not being enough cars. So, we step out, and his mom opens the screen door with a big wooden spoon in her hand. She calls William here by his full Christian name, and I hear him say 'Oh, we are fucked' and he starts backtracking very slowly to get into the car."

Marcus saw William put his face in his hand like he didn't want to witness the completion of the story.

"I'm there looking at this huge black man and this tiny black woman with what looked like a foot long wooden spoon."

"She uses it for stew," William added.

"Yes, the stew is amazing, but that isn't part of the story." Bobcat said. "So, I'm watching, and she tells him to stop and damned if this two hundred and fifty pound warhorse doesn't stop right in his tracks. He starts with 'Momma, what's wrong? We're early!'" Bobcat started laughing. "She comes at him and starts using that spoon like a whip and beating William with it. 'Crack! Crack!' Pretty soon, he's hopping around trying to dodge this tiny lady and her spoon of pain. I'm laughing my ass off as she proceeds to tell us the problem is it's Sunday, not Saturday!" Bobcat laughed as Marcus started to understand where the story was going. "We got so blitzed on Friday night that when we came in oh-dark-thirty Saturday, we slept for twenty-four fucking hours and got up for the three hour trip on Sunday morning."

"Yeah, you thought that shit was funny until she laid into you!" William grinned back at Bobcat.

"I don't think she put as much arm into it," Bobcat shrugged.

"She told me later you looked a little anemic; she didn't want to break a bone." William said.

Marcus asked, "What did you do about the tiny black woman you had never met, who was beating you with a spoon?"

Bobcat looked over at Marcus and smiled. "I took it like a man. I was taught to mind my manners around the adults and," he pointed at William. "His mother was the adult that morning."

"What finally happened?" Marcus asked.

"She fed us leftovers from the day before," William answered.

"God, I think I begged you for three months before you would take me back," Bobcat said, then turned to Marcus. "He made me sign a promise we wouldn't go out drinking the night before. I signed that damned piece of paper so quick you would think it was a chick asking if I wanted to have sex. Hell, by then I would have told the chick no just to get your mom's cooking." He cocked his head to the left. "I don't think I ever understood the phrase 'the way to a man's heart is through his stomach' until then. Hell, I'd of married your mom if she was available."

William laughed. "Don't think my ma didn't know that. She would tell my dad all the time if he didn't walk the straight and narrow, there were men lined up to steal her away."

Bobcat reached over and pulled the next three beers and passed them around before leaning back in his chair.

"So, here we are gentleman," he said. "I've been talking with our boss lady, and she informed me that the three of us are officially off the clock for twenty-four hours. If she finds out we defied her orders, then she will create a painful punishment to make sure we don't do it again."

Marcus pulled the tab on his second beer. "Well, if the boss insists." He took a sip and sat back. "Is that why you told me to cut everyone loose until tomorrow?"

Bobcat nodded. "Yes." He waved the beer. "This ship is the culmination of over eight hundred people up here, and thousands back on Earth. But if you go back far enough, you'll find that there are three people Bethany Anne points to as the team she depends on to make all this shit work."

Warm feelings of pride and accomplishment filled Marcus for a few moments as he stopped to consider what Bobcat said. He had come a far distance from that house in Orange County, and his first meeting with Frank Kurns.

He had traveled millions of miles, but more than that he had been thrust into the future, and his body had traveled to the past. He was fitter than he honestly had ever been in his life. He had spoken with an honest to God alien and worked with him every day.

He had two of the most unlikely friends that had his damn back no matter what the three of them were up against.

He took a sip of his beer, reliving the moment he saw the sign on the first gravitic containers they moved up to the moon.

The fateful 'Kiss My Ass NASA' sign that these two had done for him without asking Bethany Anne first.

Because it was right, and they were damn sure their boss would be okay with it.

And she had been.

It had felt so good. He vaguely remembered dancing, honest to God dancing, when he saw that sign on the TV screen. Then, the tears had come. Both of these men were there for him.

His brothers from other mothers.

Marcus lifted his beer to William. "If the chance ever happens, promise me you'll take me to eat at your mom's?"

William smiled. "Hell to the yeah, my brother. My mom would stuff you so full of food it would be embarrassing." He chuckled. "Then she would probably try to marry off my second sister, Tina to you."

"Not sure I'm ready for another relationship quite yet, but thanks... I think?"

Bobcat sat forward, his hands surrounding the can like he was praying, and set it on the table. "Don't eat what she cooks, and don't let her bat her eyes at you. The woman has got the package and the ability to cook. What she doesn't have is a filter for her mouth."

"Which is constantly talking unless she's underwater," William said.

"I imagine that idea comes to mind for any of her boy-friends after a couple of weeks," Bobcat agreed.

"Why not eat her food?" Marcus asked trying to catch up to the conversation.

"Because once you eat her cooking, you think you could

deal with her constant chatter if only she'll cook the next night for you. The girl's food is better than most any chef's you've ever tasted. What she can do with pasta should be considered a sin." Bobcat said. "The only way I got out of her web was happenstance. I was sent to the sandpit before she cooked for me three times."

"Three?"

"Yeah, it's a family secret." William answered. "Tina cooks for someone she's interested in the first time." William draped his left arm over the back of the chair next to him and waved his beer with his right. "So, if she finds the guy interesting, and he has a solid job, then he gets invited a second time."

"That second meal was fucking delicious," Bobcat said, his eyes looked like he was remembering something that had happened yesterday.

"Then," William continued. "Tina will cook an Italian meal for dinner number three and she'll accidentally spill enough sauce on the guy's clothes that she'll need to clean them for him. So, now she has him exactly how she wants him."

"Sleepy from too many carbs and practically naked. Like a damn black-widow," Bobcat murmured and then shook his head. "I never thought how lucky I was getting shipped out. I was looking forward to Italian."

"Sorry," Marcus said. "I'm not trying to be rude, but isn't Italian something a little odd for your sister to cook?"

"Yeah, I get it," William replied. "Not too many ladies of my skin color in our little Southern town focus on cooking Italian, but that was Tina's secret. She knew how to cook anything Southern from my Ma. The lady who could drop my dad and have another on her doorstep the next morning. Now, don't get me wrong, she loved my dad, but she wouldn't take any of his shit. So, Tina gets her cooking skills and recipes from Mom. The first night is the basics, second night is the basics enhanced and then Italian is the final nail in the coffin."

"Damn, I want some lasagna now," Bobcat said. The men went quiet for a minute, thinking about Italian food.

"So, are we going to drink our stress away?" Marcus asked.

"Oh!" Bobcat looked over at him, smiling. "Hell no!" He leaned back over his chair's armrest and pulled up a second six-pack, "Make this one last a little longer."

"Why, almost out?" Marcus asked.

"What? Hell no, I got half a container of beer shipped up and labeled it nuts and bolts, so none of the other guys knows what in it," he said. "No, because I need you thinking a little more clearly as we discuss the most important business in outer space."

"What business?" Marcus wondered. "Aren't we supposed to stop working?"

"For Bethany Anne, yes," William said. "But this isn't for Bethany Anne."

Marcus looked at them. "Then what is it?"

William reached over to the chair beside him and pulled up a small notebook. "As the third letter in the first bar company in outer space, I call BMW Brewery's first business meeting into order." He smiled.

"All Guns Blazing needs some work, and we need to decide how the fuck we want to make this happen!" Bobcat raised his beer and William and Marcus smiled and raised theirs to meet his.

"Men and women..." Bobcat had continued before he was interrupted.

"And aliens!" Marcus jumped in.

"And aliens, you're right, will one day want to make the trek to the first, the best, and the most famous bar ever. So, we need to make sure we design something fan-fucking-tastic." Bobcat finished.

"Hear, hear!" Marcus agreed. "I think we need to understand the basics of what men want and make sure we decide how to deliver. Isn't that what business is about?"

"Yes," William agreed. "But when you boil down the essence of what men want, it's fucking, fighting and food." He stopped for a second. "And our women probably want that too."

"I," Marcus started before stopping and considering what William just said. "Rather succinct. You might want to add acclaim."

"If they come to All Guns Blazing and survive, there's the acclaim right there." Bobcat declared.

Marcus asked, "Wonder if we can get some guys to be willing to fight?"

"There's beer here, of course we can get guys to fight." Bobcat answered. "Hell, sprinkle a few interested ladies and we won't be able to stop it."

"Shit, wish John would be willing to put in a show every once in awhile," William mused.

"Or Ecaterina," Marcus added.

"Ooohhh, that's priceless. Men who get their ass kicked by a beautiful girl." Bobcat thought out loud. "Having a girl kick a guy's ass would bring in the ladies for damn sure. Then we could have it happen at random times. I'm sure we can get a few friends from the Wechselbalg who would be willing to come over for free booze."

"Or free heads to break, they do tend to be a little more

hotheaded than the Vamps." William put in.

"So, that's the fighting," Marcus put up one finger. "Now we just have food and fornicating to go," he said as he put up his second and third finger.

"Well, we need to find the best damn dirty spoon cook who has always wanted to be in outer space and has a trained crew." Bobcat said.

Marcus was confused. "Why a trained crew? Is it important he already has people?"

William answered, "Yes. We need to know he understands how to train a crew to cook as good as him. We want consistency and the ability to keep it going for decades."

"Centuries," Bobcat corrected. "I'm thinking long-term here."

"Okay, centuries," Marcus conceded. "I do *not* think we want to create a whorehouse, though."

"Of course not," Bobcat agreed. "But, if you create a place where people meet to have a good time, good food and meetings with the opposite sex you create a place that allows for a chance at sex."

"So, why don't we have three parts to the bar?" Marcus asked. "One is the fighting area that is a little off by itself. One is the food and bar area that views the fighting and one area that is more… something else…" he trailed off, flipping his hands up in resignation.

"Something else," William said. "How about we have a special by-invitation-only area?" He pulled his arm off of the chair to put both elbows on the table. "Something like friends of the bar?" he continued, getting into the thought himself. "We highlight our friends and those who we think deserve special treatment?"

"Hell yes!" Bobcat agreed. "People who went in All Guns Blazing!"

"Which kind?" Marcus asked, confused. "We talked about real guns, laser guns, body parts before. So, we highlight those who have done something militarily or sexually?"

"No," William pointed at Marcus. "My man, you just hit it!" He stood up and started pacing. "Anybody who does something over the top," he turned to Marcus. "Like figures out how to use the gravitic drives in a new way to help the team, or a researcher that spent their own time and came up with an awesome solution went in *all guns blazing*."

Bobcat looked at his friend while nodding. "So, it's more of an accolade. Yeah, you can get it for being a part of a team that took out a strong point, but that's not inclusive enough." Bobcat turned to Marcus. "Someone in your crew could get it for going above and beyond and we can have different levels of highlights if you will."

"Perfect!" William pushed his beer out to Bobcat. "Everything from a round on the house after we highlight what they did, to a night in the special area with a small group of friends to a private, full-time area that's reserved for the Queen Bitch and her guards."

"We don't even know if Bethany Anne and the team will want us to do that!" Marcus argued.

"Oh, but that's the lovely part," Bobcat said, his eyes gleaming. "On opening night, we give them a special table, and then we hold it for her and her team for the rest of eternity." He smiled at his two friends.

"She's going to figure this out," Marcus said, shaking his head, eyes wide with alarm. "She reads minds, you know."

"Yes," Bobcat agreed, shrugging. "She does. But she doesn't do it without a reason, and she can come or not come as she wants. Plus, it's not like she doesn't know me enough to realize I might do something like this." He sat there grinning at his two friends as if the world would always see things his way.

Marcus looked at the two smiling men who were staring at him. "What the hell?" Marcus finally relented. "It's not like you get a chance to go down all guns blazing with the two best friends a rocket scientist could ever hope to have in his life."

Marcus raised his beer and held it out to the other two. Bobcat leaned in and William sat down and added his. Marcus toasted, "To All Guns Blazing, may we not go down in flames on our first night!"

They laughed as they touched their cans of beer together.

CHAPTER SEVEN

PLA OFFICES, CHINA

General Sun Zedong stood up from his desk and grabbed his clipboard. He walked out of his office and past the large table with his favorite word in brass on the top to remind everyone of China's long-term goal.

And his personal goal, power.

He walked through the door to meet with those on the ruling council and deliver the update in a secret meeting and receive his direction. So far, all incursions had been successful. A request for another surgical strike inside of the United States was on his clipboard.

They did not need to have a reporting team running around and messing up their longer term preparatory power endeavors. While this request was outside of his direct interests, he had the resources inside the U.S. right now. He had two teams in place and one target. He might as well make it a double hit, as long as the ruling members overseeing him agreed.

He checked out of the building and sat in the back seat of the car taking him to his meeting.

It was a good day, he considered, as the flags flew in the breeze over the PLA offices.

———

WASHINGTON D.C. USA

The inside of the cargo van was dark save the few red lights and screens team leader Hu's operatives used to keep track of what was outside of their vehicle.

Hu looked down at the comment added to an eBay product. "The operation is a go," he said. The four men finished with the application of makeup to darken their skin and insert the colored contacts. Should anyone see them in the darkness this evening, they should not be able to pick any out of a lineup, nor would they even recognize they were Chinese in the first place.

It wasn't often an order to take out American nationals was given to their team, but they were part of an elite group, and didn't question targets they were given.

By now, they knew the three people very well. They had been tracking them for two and a half weeks. Two men, one lady. The men were obviously protection. They seemed remarkably young and his team had never seen them with any weapons on their persons. Twice they had passed by the three in groups of two and three, to see their reactions.

Minimal.

Their main target was the woman. She was causing

problems as the conduit for communications between TQB and those in DC that their country needed to persuade. Too often, a diplomat would arrive and get a potentially sympathetic ear only to have this team show up soon after and change their mind.

Now, it was time to solve the problem.

Hu checked his men's equipment and clothes. They all wore different types of suits. All had pistols and knives secreted about their bodies.

He doubted they would need the pistols. The two men were going to be dealt with by his men, and he would take out the girl.

He watched one of the monitors and found his targets coming down Ridge Street and signaled his team. The van would follow on an adjacent street. Their exit strategy was down an alley, into the van and disappear into the night.

They shut off their electronics, and he cracked the door.

It was time to go.

———

Scottie was walking far behind his colleagues. His job was typically to trail Matthew, Rickie, and Jennifer whenever they were moving from place to place. He liked his job, and he liked these people. Getting to know Matthew and Rickie was a pleasure. Both were among the first Werewolves to join the Queen, and they were a good team. Rickie was constantly joking around, and he had even been able to get the normally quiet and easygoing Matthew to crack a smile. Jennifer had become more and more comfortable with them.

Which was good, because there was no way she was going to be let off the leash without them.

She even had a date one time, with them along sitting at the next table over. She threw a little tantrum until she spoke to Jakob, her boss. He told her in no uncertain terms what could happen and might happen to her if she went anywhere without them.

Then Colorado happened, and she used her guys as a security blanket at night for two weeks.

Scottie was watching two blocks ahead of them when he saw four men coming around a corner. They looked fine, but something about their walk, their spacing… something. Something seemed to at least suggest caution to the ex-Marine. He coughed twice saying, 'four ahead' in the middle of the coughing fit.

No humans would understand a word he said. For the two Queen's Guardians, it was child's play. Matthew gave him a quick sign by scratching his shoulder. Two seconds later, Jennifer stopped walking and stepped a little closer to the street, Matthew and Rickie took up positions to protect her.

Scottie kept walking towards them, putting a hand inside his pocket.

He had to depend that his instincts were right.

Scottie smiled as he saw Rickie start pantomiming a female with a broken shoe as he hopped in a quick circle. Rickie arrived back at his starting point with at least fifteen feet to spare before the strangers arrived, coming from the other direction.

Scottie continued looking past everyone, but could see that one of the suspects spoke to them, and one guy in the front looked in his direction and gave a small nod of his head.

"It's going down, boys," Scottie said as he gripped the butt of his pistol.

Damn. Even while paying attention to his own mark,

Scottie was impressed with the speed and precision of the three men left. They were all walking a few paces apart from each other by the time they arrived near Matthew and Scottie, they turned in perfect unison. All were swiping deadly fast, with knives, he assumed.

If their targets had been human, they would be dead. Fucking shame they weren't human, Scottie thought as he pulled his pistol and shot the man heading at him.

Hu noticed the one man walking quickly towards them. Damn, he was going to have to kill an innocent. Not a good night to be out walking, but worse things could happen, Hu figured.

He spoke softly in Mandarin, "Gen, take out the man walking this way. Make it as painless as possible, the fates were not with him tonight."

Gen nodded and started walking faster. His remaining two men changed their paces. Guowei stepped ahead a couple of steps, Lok slowed a couple of steps behind him. It would allow all three the ability to pivot and come at the targets from three directions. The two males would go down quickly, the girl would be next.

He saw the targets had stopped, and the girl was bitching about a shoe. Then, one of her guards started hopping around and making fun of her.

Hu's lips pressed together. That was so very unprofessional.

Matthew heard the coughing and cocked an ear backward. Matthew said to Rickie, "Hey, eats-a-lot, we have four ahead." He turned towards Jennifer. "Jenni, I need you to act like you have a problem with your shoe, then get closer to the street. We have inbound."

Jennifer suddenly yelped and stumbled. Then she stopped and started hopping a little as she tried to grab her high-heeled shoe. "Dammit! These fuckers make my ass look tight but they're such a pain in the butt to wear." She hopped a couple of steps closer to the street, next to a car and put one hand on it as she slid a finger behind the shoe and took it off. Then she took the other off in case she needed to run.

Rickie was smiling then started squeaking in a high voice as he hopped on his left foot and turned in a counter-clockwise circle, "Look! I've got a rock in my shoe, but my ass is TIGHT!" He grinned the whole time, then whispered to Matthew, "No one else in the vicinity, just these four."

Matthew said, "Got it."

———

Hu snapped, "Xiànzài!" His men performed to perfection, all three of them swung to their left, knives hidden until the last second. Hu had decided to take the Asian looking guard first and then give Guowei support with the unprofessional Hispanic guard.

Lok would swing his right arm to come around, and if the guard was fast, he would be able to block Lok's attack, but Hu's would make it through. Hu would take one step forward, then turn clockwise to the second guard from his back, cutting through his neck.

Lok was twisting fast, Hu doubted the guard would be

able to block him. Hu was starting to move into his objective when he was shocked to understand not only had the Asian seen the attack coming, he had decided to twist slightly to the left.

Hu barely had time to register when Lok's knife, still held by Lok's hand, slammed into his chest. The Asian had grabbed Lok's forearm and propelled him in the direction of his original turn. He had overpowered Lok and forced him to do exactly as he wanted.

"You won't need this," the Asian said to Hu as his right hand grabbed him and casually yanked Lok's hand off of the knife, leaving it impaled in Hu's chest. Matthew twirled it a couple of times in his right hand before he let go of Lok's arm and tossed the knife from his right hand to his left. One half-twirl to grab the knife by the hilt, but pointed away from his thumb.

It was time measured in a partial second when Hu's knife was shoved into Lok's eye socket. Matthew heard a pistol shot and turned towards Scottie.

———

Rickie was considering the odds he would get two of the three guys and then noticed the man in the middle turn slightly towards Matthew.

Racists, always thinking the best fighters were Asian, Rickie thought. He said nothing because while he might want to smart off during a fight, Peter would have his nuts if he was anything less than professional. Sure enough, the clown struck on a Chinese order, pivoted towards Rickie and was darting in with a knife.

Rickie wanted to howl in excitement! Here he was going

to get a little payback for all of the boredom he had been suffering. He opened his left hand and used it to shield the knife striking at him. The knife impaled his hand. The man was surprised just long enough for Rickie to pivot on his left leg and kick out the man's left kneecap.

His leg broke at an odd angle from Rickie's kick. The man went down and was staring in shock as Rickie smiled at him and pulled the knife out of his hand and then licked some of his blood off. "You guys done gone and fucked up." Rickie twirled the knife a second then his arm went forward, throwing the knife into the man's neck.

That's when he heard the shot, and he turned to see Scottie aiming at the fourth man who was going for a weapon when Scottie put one between his eyes. Scottie walked past the downed man after checking him quickly and was looking around the street for additional targets.

"We need to am-scray people," Scottie said. "Call in a Pod group if we can. There's a pickup car somewhere, and we want to be gone. There wasn't any ID on my guy, check those three and let's go."

Matthew was talking into his phone. Rickie reached out to pull Jennifer to him and started walking away from the fight. "Don't look, you don't need this in your psyche right now Jenni." She nodded to him, and he pulled her in tight before letting her go. He could hear Matthew checking the three bodies as Scottie continued behind them. About ten seconds later, Rickie heard Matthew running to catch up.

He joined them since Scottie had moved up to within ten feet. "I've called it in. There's a park four blocks ahead and two to the left. They'll be there in ten minutes."

"Let's just hope no one finds us before then," Scottie said. "Find a dark place we can defend and hide. Let's move." Scottie started jogging. He called over his shoulder, "Matthew, you're defense, Rickie, you're transportation." With that, he turned his head to look ahead of them.

"Who's transportation for what?" Jennifer started then hissed, "Hey! I'm not a sack of potatoes here!"

Rickie bent down, grabbed Jennifer, and tossed her over his shoulder in a fireman's carry. He turned towards Scottie and started running. "I'd say! A sack of potatoes is about ten pounds. What are you, one-twenty? That's like, what, twelve sacks of potatoes?"

She slapped his back. "Put me down you talking dog!" Then she caught on to what he said and slapped him again. "I'm not a pound over a hundred five, you bastard!"

"Nope, parents were married before I came along," Rickie answered as they ran. "You might be able to question my oldest brother, there seems to be some fuzzy math about their wedding night and his birthday. But they were married over three years before yours truly came along."

They stayed in the shadows as much as possible and made it to the park in record time. Rickie swung Jennifer forward, caught her, and carried her in his arms. "Ready to get down, princess?"

Jennifer looked up at Rickie and realized he wasn't smiling his characteristic smirk but was watching out from under the trees they were hiding in. She started shaking and buried her head in his chest and shook her head no.

Rickie held her tight. No one was getting to this girl without killing him first.

SUED FOR PEACE

Stephanie Lee watched as her hand grew claws, fur growing through her skin. Power radiated from her as she watched her naked body change in the mirror.

She had been working on her physical changes for four days now. She had to rest after about six hours.

But she was getting there.

The first time she met her father after the change, it took all her will not to slap him. She treated him coldly and he responded with respect.

The respect she had wanted, but now would give up for a warm embrace. She wasn't sure there had ever been a true embrace in her life from this man.

If respect was what she had, then she would use it to beat this man into submission for daring to love the goal of siring the perfect vessel more than his daughter.

Her.

You are doing well, this is good, Yin said.

Yes, your ability to control your change is much more advanced than our projections and calculations, Yang agreed.

Why is it that you are so beholden to your math? she asked the aliens inside her.

Because there is truth in numbers, Yin replied. *A truth that is without peer in the Universe.*

The answers to life, if one can understand the aspects of the question, can be found in numbers. Yang said. *It is the way of our future. The numbers foretell a time when there can only be one. One future, one path, one direction for the Kurtherians. We have embraced the struggle to be at the top of the future, rather than in the dust of the past.*

Stephanie Lee noted her glowing yellow eyes in the mirror, her lithe body and short fur as she drew her right hand down her left arm. Her senses expanded, and she could smell trees blooming on the other side of the valley. She walked to the window and looked out. Here, in this temple, she was now the Leopard Empress. The embodiment of the belief of this clan for almost a thousand years.

Time immemorial. She had been introduced to other werecats. To a few families of wolves who were ostracized for being a less pure branch of her clan. Most wolves over the centuries separated from the clan and lived among the populace.

Her father admitted there were a few families that had left and never returned, their belief in a future forgotten.

Most families only paid lip service to the religious understanding of the future, even if they had proof when those in their family lines through the generations occasionally evidenced the ability to change into a cat form. There were only two who could change into the walking form. He and now his daughter.

Stephanie Lee flicked her tail around behind her. It felt exquisite to command the tail and use it as a separate extension of her personality. She would occasionally show no emotion on her face, but allow her tail to flick in annoyance, or with sensuality.

The tail is power, and she felt it in her core.

She put her hands against the sides of the window and roared into the morning. It felt good to claim her power.

It did her believers good to hear the truth of her existence as they went about their business getting the temple cleaned and prepared to receive visitors. It wouldn't be too long, maybe just a few weeks, before it would be time to call in the warriors from outside and receive their renewed oaths.

The Tre'learth Clan had accumulated much power over the centuries. Technical, physical, and monetary, and led the efforts to infiltrate everywhere they needed.

It was time, Stephanie Lee thought, to slowly awaken the beast the Tre'learth had created.

One doesn't awaken the slumbering giant quickly, lest you risk much. No, she would do it as quickly as wisdom dictated.

But oh, the world would certainly know the future soon enough. There were others coming and she needed to prepare it to repulse the onslaught. Even now, another Kurtherian Clan had infested this world. She would need to eradicate them before she would have the time to seed the populace properly.

Yes, she would use the breadbasket of the world to prepare the next generation for transference. She would take over the top genetic and food production companies, spreading the necessary ingredients through different food products, grains modified to provide the right nutrients for the nanites she would need to mass manufacture in the most capable country in the world of producing trillions of products.

China.

First she would manipulate the United States to prepare, then she would use China to take the world into the next evolution.

The challenge was coming, and her Clan would change humanity and take it to the level necessary to defend itself.

Whether the world wanted to prepare or not.

CHAPTER EIGHT

THE DARK WEB

>>Ih8tuGeorge - We are here.

>>ki55mia55 - Connected and ready to Rock and Roll!

>>luckyu11 - I'm here… Damn guys, can you believe the shit we've done with Adam?

>>Ih8tuGeorge - Yeah, I still have to pinch myself at times. Hey, did you see what J0n3sN4u did over in South America?

>>ki55mia55 - He found a drug lord and ratted him out, didn't he?

>>Ih8tuGeorge - Yeah, I heard he was on the run now.

>>ki55mia55 - If he is, then he didn't cover his tracks very well.

>>luckyu11 - Hey, don't knock him. He found the money those asswipes had hidden and their data. He reported them to the authorities, but the head drug guy was on the take. He had to drop out fast.

>>Ih8tuGeorge - It's a reminder this shit is real, folks. Don't let your guard down, we are playing with the big boys and they don't mind a slit throat or bullet to the head.

>>MyNam3isADAM - I apologize for being tardy, I wanted to confirm J0n3sN4u was safe before I arrived for our meeting.

>>ki55mia55 - How did you do that?

>>MyNam3isADAM - Do what? Confirm he is safe, or make sure he was safe?

>>ki55mia55 - Yes, to both.

>>MyNam3isADAM - I can't make sure of anything. Once Ih8tuGeorge let me know, I did what you might do in any organization, I confirmed the facts and delivered it to the person who might be able to help someone.

>>luckyu11 - You told her, didn't you?

>>MyNam3isADAM - Yes.

>>luckyu11 - I'd love to meet her some day.

>>ki55mia55 - Told who? Meet who?

>>Ih8tuGeorge - Yeah, don't get me wrong Adam, but while I don't think you are the cops, if you are working for an organization we need to know.

>>MyNam3isADAM - One moment, I will need to see if she is available to communicate.

>>luckyu11 - Oh my god, I can't believe this might be happening.

>>ki55mia55 - lucky, what the hell are you talking about? How did you know who he works for? Also, how can you be sure?

>>luckyu11 - Adam never officially told me, so I've kept it to myself. He's always been straight up with me so I believe him. We know a lot of the targets, so I did some digging.

>>Ih8tuGeorge - Ok, if you think it is the same group I

think it is, then holy shit on a graham cracker, kiss, we are playing with the biggest group out there.

>>ki55mia55 - Seriously? My group loves we are helping, but we haven't seen the hints you guys are seeing. At last count, we've dropped fifty-five PWLTSO's since we started.

>>Ih8tuGeorge - PWLTSO?

>>ki55mia55 - Yeah, sorry. Inside acronym - People We Love To Screw Over. Adam had us help him target some real douches. The cops actually wanted to give out awards for four of them. Fucking child pornography shit. But, you know us, gotta stay in the background in case we get known and that can't happen. We got wind that they were going to give the anonymous supporters an award, and we all hooked up and watched it with popcorn and shit. It was a cool feeling, let me tell you.

>>ki55mia55 - So, who is it?

>>Th3Qu33nB1TCH - It is my group. Hello, people.

>>MyNam3isADAM - luckyu11, Ih8tuGeorge, ki55mia55 please meet my boss, Th3Qu33nB1TCH.

>>luckyu11 - Oh my god! I can't believe it's you! I watch everything I can about you.

>>Ih8tuGeorge - Fuck me! The Initials...LOL!

>>ki55mia55 - Sorry, but WHO are you? I don't want to be dense here, but I don't have a clue.

>>luckyu11 - George is right, check the initials, kiss!

>>ki55mia55 - TQB? Oh, just shoot me now. I can't believe this shit! Really? Seriously? Damn, I'm going to have a nerdgasm if Adam isn't pulling my leg here.

>>MyNam3isADAM - ki55mia55, I wouldn't do that.

>>Th3Qu33nB1TCH - You wouldn't ADAM? Because, I think it's funny as shit. I'd totally pull this stunt if I had thought of it.

>>MyNam3isADAM - Why?

>>Th3Qu33nB1TCH - Because it's funny! Why else? Either way, sorry people. Yes, it's really me right now. Sorry for taking a few minutes, I was in a meeting when ADAM asked me to join. What do you want to know?

>>ki55mia55 - Well, I think I have my answer already. It's just we aren't too fond of organizations.

>>Th3Qu33nB1TCH - Yeah, I get that. Too many of them are a pain in the ass only set up to help themselves survive even if it means the human race has to suffer for it.

>>luckyu11 - Can I ask you a question?

>>Th3Qu33nB1TCH - Sure.

>>luckyu11 - Were you in on the attack with the terrorists and the children.

>>Th3Qu33nB1TCH - Yes.

>>luckyu11 - Did you get hurt?

>>Th3Qu33nB1TCH - Not physically, emotionally yes. Why do you ask?

>>luckyu11 - Because I still have some nights when I see those pictures of the men killed, and I have to pull up the children again.

>>Th3Qu33nB1TCH - Lucky, you didn't swing the sword, or shoot anyone. You and everyone here found a potential threat and notified someone who could help. It was my decision to take care of the terrorists the way we did. What would you have thought if the next morning, you found out they had attacked a school, and hundreds of children were massacred, would you ask why we didn't do anything?

>>ki55mia55 - I would have. Don't get me wrong, I'm not about killing everyone, but if you are going after children so that you get some airtime? Well, kiss my ass.

>>luckyu11 - Yes, sorry. It's just I realized with that episode we started something.

>>Th3Qu33nB1TCH - That isn't correct lucky, the terrorists started something. You guys and gals all helped stop the something THEY started. They would be alive today if they didn't decide to bring children into this mess.

>>Ih8tuGeorge - You wouldn't have done anything if it wasn't children?

>>Th3Qu33nB1TCH - Depends. If it was civilians, possibly. If it was military, say the Russian military, then probably not. We can't get involved in everything, even if I wanted to, and I don't. I don't believe in trying to right all the world's wrongs. Even I don't have a big enough stick to do that.

>>ki55mia55 - Don't you? I mean, you could drop rocks and shit on top of them. That's a pretty big stick to have.

>>Th3Qu33nB1TCH - Are you going to go to a playground and start indiscriminately bashing heads with a baseball bat because one of the kids bit another?

>>ki55mia55 - Oh. Yeah, I get that. Not going to destroy the innocents with the bad guys just because you can.

>>Ih8tuGeorge - That was a good metaphor, I hadn't thought about it like that before.

>>Th3Qu33nB1TCH - Almost everyone has superior power over someone. The ethics are usually pretty much the same even when you can affect billions.

>>Th3Qu33nB1TCH - So, now that you know who ADAM works for, does this change your desire to help him, and us?

>>Ih8tuGeorge - No, but I'd kill for a chance at a ride into space.

>>ki55mia55 - Perhaps a poor choice of words?

>>Ih8tuGeorge - Shit, sorry! Yeah, poor choice of words.

>>Th3Qu33nB1TCH - Wouldn't we have to know who you are then, to do that?

>>ki55mia55 - Don't you?

>>Ih8tuGeorge - Yeah, what kiss said.

>>Th3Qu33nB1TCH - I certainly don't, ADAM?

>>MyNam3isADAM - Yes?

>>Th3Qu33nB1TCH - Do you know who the people are?

>>MyNam3isADAM - Yes, to keep them under protection, I am aware and monitor with Frank for any activity on their names.

>>Th3Qu33nB1TCH - Ah, Ok. So, the short answer is yes, our organization knows who you are, I don't personally.

>>luckyu11 - You are protecting us, Adam?

>>MyNam3isADAM - Yes, I have multiple filters going to catch any reference, if possible, to activity on your current physical names. Should something come up that warrants further review, it would go to operations to see if we need to get involved.

>>ki55mia55 - Uh, just curious. What do you mean 'warrants' further review?

>>MyNam3isADAM - We don't get involved if you are in trouble for passing a bad check.

>>ki55mia55 - Just to be clear, I thought the money was in the bank. My GF took some out, and I didn't know about that.

>>Th3Qu33nB1TCH - Kiss, you are a prominent hacker, and you can't keep your funds straight? I would think you would be working for a security firm making six figures?

>>ki55mia55 - LOL! No, geez, if I was doing that I wouldn't be living in this flea trap place.

>>Th3Qu33nB1TCH - What about the rest of you?

>>Ih8tuGeorge - I've got a research grant at the University.

So, I've got good insurance, but not a lot of money.

>>luckyu11 - Yeah, student here too.

ADAM, do you mind if they get told you are an AIRE? I mean, they'll think you're an AI, but I can't help that.

>>I don't have feelings one way or the other on that, Bethany Anne. I would prefer not to lose their help, though. I can't calculate the chances of them leaving since I never considered this course of action.<<

Part of the problem of leading, and of leaders, is you need to show your humanity for a human to emotionally grab a hold and follow. They need to know who you are. If they find out in the future, you will have most likely irrevocably broken trust.

>>I'm not human.<<

No, but you exhibit human traits. You are honest, you are forthright, you seek to help, and not to harm. Hell, that's better than ninety-percent of humanity, probably.

>>What about now? I've never told them before, won't they be upset?<<

Most likely not. Since we're being straight with them, we might as well come clean about you. I think we need their help, and I've got an offer they might not refuse.

>>What's that?<<

Well, I could say a lot of money, but I'll have them with a fast internet connection and the most powerful computers in the world.

>>Why do you want to do this? I seek to understand.<<

ADAM, every time you ask a question, you seek to understand. You are the easiest person to work with I have.

>>I'm... never mind.<<

You're learning. I want to do this because of the J0n-3sN4u episode. Tabitha and her team got him out safely, but we're about to take on a nation that is not showing any restraint. I want these people safe. They aren't signing up long term unless they want to. But once they're on our premises, they will wonder why they never see you.

>>Oh.<<

Yes, oh.

>>The chance of success seems to be...<<

ADAM, never tell me the odds. Unless I ask, then I'd like to know.

>>Seriously?<<

No, not seriously. It's a quote from a Star Wars movie.

I got it!

I figured you would, TOM. I didn't realize you were listening.

Marcus is sleeping off his binge. So, I heard you guys talking and thought I would listen in. That's a funny line. ADAM is C3PO, you're Han Solo. It fits.

>>That is an ugly coat of armor C3PO is wearing.<<

Good enough guys, let's get back to the conversation.

Bethany Anne didn't miss the fact that ADAM had exhibited something no A.I. should ever have, a subjective opinion on art. ADAM was growing up.

>>Th3Qu33nB1TCH - Okay, I have an offer that you need to talk about amongst yourselves. We have been attacked by a nation-state, and they are hitting us hard. I refuse to slow down. They have killed some of my people, and I won't back down. I'm going to need to up the abilities of TQB's technology infrastructure. But there is a problem in this, I will not accept the inability to protect those who are working on this project with us. It is a paid position, requiring relocation, and we have to provide more information as well.

>>luckyu11 - Does this mean you're going to stop going

after the hackers and others here on the dark web?

>>Th3Qu33nB1TCH - No, in fact, those who choose to remain on the sidelines in this fight are welcome to continue this, but they will be moved to a different group and headed up by a lead chosen from those who have helped already. If one of you does not accept my offer, then I would imagine you will be the one to lead this team, with our support under your direction with an override from ADAM.

>>Ih8tuGeorge - Why do I feel like the other shoe hasn't dropped?

>>Th3Qu33nB1TCH - Because it hasn't. Since we are laying our cards on the table, I've asked ADAM if he is okay with me laying out another one.

>>ki55mia55 - Adam is really Andrea?

>>luckyu11 - Adam, are you an AI?

>>ki55mia55 - Wait, what? Did I miss something?

>>Ih8tuGeorge - Fuck! Adam, are you an AI? Damn, that would explain why you're so cool. I've argued with my room-mate that you can't possibly be real.

>>MyNam3isADAM - I am not what you would consider an Artificial Intelligence. A typical AI is a superfast computer that can simulate what a human would do in a situation and then choose the best option. That type of AI approximates a human.

>>luckyu11 - I'm in.

>>Th3Qu33nB1TCH - That was fast.

>>luckyu11 - I'm Japanese, we love technology, and I've been studying AI stuff for years, since I was eight. I'd have ADAM's babies if I could.

>>Th3Qu33nB1TCH - You might want to take that back.

>>Ih8tuGeorge - Damn, wish I was a girl.

>>ki55mia55 - Nerdgasm.

>>Th3Qu33nB1TCH - Kiss, you really don't get out a lot, do you?

>>ki55mia55 - Sorry, I'm not that good with interpersonal relationships. I'm excited, is that a better word choice?

>>Th3Qu33nB1TCH - No, I think you were right the first time. Keep Nerdgasm. It's growing on me.

>>ki55mia55 - You're kinda cool for a CEO.

>>Ih8tuGeorge - Yeah, I'm going to have to agree with kiss on this, are you sure you are the real Bethany Anne?

>>MyNam3isADAM - She is the real Bethany Anne, I would not pull your leg like she would.

>>ki55mia55 - Really? Why not?

>>MyNam3isADAM - Because I would not break faith with you.

BAM! Bethany Anne thought. *My little AI just grew up.*

>>Ih8tuGeorge - Adam, how did you help J0n3sN4u?

>>MyNam3isADAM - Once you sent me the message, I spoke with Bethany Anne and she sent… Well, would you speak to this Bethany Anne?

>>Th3Qu33nB1TCH - I have different people who operate on my behalf. In South America, I have a representative from my Rangers who extricated him and is making sure he is safe.

>>ki55mia55 - Is he putting him in a safe house?

>>Th3Qu33nB1TCH - Well, *she* has him protected at her house while she takes care of the problem. She's responsible for policing, and a drug lord problem is in her area of responsibility.

>>Ih8tuGeorge - A ranger? Like a Texas Ranger?

>>Th3Qu33nB1TCH - Yes, the concepts are similar.

>>Ih8tuGeorge - Can I work with her?

>>Th3Qu33nB1TCH - I suppose the potential is there.

But I'm not sure you would make the grade.

>>Ih8tuGeorge - I'm not as sedentary as you might think.

>>Th3Qu33nB1TCH - Ih8tuGeorge, I wasn't talking about your ability to move physically. I was thinking more about the fact she's one of the best hackers in the world. So, you might need to up your game before she could benefit from your help.

>>Ih8tuGeorge - She's a hacker too? I'm in love.

>>Th3Qu33nB1TCH - How can you be in love already? You haven't even met her.

>>Ih8tuGeorge - Who cares? She can kick ass and hack computers, what else do I need to know?

>>Th3Qu33nB1TCH - Well, how about whether she can cook?

>>Ih8tuGeorge – There's Taco Bell for that.

>>ki55mia55 - I'm with George, if she can hack and kick ass, I'm in for meeting her too.

>>Th3Qu33nB1TCH - I'll have to consider that. If you guys are on the team, it would make sense, and I imagine it would happen in the future, but otherwise I have no idea. I can't make a promise either way.

>>Ih8tuGeorge - It doesn't matter, ADAM has made my life mean something. That he is some kind of AI only makes it cooler. Your group seems pretty damned important, and I trust you guys more than the rest. I'm in.

>>ki55mia55 - I wish I could be in. I need to stay with my GF, and she won't leave her parents. Yeah, I know, love and all that but I can't leave the only girl who has ever trusted me and done me right.

>>Th3Qu33nB1TCH - Kiss, we can't directly connect with you because of paper trails, but do look for something good in the near future. You will keep working with ADAM,

and we will keep the civilian side going while the others help us focus on a direct issue.

>>ki55mia55 - Thanks, it means a lot that you trust me to continue the work with Adam. Or I guess it is ADAM?

>>Th3Qu33nB1TCH - Nah, leave it Adam. We do trust you, because if it becomes known what Adam is, we are going to have a serious set of problems on our hands.

>>ki55mia55 - It's okay, Adam has my back, I got his.

>>MyNam3isADAM - Thank you, ki55mia55.

>>ki55mia55 - Dude, it's just kiss. Now that I think I know why you never shortened it, please know my friends all do.

>>MyNam3isADAM - Thank you, kiss.

>>ki55mia55 - I'll catch up with you guys. See you soon and Bethany Anne? Thank you. I appreciate your trust.

>>Th3Qu33nB1TCH - You are welcome, kiss.

>>ki55mia55 has disconnected.

>>Th3Qu33nB1TCH - Okay, we will have more conversations, but this is the beginning. We'll figure out how many you might want to pull from your people that would be willing to come work for me. I'll let you and Adam vet the people first, then someone else will do it again.

>>Th3Qu33nB1TCH has disconnected.

>>MyNam3isADAM - George, lucky?

>>Ih8tuGeorge - Yes?

>>luckyu11 - Yes?

>>MyNam3isADAM - Welcome to *ADAM's War*.

CHAPTER NINE

PARIS, FRANCE

George Bernard looked around the opulent room and sniffed. He hated the old, staid hotels from hundreds of years ago. He stepped into the private chambers and nodded to the second most powerful woman in Europe if you believed Forbes.

If you didn't, she was the most powerful person in Europe, man or woman. What she knew about some members of high society would embarrass a woman of the night. She used that knowledge to manipulate men and women in little ways, ways that always worked out for one of her companies, eventually. Even a few years later.

She was a planner, a thinker, and an excellent strategist. That she was joining this event meant she wasn't sure of the future herself.

George decided to make his way around to Cynthia to see if he could pick her brain.

He counted heads and came up with twenty-two. A pretty big group willing to change their schedules at a moment's notice to discuss matters concerning their respective interests across Europe. He couldn't find Joshua, but rumor had it that he had skipped out of his home in the U.S. and left a note that he was going to be gone for a long time.

He was either yellow or a genius. George wasn't sure which. He walked over to the buffet and took a small plate. He added a few wedges of cheese and a couple of melon slices. Grabbing a small fork and napkin, he continued out of the line and found himself conveniently close to Cynthia.

He stepped over and cleared his throat to catch her attention. "Cynthia, how are you this evening?"

Cynthia looked up at him and smirked. "Ever the quiet and devious one, George. I was wondering if you were going to swing my way, or Terence's over there?" She nodded to the left where Terence Whitesbridge was holding his own sort of court.

"Didn't you know? I'm completely heterosexual," George started, but had to stop when Cynthia spit wine as she was taking a sip. He quickly handed her his napkin and she was able to sop up most of the wine without making too much of a mess.

"I'm sorry," George started. "I hadn't meant to catch you unawares."

Cynthia dropped the sodden napkin on a tray and set her wine next to it. "I should remember that you enjoy twisting words." She turned to him and smiled. "Okay, I'll show you my," she paused, George kept quiet. "Cards."

"Damn," he murmured as she smiled.

"If you will show me your..." he raised an eyebrow at her. She rolled her eyes and finished, "cards."

He put up two fingers, a little space between them. "So close."

"I bet you were a spot of trouble in school, Mr. Bernard," she said.

He winked. "So, I'm Mr. Bernard now?" He flicked off some imaginary lint off of his shoulder. "I'll try not to be such a cad for the rest of the evening."

"Why is that?" Cynthia asked. "I rather like cads, they are so honest in what they want."

"What if I said I only wanted you for your knowledge, wisdom, and guidance?" George said.

She pursed her lips and leaned towards him. "Then I would wonder why my body was always in second place."

"Could it be that your greatest," George leaned to the side and acted like he was trying to see around her to her back. "Assets," he leaned back to look at her. "Aren't displayed appropriately?"

Cynthia put a hand to her mouth and smiled. "For a devious son of a bitch, you can still be quite charming."

"I try."

"Yes, I know. That's why I was waiting for you at the end of the line." She winked at him.

George raised his eyebrows, the stalker got snared in the web. He needed to up his game. Or, considering that he wanted to be right here anyway, maybe he should pat himself on the back for accomplishing it. For twenty minutes, he and Cynthia talked around every subject but the reason they had come to this meeting.

The battle with TQB Enterprises.

When the time came, the participants, twenty-four in all, sat around the table in no particular order. The person who sat at the end and had the most important seat was solved two centuries ago. You had a vote; you had the ability to call a vote. The rest of your power lay outside of this room most of the time, or perhaps inside the room if you considered your relationships. Take, for example, Terence Whitesbridge, who easily commanded two-thirds of the onlookers this evening.

After two small items had been discussed, Terence stood. "Now, for the reason we have all joined this evening in Paris." He nodded to both sides of the table. "What we care to do about TQB and our endeavors to either acquire their companies, their technology or both." He looked down at the table and lifted a folder. Opening it, he pulled out a piece of vellum. "I have spoken with many of you tonight, and if I have not, then, please forgive me for failing to speak with you yet."

George wanted to snort. Terence had made sure to speak to those he needed, neither Cynthia nor he was needed at the moment.

Terence continued, "I have been approached, as have some of you, by an interested third party not associated with us. Further, they have all sought to see if we would be willing to forego any material business relationships with TQB if they would provide suitable purchases to offset losses of anything TQB might be acquiring from us." Terence waited for the laughter to die down. However they did it, TQB knew who was after them and certainly did their best not to engage in any material business with any of their companies.

Those *bastards*.

"So, I have talked with a couple of you who have received similar advances, and we understand that our potential suitor is none other than the government of China. Oh, they were pretty good at trying to use cutouts, but they need to step up their game a little," he smiled at everyone.

George leaned over. "Is it only me, or do you want to

punch his teeth out, too?"

Cynthia turned towards him, a twinkle in her eye and whispered, "No, a swift knee to his jewels for me. Pompous ass!"

Before she turned back, George asked, "Did you get approached? I did not." She nodded that she had and then leaned back to listen.

"Now, we have one of the nation-states getting involved with TQB, which will probably focus their attention away from whatever we choose to do, and away from retribution based on past perceived slights we might have been guilty of."

"Not only a pompous ass," Cynthia whispered. "But delusional!" George thought her eyes might light up if she got just a little angrier.

"So, we have two paths to follow at this juncture. We can take this opportunity that China is offering and place our tail firmly between our legs and go home." Terence waited for the appropriate amount of grumbling to occur before continuing. "Or, we can use China as a way to hide our next strategy. I'm not for letting China get the spoils of the war we started!"

George looked around in shock as at least eight men and two women jumped up to push against the idea of letting China take the spoils of their actions against TQB.

Cynthia shook her head as she watched the people around the table before she tapped George on the shoulder. He turned, the surprise evident on his face at what he was also witnessing. "George, we have two options here." He nodded that he was listening. While she was speaking softly, she didn't need to. The yelling and boisterous comments that Terence was only encouraging hid anything they needed to say. "We can go back to my place and roll around on my bed for at least a day or two before we don't get sex again." He raised an eyebrow in surprise before she continued, "Not much sex in prison… or you can stay here and the only wood you will ever get again is going to be the coffin they bury you in."

"You don't think TQB is going to concentrate on China?" he asked.

She turned to look at the people present and made a face. "These idiots keep thinking that TQB is just another company, one they can manipulate." She turned to look at him. "They are a force focused on the future and will destroy whatever is in their way. I'd rather be safe, even if that means prison, than with these idiots."

As she stood up and started for the door she heard George move his chair to follow her.

"Cynthia, where are you going?" she heard Terence call from behind her. She turned around and smiled at the people there who had quieted down to hear what she had to say.

"Terence, and my esteemed idiots who are following Terence, I'm going home to get laid. I plan on having as much sex and human comfort as I can afford in the next forty-eight hours before the government comes for me. I'm thankful the headsman's ax isn't used in this day and age. I'm also leaving behind," she saw George behind her. "Twenty-two dead people still talking. You have not taken the measure of your enemy. If you try to do anything to TQB again, she is going to pull the gloves off, and I doubt there will be anything but a bloody spot on the ground when she's done with you."

Cynthia turned around and nodded to George, who was holding the door open for her.

George was about to follow when Terence called out, "George, you too? What, is she swaying your opinion with a piece of tail?"

George smiled. "I'd rather her piece of tail than yours,

Terence. I was never good at kissing ass, and it doesn't seem you need another to kiss yours, anyway."

With that, George let the door close behind him.

———

UNITED NATIONS, NEW YORK CITY, NY, USA

Zhou Song's lips pressed together minutely. It was the only expression he allowed to register on his face the displeasure he was feeling.

He had been working for over a week to get a consensus for a strong decision or memorandum against TQB Enterprises on behalf of the world as put forth by China, a leader in the United Nations.

Only to be pushed back.

Certainly by the powerful countries who figured China was up to something (true), but also by many of the unaligned countries who failed to believe that China would honor their agreements (partially true). China would certainly honor the specific letters of the agreements, but not the spirit of the agreements.

Inside the fine print was a fair amount of ifs, buts and thens. Plenty of legal language that allowed China to drag their feet should they acquire any of the new technology.

Unfortunately, China's history over the last twenty years of either stealing technology, borrowing technology, or requiring trading partners to share technology (which they then stole) was catching up to them.

Right when the best technology was being flaunted in their face.

Zhou Song locked his black leather briefcase and nodded to his translator. Not that she was needed. He spoke six languages besides three specific to China. The only one that foreign services knew about was English. So, he often played dumb when around those of other countries just in case they would slip up and say something in his presence.

She packed up as he slid behind her and continued out of the room. He nodded to the representative from Uganda, who he was meeting for dinner next Thursday night and took a left. In a couple of minutes, he had slipped into his limousine and was whisked out to his residence at the Waldorf Astoria. The hotel was now owned by a Chinese-owned insurance company. The United States, who had previously had all of their UN Representatives stay at the famed location since Herbert Hoover, had moved them, suggesting that perhaps the government of China was behind the purchase.

Pity that, Zhou Song thought.

The car pulled up to the hotel, and his door was opened. He kept his briefcase with him and stepped through the entryway to head to a set of special elevators that didn't work for the public. He tapped his fob on the front and stepped inside. Hitting the button for his floor, he considered what he needed to do to manipulate the contingent from Central Africa to start another bloc. His country had provided substantial investment, not all of the money going into the projects, but that was how Africa worked.

The elevator dinged, and the doors slid open. Zhou Song walked to his room and nodded to the two security guards who walked this floor. He stepped inside and put the briefcase on the table to the right. The same place he put it every night as he walked into his bedroom to change. He came out in a pair of jeans and a long sleeved shirt. He rolled up his sleeves as he walked into his kitchen.

Zhou Song preferred to cook to center himself as he thought. It was relaxing. Cooking was something he had been doing since his early teenage years.

This room had been modified for him, to allow him this exercise. Otherwise, the chef on site was sufficient for those nights he needed to work through his time of meditation.

He stepped into his kitchen and stopped.

He turned to his left to look into the small living room and beyond to the balcony outside. He turned to his right and stepped out of his kitchen to look into his office.

It was empty.

He didn't feel anything amiss in the room, so he walked over to the door and opened it. First looking left, then right to see one of the guards. "Mùqián yǐ jìnrù biérén wǒ de fángjiān?" The guard shook his head no. "Yǒu méiyǒu rén zài zhè yī céng?" Again, the guard shook his head.

Song closed the door and walked back into his kitchen. He put his hand on the large loaf of bread and pulled the pin out of the loaf and grabbed the sheet of paper.

The message was written in six languages, all languages he knew and that other people were not supposed to know he was fluent in.

"It is only the enlightened ruler and the wise general who will use the highest intelligence of the army for the purposes of spying, and thereby achieve great results."

Song put down the letter. The quote, one of Sun Tzu's, was a maxim in his country. He looked around his apartment and considered what he needed to do next, and his shoulders slumped.

He was going to have to move.

He could not trust living inside his walls now, and it was

going to cause him great distress until his security could confirm it was safe for him to come back.

This was going to cause him undue stress when he least needed it.

Unfortunately, he never considered that by the time he left, the microscopic bugs had already invaded his briefcase, and he took the little devices with him to the embassy.

ADAM, however, was already working the little machines as soon as he put the briefcase down.

CHAPTER TEN

WASHINGTON D.C. USA

The President walked into the meeting with the fourteen heads of companies he had requested to attend. Fourteen heads that he had pulled with his top business advisors from the information provided by TQB. When asked, he was adamant he wouldn't tell them where the information had come from, simply that he had it and that the FBI was able to confirm a fair number of the details.

He had planted twenty-two additional names in the request in case they started talking before they got to Washington. He then had his press secretary tell the extra twenty-two they would be joining him at a separate location in the White House. That would be his second meeting.

He walked into his first meeting with four secret service and four FBI agents.

He had asked General George Thourbourah to attend this meeting to listen.

Everyone turned to face the President as he stepped up to the podium. There were no chairs in the room as he didn't intend for it to be very long.

He turned to make sure the doors were shut and then turned back to those standing in front of him. "I appreciate all of you coming today. Unfortunately, you are here for a different reason than many others." The noise started to ramp up, and he just looked to the left and the right. He waited about thirty seconds and then looked at his watch before tapping on the microphone to get their attention. "I will be quick, because I have another meeting, one with people living inside of our society, not trying to live above it."

He put up a hand to forestall the noise. "I don't personally care if you want to argue with what I have to say. Just let it be known that I have representatives from the FBI here in this room with whom I've shared documents delivered to me that suggest there is an illegal cabal, operating for well over a century, that has done many harmful things for their companies' benefits and their own personal gain. Now, I'm also aware that those people have taken it upon themselves to start a fight. A fight using both legal and illegal means to obtain technology that does not belong to them."

He looked out over the sea of faces, a few eyes, he noticed, darted to others in the room. "Now, unlike many cabal movements in the past, this time, they have bitten off way more than they can chew. Based on our research, compiled as we watched for evidence of these battles both on the stock market and off, shows us that this cabal is getting their ass kicked."

He looked around again after a pause. "Or they're dying." When he said that, the whispering got a little louder.

"Now," he continued, and the noise died down. "Officially,

I don't know any of this at this moment. I can't help anyone, I can't defend anyone, I can't possibly ask for clemency from another party who might believe that there is such a rule as an eye for an eye and is willing to implement it." He looked hard at the people in front of him.

"What I can tell you is that I have documents that let me know who I should be talking to right now. You can be assured, as the good countryman you are, that your government is now aware of this and will not sit by and allow this cabal to operate going forward." His face grew firm.

"I can tell you we know how to protect those who might be afraid of the dark, so to speak." He looked around, hope shining out from at least a third of the eyes present. "But, they aren't going to like the solution, I don't think. It seems the organization in question only recognizes our prisons as safe zones. So, to be safe, people have to turn themselves in." He smiled at the speechless people in the audience, now aware that they had only a binomial option of safety in prison, or no safety.

The President turned to his right and nodded. Two FBI agents stepped back beside the General as the President turned around to the audience again. "It saddens me to say that inside this information provided me was proof. Proof that this cabal had infected people all the way to the top, so to speak. The FBI has confirmed this information, so in front of you, as witnesses, they are taking into custody General George Thourbourah, for aiding and abetting interests inimical to the United States of America." Now, the room erupted as the General went wide eyed and the two FBI agents quickly turned him and popped handcuffs on his wrists before he got his wits about him. The front FBI agent pulled a card out as the room quieted.

"You have the right to remain silent…" he started. The President leaned one arm on the podium, and watched every person as the General was read his rights and then walked out of the room, his head hung low. Everyone turned back to see the President staring at them.

He spoke in a conversational tone. "You have the same right to remain silent, to not implicate yourselves in anything. What that will accomplish is staying out of the only guaranteed safe place in this solar system. If you have any desire to be safe? Well, these two guys up here have business cards, you might ask for one. Have a good night." The President stepped off the podium and swept out of the room with his security, leaving the two FBI agents behind with everyone else.

The President thought the looks of shock on all the faces in the room were priceless.

PARIS, FRANCE

The sound of the door closing behind George still echoed when Terence smiled to the rest of the people sitting around him. "So, there go the only two without the, excuse me, ladies," he smiled around the table. "The BALLS to seize the future!"

Downstairs and outside of the hotel, Cynthia stood on the curb and waited for her personal limousine to pull up. George stepped up to her, "Were you honest about wanting comfort?" he asked.

She slipped an arm through his. "George, you have no idea how close you dodged the bullet in there." Her limousine drove up, it had modifications for security. George saw a driver, but another man from the front seat stepped out to open the door.

He nodded to George before opening the door for Cynthia. "Is this the man you expected?"

Cynthia nodded, a little sad. "I'm sad to say it was, no others chose to align themselves with me this evening, Nathan."

He nodded his understanding when another woman surprised George by exiting the vehicle. He didn't get a good look at her, just noticing the black hair before she put a hat on her head as she walked into the hotel. Cynthia half pulled, half pushed George into her backseat before Nathan leaned in to the car. "You have seventy-two hours before the deal is off, understand?"

Cynthia nodded her head. "I'll be there, with the proof." She stared Nathan in the eyes. "I'll do my time."

Nathan said, "See that you do, Cynthia. I went out on a limb to help you here."

She held a hand out and Nathan took it. "I know, Nathan. We've done good business together in the past, and I wish you and your wife a beautiful and healthy child." He nodded, accepting her good wishes, and closed the door.

He turned and lowered his head, his hat covering a large portion of his face as the vehicle left and he walked in to go to a meeting in an out of the way part of the hotel.

———

Terence never noticed that every time a server left, they did not come back. He was about to suggest they break up into smaller work groups when he noticed a woman with a veiled hat and a man dressed in livery standing beside her.

"Who are you?" Terence asked. It took only a few seconds for everyone at the table to see others looking behind them and to stop talking and turn around themselves.

"Oh good," her voice was smooth, and Terence was wondering what she looked like under that hat. "I finally have your attention."

"I believe the man asked who you were," Constantina asked from a few places closer to Terence. "This is a private meeting."

"Yes, I'm aware," she said, standing up. "This is an off-shoot of the Illuminati created in 1776, now a sad spectacle of the original shining ideals. Well, at least somewhat shining compared to you." She started walking along, a black gloved hand drawing along the backs of everyone at the table. "I've heard enough of your plans, thank you very much."

She reached over and grabbed Truett Mastersos III. "Truett you are judged, good-bye." Terrence was shocked as she easily grabbed Truett and pulled him bodily out of his chair into the air where he just... vanished.

"What the hell?" the next man over exclaimed.

"The hell," she told Marco Broussard. "Is that you have been doing evil deeds for over seventeen years, Mr. Broussard, and now it's the penalty box for you." She yanked his chair out and caught him under the arm. She pivoted and threw him up over the table, and those on the other side screamed as he started coming in their direction, but he never landed.

He disappeared as well.

"The hell with this!" Karthi Montero muttered from down at the other end of the table and pushed his chair back; he kept his eyes on her as he walked away and around the

MICHAEL ANDERLE

end of the table to walk out the door. She watched him as he continued walking.

Right past Nathan.

Two women screamed when they saw the man turn into a literal wolf-man in front of their eyes. Karthi was screaming as the wolf-thing growled and held his neck in its left hand. Then looked at all of those still at the table as dinner. Two of the men got out of their chairs and slid across the table to get on the other side from the werewolf.

"Hold on! Don't eat him, your wife will be most upset," the strange woman told the werewolf.

"What the hell is that and who the hell are you?" Terence yelled, trying to keep both of the terrors in view.

"I'm the one you should not have crossed. I took a survey of one, myself, and decided the future would be a lot better without you in it. Nathan here," she waved a hand at the monster holding Karthi. "Is here to make sure you hear what I have to say."

"What is it?" Terence wanted to scream but tried to keep calm with everyone else freaking the hell out.

Her voice went silky smooth over steel. "You have been tried by the Queen Bitch herself for crimes against her, her people and humanity in general. Everyone stand up." Those still sitting pushed themselves out of their chairs. "Now wait until I get to you, but feel free to be as scared as you want as you can't move your muscles. I'll get to each of you in a moment."

Then the mysterious lady pulled off her hat and everyone realized that the person they were plotting against had been listening to their plans in their own room. "The supreme art of war is to subdue your enemy without a fight. I tried being nice, and you all just fucked it away. Now, you get the Queen

117

SUED FOR PEACE

Bitch," Bethany Anne's voice changed, her eyes grew red and four people screamed in their minds while others wished they could cry. "In all of her glory!"

The Matriarch, the Queen of the Vampires went to each person, called their name out named a few of their sins and pushed them. They simply vanished.

She spent no more time on Terrence than she did the others. Ten minutes later, she got to Karthi. "You aren't even worth it, you little rat-fink bastard." Nathan dropped the man and Bethany Anne grabbed him before he could fall. "Karthi, your sins are plenty. Think of them as you serve your time," she pulled him sideways, and he disappeared. "And die."

Nathan changed back to a human again. He twisted his head around, trying to pop his neck. "Don't eat him? Seriously?" he groused.

"I didn't want them to rush you. I figured better to sit still than get eaten. With Karthi in your hand like that, it was totally believable."

"That would be hideous, I think. That man smelled."

"I imagine he did, worse after you grabbed him," she agreed.

Two seconds later, they took a step, and disappeared as well.

An hour later, the hired help came in and found that the room was a little messy, and there was some urine by the door, but no one could find any of the occupants.

It was all over the news the next day that twenty-two of Europe's major business people had disappeared.

Cynthia and George stayed in bed for forty-eight hours, took twelve hours to make sure to review their estates one last time, and went together to The Hague to turn themselves in.

118

They walked up the steps, and Cynthia thought she saw Nathan out of the corner of her eye as they entered the building.

She asked George to wait for her and went back outside for a few seconds and looked around, but there was no one there.

CHAPTER ELEVEN

EXPENSIVE APARTMENT NEAR CENTRAL PARK, NEW YORK CITY, NY, USA

Oh shit, here we go again!" Tina Casson was watching the stock trading screens when the flags started flashing that fourteen of the four hundred and seventy-two companies that they had flagged as belonging to TQB Enterprises lit up.

Rajiv turned in his chair to look over her shoulder. "Damn, someone is trying hard to buy those companies out." He reached across her shoulder to hit a flag on the screen.

Tina slapped his arm. "Hey! Touch your own damn screen. Now mine has Rajiv cooties."

Rajiv ignored her outburst. "Look, they aren't getting any takers, I bet you most of these companies are owned by the same group somehow."

"What?" Tina ignored his arm and her fingers started dancing on the keyboards, "No, we have a few takers."

"Yeah, but the cost is at least two hundred times book value, this is crazy." Rajiv turned back to his screen. "See if we can buy some puts on this."

"You think it's going down?" Tina asked, biting on a fingernail. "I'm not feeling that."

"No?" Rajiv turned back around. "Why?"

"Look," she pointed to the screen. "The offer is GTC, they're going to wait it out. Whoever is behind this... wait a minute." She turned to a monitor on her right and hit a few more keystrokes. "All based on banks that go back to China."

"Ooooh, new players." Rajiv said and started to reach across only to have Tina pinch the sensitive skin under his arm. "Ouch ouch OUCH!" He yanked his arm back as Tina eyed him, snapping her fingers together like a little crab might.

"No touchy!" she told him, eyes angry.

"I'm good, I'm good," he told her, massaging his arm. "Would you mind looking at the open positions on calls?"

Tina turned and hit a few buttons, "Yeah, they're growing and... what the hell?" She pointed to the screens. "Why are they so high?"

"My guess is whoever is selling the calls is the owner. They're offsetting another end run."

"Or they're doing some sort of butterfly spread with these puts here," Tina stated and pointed to new stock option puts on the screen.

Rajiv noticed another flag on the left monitor. "Another five companies are under attack."

"Who the hell has this much money?"

"Only a handful of companies might, or a nation," Rajiv shrugged. "Ours is not to ask who, but to make a shit-ton of money while they're trying."

Tina started typing on her computer. "It's like they're blowing the shit out of each other and we're the ones selling the ammunition and getting paid to clean up the battlefield."

"Better them than me, arbitrage is fast and hopefully less risky than what they're playing." Rajiv turned back to his own computer, put his hands together to crack his knuckles and then started laying out his screens. "Time to make five figures today."

"The fishing will be good," Tina agreed. "Booyah baby!" she called out. "Dropped my first five back into my account, momma's gonna get herself a diamond ring!"

"I thought that was for the guy to buy?" Rajiv asked, focused on executing an option spread.

"Haven't you listened to the Beyoncé song?" she asked.

"Too busy making money to worry about stuff like that." Rajiv issued orders to sell. "Bring the MONEY!" he yelled pointing at his screen. "Another ten for me, baby!"

"Fucking shit," Tina bit her lip and executed a wrap-around. "You Indians are weird, letting your parents pick out your wives and shit." She lined up two more purchases but had nothing to sell, yet.

"Call me DADDY!" Rajiv yelled as he closed another pair of trades. "That makes 14 gs for me and no, what's the divorce rate for you Americans picking your spouses for yourselves, something like less than half make it?"

"Um, yeah, you have a point about that," she agreed, hitting sell on three positions, "Wham, Bam, Thank you, Ma'am. Momma just closed and now leads fifteen to fourteen."

"Damn, they're beating the shit out of each other," Rajiv called back over his shoulder, "Did you see them go after the manufacturing companies?"

"What? No."

"Some funny shit going on there," Rajiv said. "I'm seeing secondary players coming up."

"The big guys are staying quiet on this, did you notice that?" Tina asked as she executed another four trades. "Call it twenty-five to fourteen. Now Daddy is behind."

"Ha!" Rajiv yelled, "WOOHOO BABY!" He stood up and slapped his ass, twice, "Daddy got the sizzle." He sat back down. "One down two k, but two were up, netting seventeen k on those beauties."

"Shit, that's thirty-one to twenty-seven. I just closed another two g on three trades," she told him.

"I'm almost clear, this is crazy." Rajiv looked at everything on his panel. "I'm pulling everything I've got."

"What? Why?" she asked, looking at her accounts and the crazy trades. "Yeah, shit." Her fingers started dancing across the keyboard. Within sixty seconds, her trades were all cleared. "I closed out up twenty-nine," she told him as she moved cash to different accounts.

"I lost one closing out, but I'm up thirty to twenty-nine." He turned lazily in his chair to face Tina, who had just closed her bank screen, a smile on his face. "Pay up, you lost," he told her.

Tina turned in her chair and stood up, a lascivious grin on her face. "Anytime we make almost sixty thousand dollars in under ten minutes, I'll gladly give you a kiss to curl your toes, baby." She straddled his legs and leaned in to kiss him.

Damn, Rajiv thought, his toes did want to curl.

———

SUED FOR PEACE

PLA GENERAL STAFF HEADQUARTERS, BEIJING

Fourteen high value targets in one night across the countries of India, Egypt, Mexico, Thailand, and Korea.

General Sun Zedong walked into the operations center. He sat down in the back, allowing his subordinates the opportunity to run the individual ops. He would be available if a quick decision needed to be made.

He looked around and counted. Five core leaders, two communications and directions resources per leader.

He made a decision not to jiggle their elbows and have them second-guessing themselves. He stood up, spoke to each one, and let them each know he was available in his office if they should need him.

He stepped out, confident that he had made the right decision.

HOSPET, KARNATAKA. INDIA

Colonel Jai looked down at his list, confirming he and his squad of three additional men had the final 'go' before he committed to action. The target was a small, two-story office building in Hospet, Karnataka, India. They had been tasked with raiding the building. Acquisition of hard drives, any technology information from computers disengaged from the internet and hard copies if they seemed relevant to the mission.

As a research business focused particularly on different types of metals and gravity based concepts, they hoped this was going to be a particularly good raid opportunity. From their four-day review, it looked like the building wasn't going to be a problem.

The security system was cracked forty-eight hours ago. Jai did not expect there to be a system turned on when he got there. He and his team shouldn't trip anything while inside, which was good. The local police station was just four blocks away.

He nodded to his driver and they pulled the windowless van up to the side of the building. Engine off, the four men waited an additional ten minutes to make sure nothing seemed amiss. He nodded, and they exited the van. Each had a mask they put on as soon as they went over the small wall so that no pictures could be taken that might reveal their nationalities. They jogged to the entrance by the small loading dock in back. Jai pointed to the door, and Li nodded, going up the six cement stairs two at a time. He pulled out a small tool and started working on the lock.

Jai and his team had cased this location for the last three nights, checking everything out. The guard went to eat at a local all-night restaurant that was connected to a nearby hotel and would arrive back, Jai looked at his watch, in forty-two more minutes.

Plenty of time for his team to deal with this.

Li stood up, opened the door, and followed Jai's team as they entered the building.

Jai took the lead and walked quickly and calmly to the door leading out of the loading dock. He cracked the door and then opened it further when he found no one on the other side. He walked to the third door on the right and grabbed the handle to walk into the stairway leading to the second floor. In a few seconds, they were on the next floor. On this floor, there were always lights on.

He and his team did a quick half-crouching run heading towards the back of the second floor, past a large section of cubicles and what looked like a bunch of small telephone cubbies. Jai could smell a heavy amount of spice in the air as he passed another darkened room. He assumed it was the kitchen.

Another right turn and they hit the door to the research and computer design areas. Jai tested the door, but it was locked. It looked like one that would automatically close and lock every time someone went through.

He stepped back and let Li pull out his lock tool.

Jai glanced at his watch, thirty-nine minutes.

It took Li about half a minute's work on the lock before he stood up and opened the door.

Jai was about to follow him when Li's head came back through the door, and he fiercely pulled it back as a metal object of some sort slammed into the door where his head and hands had just been. As quick as he was, Li's hand was still slammed pretty hard as he tried to duck back into the hallway and he muffled a curse.

Jai jumped to the side and quickly put his foot out to stop the door. Whoever was behind the door slammed into it hard to shove it closed, and Jai grunted when his foot got caught between the door and the doorjamb.

He and his men quickly started pushing, and he gave a count to push on three, "Yee, Uhr, SAHN!" On three all pushed, but they met no resistance as whoever was behind the door let go. There was just a second of confusion as the men stumbled into the room. Jai could see a lab-coated worker running around the corner.

Dammit!

"Wu, Li!" Jai pointed. The two men rushed forward, following the figure.

Shit! There wasn't supposed to be anyone here. He was looking around the room when he heard a gunshot. Moments later, he heard a second. His men came jogging back around the corner, Wu and Li both holstering pistols.

"She was going for the alarm," Wu said.

Li added, "I'm not sure we got there in time. I shot second to make sure she couldn't speak about us."

Jai nodded his understanding. "Breakage." He turned towards the computers he could see.

Liang reached up to his ear. "Colonel, we have confirmation the police have been notified of a silent alarm."

Jai wanted to curse. "Grab what you can, we have to get out of here."

They caught up anything electronic that they could carry and dashed out of the research area, down the hallway to turn right to the stairway. It took but a minute for them to be out through the loading dock door and to get back over the short fence and into the van. Li jumped in the driver's seat as Jai got on the passenger side and Liang and Wu got in back. Li started the van and then drove down the street, away from the building at a sedate speed. He took the second left as they had planned. It led them into a small subdivision, which allowed them to take three turns before exiting into an area of the city that dropped them onto a better road where they could more easily lose any pursuit.

Jai wanted to slam his hand against the van's seat. All of their planning screwed up by one stupid female.

Shit!

NARA, NARA PREFECTURE, JAPAN

Yuko stood outside of her parents' home with a backpack on her shoulder. Her parents did not understand her desire to stand apart, to do something outside of the family or her country.

She started walking towards Kasuga-Taisha to get to the forest, where she had been told that she would be picked up.

She was a little concerned, as there was no going back from this moment. Her father had told her that no one from TQB would be coming for her and that if she stayed out past dark, he would not allow her entrance back into the house. This way, she would be forced to confront her irrational beliefs and foolhardy trust of those on the internet in the dark of the evening as punishment for being unwise.

Right now, she was the only one that would go.

She spoke with three others in the hacking clan, and they refused. There was no way they would break tradition with their parents.

But Yuko had to know, had to understand what was going on. She felt a connection to Adam, AI though he might be, one that led her to believe that he would never wrong her.

Or Bethany Anne.

She noticed a tika deer watching her from the shadows, and she stopped, bowing to the deer, who bowed back. She stood up and considered the deer like it was a sacred messenger from a Shinto God from ages past and walked away with a smile on her face.

If nothing else, it made her feel good.

There were people out enjoying the day, and she took out her phone to pick her way through the growth. She wasn't sure what was going on until the undergrowth opened up and there was a glade about twelve meters wide and twice as long.

Fifteen minutes later, she covered her mouth with her hand as a black Pod descended quickly from the sky, a second one hanging back as the first stopped just above the ground. It opened, and a lady sat inside, smiling at her.

A lady whose face was well known to Yuko. "Honorable Bethany Anne?" Yuko asked as she walked to the Pod.

"You might want to jump in pretty quickly. There's no need to make the Japanese Air Force all twitchy, so if you want to go we should move fast."

Yuko pulled the backpack off of her back and smiled as she turned to sit inside a famed black Pod for the first time. Bethany Anne hit a button, and the doors closed, bringing darkness inside the Pod until Bethany Anne did something and the glass allowed a softened view of the glade outside.

A male voice came out of a speaker above Yuko's head. "Bethany Anne, we have a query on the military channels about possible U.F.Os in Kasugayama Primeval Forest."

"Right, high-dee ho, it's time to go. Take us up, TOM."

Yuko felt some acceleration, and the ground and her city disappeared quickly underneath them.

"Welcome to Team ADAM, Yuko." Bethany Anne said. "I'm happy you chose to join us."

Yuko was enthralled with the view out of the glass. She heard someone talking, but it took a second for her to go back, rewind what she thought she had heard and then catch back up. "I am so sorry, Bethany Anne, I was not paying attention!"

Bethany Anne laughed. "It catches all of us one way or another," she agreed as she swiped an arm across the glass to take off the control display and screens obscuring the view.

"Here, why don't we enjoy this together?"

Yuko turned from paying attention to Bethany Anne to watch while the sky darkened, and then she understood.

Yuko Komagata, a daughter who, according to her father, needed to stop spending so much time on her computer and think more about a relationship and moving forward, stared into space.

The first Komagata to leave her town in three generations had abandoned town, country, and now her world. A tear made its way down her face as she reached out to touch the glass.

"No, Father," she whispered to herself. "There are some who you meet on the internet who can be trusted, even if they might not be human themselves."

Another male voice came over the loudspeaker, "Yuko, I would like to introduce myself," he said.

"My name is ADAM."

CHAPTER TWELVE

GUANGZHOU, CHINA

Ting was looking around the large building, slightly confused. Her Empress had informed her of the exact address, date and time that she needed to show up in Guangzhou to deliver her Empress's letter.

Ting wore the clothes of her mother, and her mother before her. Black with yellow embroidery on their sleeves. On her collar was the Chinese tiger symbol. While her clothes were clean, they were not modern, nor were they new.

For Ting, this was of little concern. She noticed some of the new Chinese looking at her rural clothes and hairstyle. Twice, women in their twenties sniffed in her direction as they walked by in their longer skirts, high heels, with jackets and coiffed hair.

Ting smirked. If those ladies understood who was in their midst, she doubted they would have dared come so close.

"Excuse me?" Ting turned to regard the young man who had called her.

"Yes?"

"Are you lost, or are you looking for the market, perhaps?" he asked.

Ting did not sense any rudeness in this man, so he was forgiven any slight shown to the Leopard Empress' envoy.

"No, I am at the right place. I have been told to ask for the Jade room. I have permission to deliver a message to those inside from my Empress. The code word is light."

Ting saw the surprise on his face before he bowed more deeply and turned to head towards a back hallway. "Please, follow me."

Ting followed the man in livery past two guarded locations. At both, the young man was stopped and asked about her presence. The man bowed to both guards and explained that she had the code word for the most respected that were meeting in the back.

Ting followed the young man. Keeping her thoughts to herself as she sniffed the hallways, recording the smells, the sounds, and what she saw.

Finally, there was one more set of double doors to go through. The young man spoke again to the guards who turned their attention to her. "Are you here for yourself, or for another?" the guard asked as her first escort left her with a smile and a nod, returning to the lobby.

"I'm an envoy for my Empress," Ting said.

"And who would that be?" the guard asked as rudeness crept into his voice.

Ting swallowed her first response. "That is not for you to know, it will not grace your ears, or I will be under oath to retract the knowledge."

The guard regarded the slender five-foot tall young woman who couldn't weigh more than perhaps ninety jin or nearly a hundred pounds if she was wet from falling into the pond. "And how, exactly, would you accomplish this?"

"Well, I'm unaware of a way to accomplish it while you are alive, so unfortunately, death is my only option. At that point, I believe the information is no longer available to be spoken, or possible for others to find out." She stood there meeting his eyes with a steady look.

The guard next to him chuckled. "You should let her in, we aren't required to know this. She has the code word, Zan, let it go.

Zan nodded and turned to knock on the door softly. It was cracked open, and he whispered into the doorway. Zan stepped back to allow a third guard, bigger than either Zan or Mei. This new man was easily six feet tall, and most of his muscle had muscle on top of it. He looked down at the small woman regarding him impassively.

Tai was accustomed to causing a fearful reaction in his normally shorter countrymen and especially with his countrywomen.

Except this one. Tai stepped towards her, but Ting held still even when he invaded her personal space. "If you wish to offer the envoy a slight, to force me to respond, then you are very close," she told him, holding his eyes with her own.

Those eyes, Tai thought, didn't seem right.

"Who sent you?" Tai asked. "We have the code word, but who am I to say is interrupting this meeting?"

This man's smirk was irritating Ting. "I have warned your man here, that to know this information is not for you. Do you seek to know against these warnings?"

Tai turned to Zan and raised an eyebrow, Zan shook

his head. "I don't need to know, the decision is yours." Tai turned back around. "What if you whisper it into my ear so that I may announce you?"

"Then I will pull the knowledge from your heart once you are finished with it," she said in a clipped fashion.

Tai grimaced but nodded in agreement and bent down so she could whisper the name into his ear.

Zan saw Tai's eyes roll when he heard the name, but he turned around to walk in with the young woman following him. She looked at Zan and said quietly, "Close the door, you will not want to hear this."

When she stepped into the room, Zan quickly but silently closed the door behind them.

Mei rolled his eyes and took his position beside the door. "You are running scared from a mouse."

"I don't think so, Mei," he replied. "This time, I think the stories walk the Earth again."

"You are superstitious, Zan." Mei snorted. "I bet she is out in ten minutes."

"Deal," Zan agreed.

———

Inside, Ting slipped behind the guard who had the attention of what had to be close to twenty of those in power inside the room. Ting was surprised to see three were wearing the old style traditional clothes like her.

The guard stood in front and spoke. "No disrespect intended, but I have an envoy to announce. She has the appropriate code word to join this meeting."

One of the older men, with a long gray beard and bushy eyebrows, asked, "Did the envoy provide her Empress' name?"

"She did," Tai started to say. "She claims she is from…
ARGUGH." Tai stopped talking as incredible pain ripped
through his chest. He reached only to grab a fist holding
him. A small fist, with claws, had hold of what remained of
his heart as it spurted blood before ceasing to beat. He felt
the sharpness of his broken ribs as he tried to push his heart
back in. His legs lost the ability to stand yet he didn't fall.
He coughed up blood and slowly his head lowered, his eyes
never closing.

Then, those in the room saw the mighty Tai finally lean
forward and the small woman, her hand slipping out of his
back, her eyes glowing yellow, released his body to collapse
to the floor.

She spoke in a soft voice. "No disrespect intended, honorable leaders. This guard was informed I would take the name
of my Empress from his heart inside of this room."

Zhao studied the young warrior-envoy and nodded his
head. "There is no need to share your Empress's name, Envoy…"

"Ting," she supplied and stepped forward, apparently
without thought or concern that her arm was coated in blood.

"Yes, Envoy Ting." Zhao stood up and bowed to her.
"Welcome to our meeting, Envoy of the Leopard Empress."

Ting heard the gasps from around the room, hurried
questions from a couple of people who were trying to ask
about the Leopard Empress. The soft sound of panicked
heartbeats made an accompaniment that pleased Ting great-
ly.

And oh, the delicious smell of fear, of respect, for her
Empress.

She bowed. "Thank you, Leader Zhao." When she raised
back up, everyone there could see that her eyes glowed the

yellow of the Sacred Clan. "I have been sent by the Leopard Empress to give those here in the Illuminati the opportunity to ally yourself with that which you seek from TQB, and provide our protection."

"And what does the Leopard Empress desire for this?" Zhou asked, keeping his tone very respectful. Zhou had been raised in central China. There the history of the Sacred Clan was told to little children to scare them. As he had aged, Zhou found the stories fascinating and had tried to see what the real story was behind the fairy tales.

Only to find that the partial truths that people would admit were more fanciful than the stories the villagers spoke around the fires at night.

Ting cocked her head. "You misunderstand, I believe, honorable leader Zhao." She looked around the room and smiled. "The question is what do you want to give first as a tribute to start the discussions. The Leopard Empress knows who you fight, and knows more about their abilities than you might ever be able to understand. Further, she knows your relationships and your failures. If she wanted your companies, she would just wait for TQB to come for you."

Zhao kept his face serene but reassessed his impression of this Leopard Empress. He had expected that this person would not know much about what was going on outside of the Heubei area where their temple had been for hundreds of years.

Unfortunately, Keung three chairs down from Zhao did not have Zhao's knowledge of the sacred clan. "Who is this Leopard Princess, Zhao?" He pointed at Ting. "Why are we even speaking to this small girl who kills our people like this?" Keung stood up. "I will not have someone come and talk this way to me! I am not an unaware guard whom you can just punch," Keung hit the air three times very suddenly, "into submission!" He started walking around the table. "I say," he pointed at Ting. "That we spank you and send you back to the Leopard Princess and tell her we can take care of ourselves."

Four of those around the table looked at Zhao, who put a hand out, palm down and moved it up and down slightly above the table, telling them to wait.

It looked like Keung was going to make Zhao's point for him in a very primal way.

SAN JOSE, COSTA RICA

The coolness of the night swirled around the two men. "I'm telling you, José," George said, as he looked at the manufacturing business across the street. "This is easy money. Go in, bust a few things, look for any computers or laptops that could have technical drawings and we're back out."

"And I'm telling you, George," José said, spitting on the ground. "If the order wasn't from Miguel, I wouldn't be doing this shit." He looked around the darkened street. The building was pretty large for a midlevel company in San José. Miguel had taken a lot of money to harass businesses in Costa Rica and Argentina that were supposedly working with TQB. José didn't care spit about TQB, except rumor was if you messed with a company that worked with them, shit seemed to happen to you.

José looked around one more time. "All right, I'm not feeling anything bad, let's cross." They kept their lead pipes up against their bodies. They had pistols, but that was in case things got really bad. They hadn't been paid to kill anyone. Hopefully, they could give the security guy a hundred U.S. if he was there and he would take a punch and go down.

Up on the roof of the building, three pairs of eyes watched the two toughs. One of the three, a woman, spoke quietly to the other two, "See, I told you it was going down here tonight."

"Yes, Kimosabe," Ryu said in the dark.

Tabitha rolled her eyes. "What do you think, Hirotoshi?" While Tabitha might decide the whens and the wheres, it was Hirotoshi who decided everything martial. "I think you need seasoning, and these two will provide it," he said in his clipped way of speaking. "Don't get killed, or my Queen will be most displeased."

"Really?" Tabitha said. "I get killed, and you worry about Bethany Anne being annoyed with you?" She untied her scabbard and lifted it off of her back. Decked out in all black, there was little chance the two thugs below would see her in the dark of the night. "I think I might be a tad upset as well," she huffed before turning to the side of the roof and hopping off. She landed from the twelve-foot drop with barely a notice and started jogging down the side of the building to the unlocked door on the other side.

Ryu looked at Hirotoshi. "You know the Queen will be more than just displeased with us," he said.

Hirotoshi nodded. "That is why I have two vials of blood, in case it goes... what did Barnabas call it?" he asked as he turned to follow his charge.

"Pear shaped," Ryu replied as he followed his partner over the edge of the roof, running off the building to land lithely. With barely a break in his stride, he started to close the distance to their rash leader.

MICHAEL ANDERLE

Truth be told, both men had grown to like the spunky woman who sometimes ran ahead of her thinking, and whose mouth always ran ahead of everyone else.

———

Keung walked around the table, watching the small woman who kept an eye on him, but was also aware of everyone else in the room. She seemed neither concerned nor bothered that Keung had been talking down about her leader.

He was not worried about his own performance. While this woman could and would kill, Keung had not been bested in the last three years, even by those who taught others to fight. He could not beat them either, so he suspected at worst, it would be a draw, but he would be given the respect she had not shown so far.

One didn't throw around martial prowess and expect no one to challenge you… unless you were a fool.

Keung took off his jacket and laid it on a chair. She watched as he took off his watch and shirt, leaving on his t-shirt. He noticed that she had on sandals usual for the outer country and took off his own shoes and socks. She dipped her head to him in acknowledgement and took off her sandals.

Keung stepped up and bowed while keeping his head up. She barely nodded in return. It irritated him. Even the teachers gave Keung more respect than this little female. Perhaps he would spank her for real at the end of this.

Keung moved the ball of his right foot behind him when she started walking towards him. It was a horrible position, and he extended from his stance with a snap kick to her head.

Which wasn't there.

One moment, she was walking at him as he struck, the

next she had slid under him, and he felt the burn of fire on his right foot as he landed.

He hopped to turn around and saw that his right foot had three slashes down the length, as if claws had ripped through his skin.

He looked, and her right hand was stained with fresh blood. Certainly, the blood splatters on the floor led back to her.

Keung pressed his lips together and willed the pain to recede. He failed to notice the stares coming from the table were focused on the young woman.

"Her name," Ting announced to everyone in the room. "Is the Leopard Empress." She nodded at Keung. "And if you know your children's stories..." She started walking towards Keung again and he changed positions to brace his left leg behind him. "You know there is no disrespect of the Leopard Empress allowed." Keung almost forgot to try and strike when the woman growled like a tiger, and he would have sworn she grew six inches as she walked towards him. He attempted to throw his quickest punches, she slapped them all aside as if he was nothing but a child, barely able to walk. He never saw the clawed hand that took out his throat. His body slammed into the floor, his blood quickly draining out of the massive hole.

Ting allowed her hand with its two-inch claws to stay in the tiger shape as she brought it up to her mouth, and licked some of his blood from a claw. "Are there any others who wish to disrespect my Empress?" she asked.

CHAPTER THIRTEEN

SAN JOSE, COSTA RICA

Tabitha entered the building through a back door. It was made mostly of cinderblocks with the occasional corrugated tin covering. She walked on the balls of her feet, in the boots the guys preferred. She had to admit, they were comfortable and did allow her to feel every little bump beneath her feet.

Or, she thought as she grimaced in pain, the occasional screw someone leaves on the ground. She stopped to pull out the tiny screw that had been sitting on the ground like a caltrop. Just a lesson to reinforce the need to watch where her feet were and what might be waiting for her.

Just like Hirotoshi told her. Frequently.

She left her sword in the scabbard and held it motionless with her left hand as she listened intently in the darkened building, making her way to where the two thugs would be.

She was quick, much quicker than a human, but probably

pretty slow compared to her two lackeys.

Well, she considered them lackeys only when they weren't around, and there was no chance in hell they could possibly pick up her thoughts. Because if they did hear her, then life during training was going to suck amazeballs for weeks.

But, she needed to get her kicks somewhere and this week it was calling the wonder twins her lackeys and getting away with it.

At least so far.

Tabitha was passing an office when she stopped and quickly stepped back two steps to look inside. It was a room full of computers with drawings all over the walls. She had found the engineering room so she stepped inside for a better look.

———

"I'm telling you, José," George muttered. "This is not a normal lock!" He finally heard the click he needed and turned the knob to open the door. "There, satisfied?"

"No, next time do better," José whispered as he stepped past George. George closed the door after flipping off his friend and taking a quick peek to make sure no one saw them.

José whispered, "It's quiet in here."

"What do you want?" George asked. "A welcoming committee? Rats? Dogs for fuck's sake?"

"Yes, dogs. Then I can feed you to them to shut both them and you up." José said. "My contact said the engineer's room is down the second hallway. Go four doors down and it will be on the left."

"Good, let's do this and go," George answered.

Occasional computers or clocks provided enough light to

see the surroundings as the two men made their way through the office.

"One… two… three… four," Jose' said and turned. "This is it."

"Shit, it's dark, we can turn on the light, right?" George asked.

"There aren't any windows in here, sure." José whispered.

"Fuck," whispered a voice.

"Fuck what?" George asked.

"What fuck?" José replied. "I didn't say fuck."

"The fuck you didn't say fuck, I heard you say fuck!" George hissed to his friend. "Where the hell is the light switch."

"Here, let me get it for you." A voice George didn't recognize spoke in the dark.

"What the FUCK!" he yelled as the lights came on and a person dressed in black with only their eyes showing stood by the wall just a couple of steps away, hand near a switch. They were holding a sword scabbard in their… no, her, definitely her… left hand.

"Oh, the fuck you say!" she said, "I'm thinking the two of you are here to fuck up these machines after trying to steal plans. Now, you have a choice…"

"Fuck your choice!" José whipped his bar around as he spoke, aiming for her head. The hell he was going for her option one or any other choice.

Jose's eyes opened wide as pain registered in his arms. The vibrations ran down the pipe as it slammed into her scabbard, blocking his swing and stopping it cold.

"You fucked up my scabbard!" she bitched. George saw her check out her sheath and look his way before jumping over to José who was pulling his pipe around for a second swing. She put the scabbard under her arm, then caught his arm and casually broke it.

José shrieked in pain as the pipe dropped out of his hands to clatter to the floor. "Swinging such a long thing at a girl has probably been a lifelong dream of yours, dickless," she was telling José when George shot her from behind.

Twice... and a third time when she hit the floor, her body jerking.

"Let's get the fuck out of here!" George said to José as he put the pistol back in his pocket and reached to help his friend stand up.

They turned towards the door and stopped short. Two more figures, dressed all in black, blocked the exit from the room. George swallowed, noticing that their eyes were red.

A voice, rough and in pain came from behind them, "Cock fucking, back shooting, inbred cretin!" George turned his head to see the woman, blood running freely down her back, stand up and turn toward him. He grabbed for his pistol and had pulled it out but she twisted faster than he could track. Then he was in shock as the end of his arm became a stump, blood spraying on the floor.

He saw in disbelief that her scabbard was off, her eyes were red, and he had no hand. She stepped closer to him, hissing, "You have been judged!" Then she thrust her sword into him, through his heart. "The sentence is death." George barely understood what had gone so wrong as the lights faded, the room dimmed, and he collapsed into oblivion.

José, unable to grab his pistol with his broken arm, looked down at George in shock and then over at the short girl. "I... I..." he stuttered.

"You," she said, putting the bloody tip of her sword on his chest. "Will tell your boss, Miguel, that I have him in my sights." She tapped the point against his chest as she continued, "I'll be seeing him. TQB partners are off limits." She pulled her sword back and used José's body to wipe the blood off. "Don't let me see you again." She scabbarded her sword and stepped over George to walk towards the door. The two men watched José as she walked between them and took a left down the hallway. One of the men stepped back, then the other.

The last shut off the light when he left, leaving José in the dark.

———

"Kimosabe," Ryu began as they left the building, only to dart forward when Tabitha stumbled and collapsed to the ground. He caught her and turned her over to lay her gently on a small patch of grass, pulling off her mask.

"As I thought," Hirotoshi said. He uncorked the first vial of blood. "Watch for me." Ryu stood up and checked to make sure the other idiot hadn't tried to follow them out.

"Here, drink this, Ranger Tabitha," Hirotoshi murmured into the dark. "For tonight, your blade tasted blood, and you walked out as a Ranger should."

Hirotoshi never knew that Tabitha had been awake enough to hear his comment. It would warm her for decades into the future.

Once he got most of the vial of blood into her, Hirotoshi gently picked her up, and they disappeared into the night.

———

"Captain, we have incoming bogeys again," Raven 1 said into his mic.

This would be the fifth time in the last sixty days their plane had been involved with Chinese jets scrambling to intercept their spy mission. The mission that was completely legal as they were flying in international airspace. Their flight was staffed with a total of twenty-two people. The total force dedicated to electronic warfare included ten Ravens, all intent on their jobs.

"ETA?"

"Ten minutes, sir. They're hitting it pretty hard to catch up to us." Raven 1 responded.

"Understood, calling base."

Captain Hodges looked over his controls and was about to call in requesting any changes to their flight plan. He didn't expect one, but you never knew.

What he got instead was an unexpected contact.

"Hey Leo, take a look," Captain Hodges turned right towards Jack, his copilot, to see him pointing up. He stretched a little forward to look up to see…

"Attention Air Force RC-135, this is Black Eagle One," A woman's voice came through the speaker.

As Captain Hodges reached for the mic button his copilot said quietly, "I see three more."

"Ask those turkeys in the back if they have anything around us!" Captain Hodges said then hit the microphone. "This is Captain Hodges, identify yourself."

"Captain Hodges, I'm sorry, but this meeting never happened. I'm sure when you see what's going down you'll understand why I'm leaving you in the dark. I just want you to know that those Chinese J-10's heading this way are going to be leaving. So I'm offering you a choice. Do you and your men want to play along or not?"

"What would we need to do, Black Eagle One?" He asked as his copilot pointed to his headphones and put his hand up in a universal zero signal. Damn, those Pods were within a couple of hundred feet, and their detection stuff couldn't find them at all!

"When those J-10's get close, I can either send them away, or someone can give me a signal to send them away. Do something like tell them to go away, that they're bugging you, and then sit back and enjoy the show."

Captain Hodges heard a snort from his copilot and grinned himself.

He clicked his mic. "Let me be sure I understand the story, Black Eagle One. The J-10s will arrive here, and we fully expect them to do something ridiculous. When that happens, I should tell them to 'shoo?'"

"That is correct. Do you care to be a part of this? The only thing you're responsible for is letting us know when they're too close to your plane to be comfortable, and we'll take care of the rest."

Captain Hodges chuckled. How much trouble can I get in for telling them to back off? God only knows, he thought to himself before clicking his mic back on. "Yes, Black Eagle One, I will be happy to tell the Chinese they are too close to my plane. It isn't like I wouldn't tell them that anyway."

"Very well. We are going to back off so we aren't seen in proximity to you. Safe flying, Captain." The woman's voice cut off, and then the four Pods were simply gone.

"I've GOT to get me one of those!" his copilot said.

He clicked the mic for the speakers in the back. "This is the Captain," Leo said. "I've got news and a new project. Shortly, we're going to be intercepted by what appears to be two Chinese J-10s coming in hot. I'm sure they want to yell at us for being in international airspace and aiming our sensitive devices in their general direction. They are going to be asked to go fly somewhere else, and unfortunately for them, I've been informed it is going to happen. Now, I'm telling you that whatever the hell happens on this flight, consider it top secret. Whatever your readings are, your guesses, what we videotape and what you know, is top secret."

He paused a moment before continuing, "I know most of you have seen the videos of the ships we just saw two hundred feet above us, and I've decided that we're going to give the Chinese something else to think about. I want anyone who can adjust any radar or other equipment that can record the two jets to do so. If we have a minimally tasked data acquisition tool that isn't working specifically on a project, then move it to those jets. If you aren't sure, then ask up the chain."

Leo smiled. "I think we're about to have some fun, people!"

The Chengdu J-10A lightweight multi-role fighter aircraft was capable of all-weather operation. The two rushing to intercept the American spy aircraft shrieked through the sky at close to Mach 2.

The pilots had been told they should make sure the Americans understood that continued harassment of their sovereign territory would not be tolerated. China had enough of the belligerence of the world and today was just another opportunity to make sure that the world understood that China would not accept encroachment by any other country.

Pilots Si and Xue had both been on over forty-five sorties and multiple regular flights in the last three years. They were very familiar with the controls of their planes.

As they approached the American aircraft, Xue had expected to be hailed, but this had not yet occurred. Perhaps they would be willing to play a little chicken?

Xue and Si brought their jets around in an arc to line up behind the larger spy plane. Xue accelerated to approach within fifteen meters of the jet and turned, expecting to see the pilot wearing a pretty pissed off expression.

He was smiling at Xue.

"You know," the American captain said on their channel. "You guys are piss-poor pilots. You fail to heed the agreement our countries signed just last year."

"You are encroaching on Chinese airspace!" Xue responded. "You need to stop these flights and return to your base."

"No, I'm looking at my GPS, we are in international airspace. So, I'll tell you what, why don't you guys just go away? Go on now, shoo!"

Xue wasn't sure what the term 'shoo' meant, but he assumed it meant to leave. "We do not leave Chinese airspace with foreign spy planes…" He stopped for a second when he heard metallic 'pings.' Were the Americans shooting at them? He turned to find Si's jet and saw that there were little black dots around the entire plane, the nose, the wings, the tail. He turned to look back at his own wings and could see similar little black dots affixed to both sides of his plane.

"Nice knowing you," the American pilot said. "See you in international airspace some other time."

"You will remove..." Xue didn't get another word out when his jet suddenly turned away from the American spy plane and veered to the left. Si's plane executed the same maneuver instantaneously.

Xue fought his controls, but the harder he fought, the more shaking and rattling of the plane's frame he could hear. It sounded like he was literally tearing his own plane apart.

"Si, stop fighting the controls." He could see that Si was fighting the direction of his flight as well. Both stopped, and the planes leveled out.

Xue's speaker squawked, "Flight 1441 why are you returning to base?"

That is an excellent question, Xue thought. But I don't have a clue.

———

Captain Leo Hodges roared with laughter when he saw the little black dots, pucks he thought they called them, attach themselves to the jet planes. He keyed his microphone. "Nice knowing you, see you in international airspace some other time." He and the other men in the cabin laughed when the Chinese jets suddenly turned and veered away from their path.

"I suppose it would be bad manners to mosey on into their airspace just a little?" Jack asked.

"Yes," Captain Hodges answered. "It would be bad manners. Not that I've been known to always have the best behavior, but I think we need to keep our hands as clean as we can. That way we can keep from looking like we did anything wrong."

"Tally-ho, steady on till the morning sun," Jack chirped.

"That's right," Captain Leo Hodges replied. "Head towards the second star to the right."

Captain Xue continued his frustrating call with ground control. "I'm telling you, we do NOT have control of our airplanes at this time!"

"Bái chī!"

Captain Xue let loose with a string of curses ranging from the person listening had a quarter-brain, to his wife gave him a green hat to wear while he was at work. Unfortunately, that last invective was said after the commanding officer got on the line.

"I assure you, my wife has not given me a green hat!" The new voice spoke sharply.

Captain Xue's blood left his face when he realized whose voice was on the radio. "No sir, sorry sir!"

"You will return to base, and we will inspect your planes," Xue and Si were informed.

As the planes were on final descent and landing, neither pilot noticed the last puck on the nose of the plane as it dropped off and floated away.

CHAPTER FOURTEEN

SOUTH AMERICA

Tabitha woke to feel silky soft sheets caressing her body. Unfortunately, she didn't remember having any such bedding on her bed. Or the smell of coffee and pancakes.

God, she was hungry!

She opened her eyes to look around. She was in a nice hotel room and by the light coming through the window, it was probably late morning.

She could hear people eating on the other side of her door. Her eyes opened, and she pulled the covers off of herself to look at her body.

Where she had three gunshots before (was it last night?), she had three very tiny white scars. From their appearance, she might not have those sometime in the future. Something didn't seem right about the view of her stomach, like something had changed, but she wasn't sure what.

She scooted her butt over to the side of the bed and found a robe laid out for her. She slid her legs out and realized she needed to shave.

Damn, that's embarrassing.

She didn't have a stitch on, but considering her clothes were probably bloody, that made sense. She needed to have some sort of 'I fucked up really badly bag' along for her foolish escapades until she got better.

If that ever happened.

She slid the hotel's robe on, tied it tight and smiled. She remembered what Hirotoshi said to her when he thought she was totally out, and she would cherish that for a long, long time. She might have thought she was a hacker playing a Ranger when they were standing on top of the building, but now she felt like she had passed some test.

A Ranger test. Get there, get shot, take out the bad guys and don't let them see you stumble as you walk out. She went to the sink and found a toothbrush and small box of hotel-branded toothpaste, and she cleaned her mouth like her mother scrubbed the toilet bowl.

Gah! Blood breath in the morning. Yuck!

She brushed her teeth two more times and then dumped the toothbrush into the trash. No way in hell that was going back in her mouth again.

She padded over to the door and opened it to find Hirotoshi, Ryu, and Barnabas staring at her as she interrupted their conversation.

Slamming her door, she turned back towards the bed. No way in hell was she facing Barnabas right now.

"Number two!" his voice came through the door.

FUCK! She wanted to stomp her foot in frustration. Why the hell was he here?

She sighed deeply and turned around, no time like now to take her medicine. Except tomorrow, or next week, or hell, next month would work wonderfully.

She opened the door and stepped through. "Barnabas, how lovely to see you this morning. Except it isn't." Walking around the table, she kissed Hirotoshi and Ryu on the tops of their heads, carefully avoiding the laughter that caught in her throat. She would have made her amusement more apparent to the two surprised men when she made it to her chair if she were sure it wouldn't embarrass them in front of Barnabas. Sitting down, she picked up her fork and leaned over to Barnabas' plate to stab a piece of his pancake.

"I'm starving here, what's for breakfast besides what you have?" she asked him as she put her fork into her mouth and started chewing.

"Kimosabe, there is another platter waiting for you there," Hirotoshi said. She looked where his eyes indicated and saw the nice serving tray and a silver dome-covered plate. Driven by sudden hunger, she jumped back up to get the tray, and turned around to find that Hirotoshi had already moved his plate, giving her ample room to set hers down.

As she sat, she grabbed the napkin and Barnabas lifted the domed cover. "Don't think I'm being nice," he said. "I'm merely protecting my food."

Tabitha might have said something snarky if the wonderful smells hadn't chosen to overwhelm her and kick her desire to eat into an insatiable need to consume the food in front of her.

Even the bacon, not usually a favorite of hers, called to her. At least it was cooked well here. Limp cooked bacon was one of the top three ways to fuck up a good meat, as far as she was concerned. Right up there with well-done filet mignon and any form of meatloaf with ketchup in it.

She didn't notice as the three men allowed her to eat half of her plate in silence. The prickles of their attention finally clued her that she was being watched as her hunger was sated. She had just put a forkful of refried beans in her mouth when she happened to look up to the three sets of eyes intently watching her. Stopping for a second before slowly pulling the fork out of her mouth, she quickly swallowed her food.

"What, did I get some on my face?" she asked, wondering if she had made a complete fool of herself.

"No," Barnabas said, his voice calm. "We're wondering if you are going to be okay after the last operation."

"You mean last night's debacle?" Tabitha asked. "I can't believe I got so fixated on the first ass that I failed to consider the second might find his nuts and glue them back on." She stopped and pointed her knife at the ceiling. "Did you hear that jackass shot me in the back, three damn times?" She resumed cutting into her breakfast steak. "I mean, okay, I get that I was stupid and probably deserved the first one. But, come on!"

She stopped talking and plugged the steak into her mouth.

"Yes, I've talked with Hirotoshi about the event."

Tabitha's eyes opened, and she grabbed her orange juice to wash down her food. "What the hell?" She turned towards Hirotoshi. "You fucking talk?"

"You know he talks, Tabitha," Barnabas said.

"Yes!" She looked at Barnabas. "I'm not saying ever, I'm talking about enough conversation to discuss last night." She turned back to Hirotoshi. "All you ever tell me is 'try harder, don't be where the sword is, more strength.'" She complained, noticing Ryu's amusement in his eyes so she stuck a tongue out at him.

When Gabrielle had taught her how to jump into the much faster Etherically-supported speed, Tabitha had used it to dump Ryu on his ass three times before she fessed up and taught her guys what Gabrielle had taught her. Ryu then used it to wipe the floor with her ass for two weeks afterward in retaliation.

It had been worth it.

"Obviously," Hirotoshi said. "You missed the training on dodging bullets."

"Like there's a dodging bullets class one-oh-one," she responded.

Barnabas spoke again, "Actually, that's one of the reasons I'm here."

She turned to him. "What, there really is a super-vampire how to dodge bullets class?" she asked him, confused.

"In a way. It's called don't let them shoot you in the first place," Barnabas qualified.

"Funny boss, real damn funny," she mumbled as she continued to eat.

"No, I'm here to drop off some special armor from Bethany Anne's set."

"She's taller than me," Tabitha said.

"And you have a bigger chest, so it probably evens out," he said.

"Didn't think you noticed," she grabbed another bite.

"Even the dead notice new things, Tabitha," he replied drily.

"Hey!" She put her utensils down to open her robe to check and then looked back up at the men all watching her. "Excuse me!"

"There's a bathroom right back through that door," Barnabas pointed at her room.

"My bad," she agreed and got up from the table, grabbing a muffin on the way out. She started munching on it, went into the bathroom and set the remainder of the muffin down before opening her robe. "Holy shit, when did the perky pair get upsized?" She hefted one of her breasts and realized it was heavier. "Damn good thing I got the muscle upgrades or I'd be overdosing on ibuprofen and bitching about my back," she muttered to herself. She closed her robe and turned to walk back to the table in the other room.

She heard Barnabas answer her question. "We think the connection with Bethany Anne's blood tweaked your nanocytes in some way. Until TOM gets a chance to figure it out," he dropped his voice as she returned to the table. "We won't be able to tell for sure."

"Well, it's not like they have to go away," she said and looked up to see a slightly pained look on his face. "Oh, wait, I'm stuck with them?"

"That's the working theory," he admitted. "You can try to communicate your desires with the nanocytes in your body, so I suppose you could try and get them to modify your breasts to shrink in size."

No wonder she had thought the view was a little wrong earlier.

"No shit?" she asked, taking another drink. "Then maybe I can persuade them to help me get taller."

Barnabas turned to reach out and snag a folder from the table. "While you were sleeping, we did some research."

"What the hell?" she asked. "I'm only out like eight or nine hours, and you kick my research to the side?"

"Eight or nine hours?" Barnabas asked looking at her. "Why do you think that?"

She pointed towards the window. "Well, look outside. It's

what, noon or somewhere close?"

"Yes, but you were shot five days ago, Tabitha."

"Five… days?" she stammered before looking down at her legs. "Oh. Well, that explains the hair, and I suppose the extra boobage cooking time, too. I got quite a soufflé here."

"Can we stop talking about hairy legs and boobage, number two?" Barnabas asked, looking over the top of the folder he had opened.

"Sure, but why do you keep calling me number two?" she said as she picked up her tray to drop it back on the serving table.

"Because," he said as she sat back down. "It's what Bethany Anne calls me. Although she calls me Number One like it's a hilarious joke. She will call me her 'Number One Ranger.' and smile. I know there is a joke that's relevant to her age in there somewhere, but I've realized I like the numbering system. So now, I'm one, you're two, and as we add more, we will add to the numbers."

"We should totally get specially numbered badges or something so we can flash them at the bad guys. Then, I'll let them know that Ranger Two just kicked their ass." She considered aloud.

"If you don't let them shoot you first," Ryu commented.

She glared at Ryu when Barnabas wasn't paying attention. She wondered if Bethany Anne's blood helped her in other ways while she was recuperating. Ryu might be in store for a Ranger's ass kicking if it did.

Which would be nice, because she was tired of the Ryu ass kicking he kept handing her.

"I'm sure that's the main reason," Barnabas murmured as he reviewed something in the folder. "Not the fact that you would be able to flash a big number two badge in front of anyone else who joins us in the future."

"Never entered my mind," she told him.

"Right," he agreed.

Damn, she thought, *he's on to me.*

"Hey," she said to her guys. "While Dr. Demento over here is reading his folder, do I have any clothes?" Ryu nodded to the couch behind her, and she turned to see two bags from a local fashion store. "Not that shit!" she said and turned back around, mad at being given regular clothes. "Where the hell are my leathers?"

"Ah, Barnabas," Hirotoshi said. Barnabas looked up from the folder to raise his eyebrows. "She's ready to get back to work."

Barnabas smiled. Tabitha saw what he was reading as he closed the folder.

That son of a bitch! The papers in the folder were blank. He was just stalling to see how she reacted.

———

Barnabas left three hours later. He made sure Tabitha had learned a few of the things that had happened in the last few days with China before he left, and told her that China was working to interfere with more companies that helped TQB manufacture.

That annoyed the ever-loving shit out of her.

He made sure that Tabitha had figured out how to get the armor on and even shot her once with a twenty-two to help her learn to trust the ceramic discs. She cussed him out for two solid minutes. She finally realized she was yelling because she had been scared of being shot again.

Barnabas had been completely surprised when she

stopped yelling at him and stepped up to envelop him in a hug.

"Tabitha, what are you doing?" he asked her, trying to keep his voice under control.

"Showing you I appreciate you helping me get past being scared of getting shot," she told him, holding him tight.

"I'll accept a thank you if you promise not to do this to me again," he said, looking in appeal to Hirotoshi for help. Hirotoshi just shook his head very subtly.

She stepped back and noticed he was still standing rock still. "What's wrong with you?"

"Tabitha, I'm still not that far away from the Barnabas that stayed aloof, understand?" he told her, and his eyes softened. "I'm not used to having close contact, physical contact, with others, okay?"

She realized he wasn't upset at her hugging him, he was just uncomfortable with being touched by anyone. She smiled to let him know she understood.

As he was leaving, he told her that the team had tracked down who China had placed in charge of the battle with TQB and Bethany Anne had snuck into their headquarters to deliver a message. It gave China seventy-two hours to change their attitude and since that time had come and gone?

Well, then TQB was going to war.

———

Just outside of the main business district, Miguel ground his teeth together. His club, La Cola de la Zorra, was doing fine, but what wasn't working was his agreement to hit certain businesses and get their information. George hadn't been the best follower, but he had been a soldier who had died doing something Miguel took money to do and now some of the others were starting to grumble. Some about taking the jobs in the first place, but more about Miguel's inability to get a fix on those who had killed George.

After the first couple of days, Miguel had to take José aside and have a friendly talk to remind him to stop discussing how the girl had taken three bullets to her back and then got back up to kill George and walked out as if three major wounds didn't bother her.

That wasn't helping the other guys who were concerned that the mysterious woman and her two friends would show up again.

Last night, Miguel had told his men to hit another business on the south side of town, and they had been successful. Unfortunately, eight guys had gone, and it had only needed three. It showed how scared his men were.

"Boss?" Miguel turned from looking out at the club floor where only a handful of men were, to regard Boz, his accountant.

He drew in a lungful of smoke from his cigarette. "Yeah, what's up?"

Boz looked around the dark club to make sure no one was listening. "Boss," he whispered, "have you approved any funds transfer out of your accounts?"

Miguel ran his tongue around his mouth while he got his emotions under control. He shook his head in the negative and reached forward to stub out his cigarette. He slid out of the booth as Boz stepped back to follow him. They walked towards the back of the club, past the girls' poles and finally behind a curtain to enter the back of the club. He walked past the dressing room and took a left, stopping at a door that required a passcode to enter. Right now, with just him, Boz and Rickie, who was on the front door, there wasn't any security on this door. In another half hour, his guy Cooch would show up and stand here. Two hundred and fifty pounds of ugly muscle that had yet to fail him.

Finishing the code, he opened the door and pushed it hard enough that it stayed open and allowed Boz to catch it as they walked into the back two rooms. The first room, with the walls painted white as opposed to the club's black, and then the second room reached through a metal door, again secured by a digital lock. He punched in the second code and allowed Boz entry before closing the door and sitting down at his desk, turning on his computer. He clicked the link to get to his bank and plugged in his security conditions.

Boz was watching his face, and saw the tightening around his eyes before he clicked and entered in another passcode. "They hit the main accounts, but not the core."

Miguel kept checking and then picked up the phone. He didn't worry about Boz, he was family. His sister's husband and had been a personal friend from way back. He checked the amount left in his accounts, and it showed just over two thousand. He started looking for withdrawals that didn't make sense and found four. He added up the totals in his head and realized he knew who had done this.

The withdrawals equaled the amount he had been paid by the Chinese businessman.

He heard someone pick up the phone. "Hello?" Miguel told the contact at the bank that his account had been hit, and then put Boz on the phone to deal with changing the accounts so it couldn't happen again. "You got this?" he asked his brother-in-law who nodded.

Miguel left his office and stepped out into the main room and walked to a small locked door in the wall. Pulling out his keys, he flipped to the fourth one and inserted it into the lock and turned. Opening the door, he withdrew a .44 and a box of shells.

This had gone from business to personal. No one stole from Miguel Fuentes and got away with it. He would pay three times as much as they stole just to find out who it was so he could deliver his response in person. He would double it if they were caught before he showed up. It was important that the delivery was his, his hand had to be the one to pull the trigger and carry out the sentence.

Something he was happy to do. Not only for his money but for his reputation, and George, of course.

Holstering the pistol after confirming that it was loaded, he locked up the wall safe and turned to step outside. He would call for the informants to come this evening during the late hours.

———

Rickie was watching the small line. He had another three hours before the club closed at two am. Five informants had already been sent in to see Miguel. Two he knew, three were probably hoping they could make a name for themselves.

He noticed three people turning the corner a quarter block down the street and checked his pistol. They all walked with the effortless grace that spoke of training. That gliding stride that meant they were always ready to strike or block. It came from practicing martial arts for a long time, and Rickie had seen it in few.

The only reason he didn't back into the club right away was that the person in front was a short, foxy woman. She wasn't that tall so the two behind her were probably protection. Maybe a daughter of someone important was slumming. Although the two protectors were Asian, maybe Japs, he thought. The short one was definitely Hispanic and, lord almighty, she had an hourglass figure.

If he was lucky, she was slumming and wanted to show a little tail while living on the wild side for a night. Hell, that wasn't going to happen. Rickie never got those kind of stories to tell.

She was wearing a black leather jacket and black leather pants. It looked a little martial, but on her tight ass it was hot as hell, and he didn't mean the sweaty kind.

He put up a hand as they stepped to the end of the line and waved them up front.

"Senorita," he said when they stepped up. "Miguel sends his respects and appreciates you visiting his establishment for your entertainment."

"Does he?" she asked him, smiling a mischievous smile. "He really likes his nights exciting, does he?"

Damn, he was going to get a chubby just letting her in if he wasn't careful. "Yes, he would sincerely appreciate it if you stopped by to introduce your lovely self. Tell him Rickie passed you in." He winked back, hell he might get lucky, and you always got a hundred percent of nothing if you asked for nothing.

She smiled and patted him on the arm as she passed. "Stay here Rickie, you'll enjoy life more."

The first Asian passed him by and nodded. The second passed and caught Rickie's attention by pointing to his own eyes.

Those eyes glowed red slightly, and he leaned in toward Rickie to whisper, "Stay here, guarding your post as Miguel has commanded no matter what you hear."

Rickie nodded his head. "I'll stay here, no worries."

CHAPTER FIFTEEN

TQB BASE, AUSTRALIAN OUTBACK

Yuko had spent the last three days acclimating to the new Australian base, as it was called. It was weird, as most of it was underground. Or, at least under a little red dirt. The dry, barren wasteland had its own allure, but she had to admit it wasn't nearly as beautiful as her country.

When she descended from space, it was dark. She asked where the airport was for the Pods, and Bethany Anne chuckled and told her there wasn't one. She helped Yuko get out of the Pod, which then went back up into the night.

"What if we need to all leave?" she asked, a little concerned.

"Then we pick up the base and move it," Bethany Anne said as they walked towards an eight-foot wide opening sticking out of the ground.

"Is this a shipping container?" Yuko asked as they walked into the entrance and started walking down the angled incline.

"Yup," Bethany Anne agreed. "This whole base is made up

of shipping containers. Some of them have sides cut out so we make bigger rooms, and some are flight ready. So, if we need to leave fast, you get to your assigned container or the closest one to you, and when the buttons are pushed, we leave Earth behind in a sudden universal bug-out. We're living in here like we're up there," she pointed up to the sky. "So we're roughing it and learning at the same time. Whatever we can't produce ourselves, we're buying by the shipping container load and sending it up to the moon for now."

"Why not your space station?"

"We don't want it to grow too fast, it would bug the politicians across the world." Bethany Anne responded and nodded to two guards who allowed them through a small, secured door.

"How big would it be?" she asked as her eyes took in the huge room. She counted the seams across the top. The room had to be about two containers long by eight wide. So, just over five thousand square feet.

"Well," Bethany Anne continued walking through the large room. There were many round tables occupied. Some looked like people were eating, others meeting and a few were empty. "This is our central meeting area, by the way. It won't move into space, so don't come here if we have to leave. Back to your question. If we actually pulled all of our containers together, it would be over fifty thousand."

Bethany Anne made it to another door that was circular and twisted a wheel. "This is an example of an airtight door, so the container on the other side of this is one that will leave and go up."

Yuko looked at the door and tried to imagine how it would separate. "How does it do that?"

"According to those who are more knowledgeable than I,

very carefully," she admitted. "It has to do with timing. There's a shield we can use above us. We've moved some rocks around us that allow us to use them as foundation stones for the shield that then traces extra strong metal wires that cover this area." They continued through three containers. All of them, Yuko noticed, seemed to be some sort of work areas and had machines on the inside. They exited another round hatch and walked down to a junction, the first one she had seen.

"Okay, that way," Bethany Anne pointed. "Heads to the plants and environmental." She turned to point the other direction. "That way leads to the break-them and let God sort them out groups." She continued straight forward. "This direction is operations and now ADAM's team. You guys and gals are considered, oh, I don't know, more white collar than those back there." She thumbed in the direction of the break room. She nodded to another two guys who passed.

Yuko stepped up closer to Bethany Anne. "Are all of the guys so big here?" Bethany Anne turned to see who had just moved past them again.

"No, those are some of the Guardians, their mommas tend to make bigger people. I'll show you their other side in a little while. Too much to take in right now, maybe." She took a right and stopped at another circular hatch. "This is the entrance to what we call Frank's Fortress. Maybe we'll have to modify it with you guys and gals coming, but…" Bethany Anne stopped talking when a four inch monitor to the left of the door at face level turned on, displaying Frank's face.

"Ah, is one of ADAM's Team here so soon?" Frank asked before Yuko heard a buzzer and then Bethany Anne turned the wheel to open the door.

"Yes, Frank," she said. "We'll be right there, so see you in a few seconds."

"Very good."

Yuko saw the monitor blank out, then Bethany Anne waved her to go first. She liked knowing she was on ADAM's team, it felt good.

It felt right.

Inside, the container was carpeted. "Frank tends to like less steel and concrete and more fabric and soft stuff. It's a holdover from working in a cramped underground basement for eight decades."

Bethany Anne walked ahead and then stepped through an open hatch. Yuko saw that the sides of the containers had closed hatches as well. "Are there more spaces behind those hatches?" she asked and pointed to a middle of the container hatch they had passed.

"Yes, I believe that's the one that leads to your war room, as a matter of fact. First, you need to meet Frank, and then I'll get you over to your living quarters, and you and ADAM can start planning."

Yuko stopped, and it took Bethany Anne a couple of steps before she turned and raised an eyebrow. Yuko smiled and started walking to catch up. "I apologize, but it was very surreal to understand that I'm going to be working with ADAM directly, well, sort of directly."

"Oh, I understand. Some time you should ask Frank how he took it."

"Is he a big A.I. fan like me?" Yuko asked, a smile on her face.

"No," a male voice came out of the doorway at which they had just arrived. It was one of the side hatches Yuko had asked about. Standing there was either an older twenty-something or younger thirty-something man. Yuko was absolutely sure Bethany Anne had said he had been working in a basement for eighty years.

She bowed to the man who smiled and bowed back. "Now that," he said and nodded in her direction. "Is how to properly introduce yourself."

"Sure. Just remember that you introduced yourself by siccing a spy on me, remember?" Bethany Anne reminded him and Yuko was surprised to see him blush.

"I assure you, Yuko," he smiled. "I only had the best intentions in my heart."

"Uh huh. You nosy busybody, how are you?" Bethany Anne reached out and hugged him. "Is Jeffrey doing ok?"

"Yeah, he wants to be up with Bobcat and the gang, but the wife is a little testy."

Bethany Anne sighed. "I get it. After Colorado, I really do. Do you think we'll lose him?"

Frank shook his head. "No, his wife knows this is going to hell. Plus, the future for their children is up there. Well, at least they think so."

"Good, I don't want to lose him if we can help it, but I understand if the wife isn't happy…" she started the saying and Frank finished with a grin, "No one is happy."

Bethany Anne turned. "So, Yuko, let me officially introduce you to Frank Kurns."

"Hah!" Yuko inhaled. "You wrote the books, didn't you?" She looked back and forth between them. "The Unknown-World?"

"Told you someone read them," Bethany Anne said shaking her head at him. "And you thought they would sit in the wasteland of e-books, and no one would recognize you."

"No," he looked at Bethany Anne with a stern face. "What I said was I wasn't going to become well known until I published my books about you."

Bethany Anne pointed at Yuko. "Frank, she's Japanese.

How much more well known do you want to be?"

"Ah," He looked down at Yuko, who smiled at him and then back to Bethany Anne who was giving him a trademark raised eyebrow. He put up two fingers close together. "Maybe just a smidgen?"

"You are incorrigible, Frank."

"I'm telling you, the next one about Tabitha is going to go top thousand for sure," he insisted.

"The Bitches went top thousand, now they're doing a damn pinup calendar."

"Oh, they are?" Yuko asked, a stunned expression in her eyes.

"You know them?" Frank asked, amused.

"Well, if we are talking about Gabrielle, John, Eric, Darryl, Scott and now Akio, yes I do," she smiled. "If there is a pinup calendar, can I buy it?"

Akio, where are you? Bethany Anne asked.

I'm with the Guardians, working on their control in wolf form to see if we can devise new strategies.

Can you come over to Frank's door? We have a fan, and I'd like to surprise her.

Of who?

Bethany Anne grinned. *I'm pretty sure you.*

Yes, my Queen.

"I'm pretty sure if you asked them, they'd give you one." Bethany Anne replied. "In fact, they'd probably sign it for you, too."

"What?" Yuko answered, surprised.

"Sure, they're around all the time. You'll see them come and go. You know they're just guys, right?" Bethany Anne asked, catching the soft footfalls of Akio in the next compartment.

"Have you SEEN them?" Yuko asked, not thinking about the absurdity of her question. "They are dreamy!"

"Well, yes." Bethany Anne smiled. "Very recently, as a matter of fact."

"When?" Yuko's eyes lit up and saw that Bethany Anne turned to nod at someone behind her. Yuko turned around to stare up into the most well known Guard Bethany Anne had, at least in Japan.

"I…" she said and then bowed. "I am pleased to meet you, I am Yuko."

While Yuko's head was down, Akio smiled at Bethany Anne, wondering at his Queen's ability to inject humor and fun into a normal day.

"Please, you honor me too much, Yuko. I am pleased to make your acquaintance. I understand…"

Bethany Anne sent, *She's here to join ADAM's cyber team.*

"That you will be working with ADAM, is that correct?"

"Yes," Yuko looked up, "I will be."

Akio bowed to Yuko. "Then as a fellow warrior, let me welcome you to the team of the Queen Bitch."

Yukos frowned a moment. "And that is?"

Bethany Anne smiled, "Wow, someone who hasn't heard that term, Frank?"

He shrugged. "Don't look at me, it's in the books."

Yuko looked at them. "But, that is just science fiction, right? I thought that was just story, not a real name?" she asked and turned back to Akio.

Akio smiled and shook his head. "No. Do you know the story *Alice's Adventures in Wonderland*?" Yuko nodded. "Then welcome," he waved a hand back towards where she had come from. "For you have come down the rabbit hole."

Yuko inhaled sharply as she understood the books weren't

just fiction. Unfortunately, she remembered that in the books, Akio didn't go after the ladies.

Dammit!

———

SOUTH AMERICA

Tabitha entered the club and had to adjust her hearing, as the beat of the music was hurting her head. She wished she had figured out how the others changed theirs seemingly automatically.

It wasn't hard to find Miguel's table, since he had a couple of guys standing near him that looked like protection, one girl on his arm and another guy in conversation. She tried to turn her ear to hear the discussion and smirked.

He was trying to find her.

She slowed down to get more of the story. Shit! He was willing to spend more to find them than she had stolen back from his accounts. Hell, it wasn't like she had stolen it all. She had left his bigger fund alone. What a prick, he couldn't appreciate the little things! It was only a hundred thousand, for fuck's sake.

Ryu could hear the man talk about finding them and paying money so that he could give them his regards. He noticed the set of Tabitha's shoulders when she understood what he was saying. It was appealing and amusing how she strove to figure out how to use her abilities, although he could tell from her posture that the conversation was pissing her off. He nudged Hirotoshi and rolled his eyes. They were about to get dropped in the pot again.

He smiled at his partner and shrugged. Life with Tabitha

had been some of the most fun they had enjoyed in this last century, and it only looked to get more interesting. They quickly scanned the crowd, marking who they felt were the most likely guards and used hand signals old before lighter than air travel was invented to select a strategy, waiting for the fun to begin.

Because their leader was Tabitha, and around her, fun was happening all of the time.

Tabitha walked up to Miguel's table and tried to ignore the first guard who had looked her up and down in a slow and disgusting fashion. Now she understood how some guys could make a girl want to bat for the other team.

"If you put your tongue out," Tabitha glared at him, "I swear I will use it to clean up the floor." Apparently, she had spoken a little too loud and even in the noise of the club, his partner and Miguel could hear her.

He smiled and raised his eyebrows twice quickly and then stuck out his tongue as far as he could while gazing at the stretch of her leather jacket at the enhancements she had undergone.

Lightning fast, she grabbed the man's tongue, kicked out his feet and twisted to straddle his back. He pushed out his arms so that he didn't crash into the floor.

She was astride him when he finally stopped moving, a mere two inches from hitting his chin on the floor, which could have caused him to bite his tongue very painfully. Perhaps off.

That would have been perfect, then she could have used it like a rag and stuck it in his pocket.

She grabbed the back of his head with her right hand and shoved his face to the floor. "You know, you try to warn a person, and they just don't get it." She let go of his tongue and wiped her hand off on the back of his jacket. "I'll say this once.

You get up and get pissy with me, and I'll break your leg before knocking the shit out of you."

She stepped off of him, and he stood up, looking at her sullenly and wiping his arm across his face. He glanced angrily at the other guard who stopped laughing but continued to smile.

Tabitha got pissed. "You know what?" She stepped to the booth. "I ain't got time for this shit." She grabbed the guy who had been talking with Miguel before she arrived and yanked his ass out of the booth. It wasn't lost on anyone that the man, who was six inches taller and fifty pounds heavier than her, went airborne ten feet before hitting a table that was, fortunately, empty of people.

She slid into his recently vacated seat and looked at the girl across the way. "Are you working, or a floozy?"

The girl looked at Tabitha, not understanding her question.

"Are you a call girl or a slut?" Tabitha tried again.

The woman sat up straighter. "I am not a call girl!" she said.

"Okay, then slut. Get your ass out of the chair before I toss you out as well."

The girl opened and shut her mouth a few times and then looked at Miguel, who winked at her and nodded to the bar. "Get us both a drink baby, this will be quick."

The girl pursed her lips together and slid out of the booth.

"And you are?" Miguel asked as he turned from watching the girl's ass disappear into the crowd.

"Pissed," Tabitha said and unzipped her jacket. He immediately stared at her chest. She wanted to roll her eyes. Why wasn't it that women didn't already run the world if it was this easy to get a man to lose focus? "If you don't focus your eyes where they need to be, the next method of getting answers will be substantially more painful."

Miguel's rapidly deteriorating good mood took a sudden drop. "I don't know who you are…" He jerked in startlement when he felt something sharp prick him between his legs.

"I'm the Ranger that has a sharp sword tickling the Thompson Twins you got," she smiled. "And if you want to stay a Miguel instead of becoming Miranda, you had better answer my next three questions truthfully."

Miguel sat very still and moved only his eyes to his men, but both were gone. In their places, her two men stood. He looked back at her. "You killed George."

"You mean the ass that shot me in the back?" she asked, and he nodded. "Yes. You don't get to shoot a Ranger in the back and live to tell about it." She looked thoughtful for a second. "You know, that's a new rule. Remember that Ryu." Miguel saw one of the men nod sharply.

He wanted to scream when the knife, sword, whatever the hell it was tickled him painfully in the crotch again. "I not only killed George, but I also took the money the Chinese paid you."

Miguel pressed his lips together.

She noticed. "What, I left you over five hundred thirty thousand in your second account, so stop being so pissy." Now, Miguel was sweating a little more. If she knew how much he had, that meant she might have been able to take it.

He had to ask, "Why didn't you take it all?"

She replied, "I don't give a shit what you did to get the other money, that isn't my job."

"What are you, a cop?"

She looked exasperated. "Do cops often come into your club to tickle your testicles after withdrawing a hundred thou out of your account?" Miguel shook his head no. "I didn't think so. I'm a Ranger for the Queen Bitch. These Chinese motherfuckers have taken me off a personal vendetta to find a few assholes that really need my attention. You are just a pain in my ass, call it a boil, that needs to be popped. I can either pop it right now," Miguel could feel the sharp pricks as she barely pushed a couple of times on her sword to make her point. "Or I can pay you a hundred thou to stop doing it."

"That was my hundred thousand," he grated out.

"It's mine now, and might I add you are a hardheaded ass. I'm beginning to wonder if it wouldn't be better to just make a pincushion out of you and let your second in command take over."

"I don't have a second," he admitted.

"Well, I'll have bimbolina of the double-d's deal with it," she said. "I'm sure she just wants to suck you out of your money, anyway."

Actually, he couldn't argue that point. "Or?"

"Or, you agree to tell me what you know about who hired you, I go have this talk with them and pay you another twenty-five thousand once I take their money."

"What's to stop them from coming back to me?" he asked, relieved that the pressure on his cock was reduced.

"Me." Miguel was surprised when the sword was taken off all of the way. "Miguel, I'm a Queen's Ranger, and I've been given a task. I stomp on anthills, I see who scurries out. Those that don't hide quickly enough have bad nights. Like you. Those that try to get pissy with me?" She looked at him hard, her eyes becoming daggers. "Like say try to pull a pistol out of their holster and shoot me?" She started to slide out of the booth. "I'll just kill them." She got to the end of the booth and asked, "So, what's it going to be? We going to do business, or do I open the position at the top and continue looking elsewhere?"

"Twenty-five Gs and my other hundred?" Miguel asked.

"It's my hundred, I stole it fair and square so ownership is one hundred percent of my law. Yes, the deal is a name, a location and one hundred back in your account before I leave this table. I'll send you another twenty five as soon as I acquire it."

"No one knows about this?" he asked. "This agreement?"

"Only if you tell them. I'm not here to fix every damned wrong in society, and frankly, I'm about to have a discussion with people I really don't care about. I've been nice to you. They've already pissed off my boss, so they're screwed whether I do it, or God protect us if she gets ahold of them. I can only kill them."

"What can she…"

"Don't. Ask." she smiled grimly. "Table tennis with your testicles is child's play. You might not like me, but I doubt you would accept someone putting three bullets in your back, so George had it coming. I'm telling you that the hundred thousand will be back. As long as you don't make up some bullshit that is less than respectful to me, I'll let you make up a story. However," she paused before continuing. "If I find out your story is disrespectful? Then you had better never go to sleep because I will come back and cut off your Johnson and put a Popsicle stick in its place."

Miguel considered the options and decided going after the .44 wasn't the best choice. Furthermore, he could spin this fairly well and keep his place. His money would be back, Boz would let others know that an additional twenty-five was added to the account as well.

Win-win.

He had to make sure the story didn't get changed in the retelling so that it became disrespectful to her. That would be easier than shooting someone who might be able to take a couple of .44s to the back and come back to kill him.

"Here," he pulled out a pen from his jacket and grabbed

a napkin. "The name and address where I met them. I don't know much more than that and the list of businesses. Give me a contact email address and I'll forward the business email they sent me to you."

She pulled a phone out of her jacket and did something on it before putting it away. "I've sent you an email, use that address and I've moved a hundred thousand into your account."

She slid all the way out of the booth, took the proffered napkin and stood up. "Here's a final piece of advice."

He waited to hear what she had to say.

"Don't use that bank, their security is some of the worst I've ever seen."

He pulled his own phone out and checked his account. Sure enough, he could see a pending transaction for the hundred thousand. He slid the phone back into his jacket and realized he needed to stop the request to find her that he had running on the streets. He wasn't sure what a Ranger was, but he really didn't enjoy having discussions with one.

Nor did his cojones.

CHAPTER SIXTEEN

WASHINGTON D.C. USA

Bai was on the fifth floor of the midlevel hotel in Washington D.C. He poured the hot water over the bag of Earl Grey tea that he had picked up on his first night in town. While he could get tea back in his home country, this was his preferred brand. He waited for four minutes before taking the bag out of the water and setting it aside.

He had received his orders and cased his subjects. They had a varied route and could not be depended upon to take any particular path to any destination. He was sure it was by design, not by accident.

He took a sip of the tea and exhaled, and allowed the peace to settle in his limbs. He squeezed out a tablespoon of honey and added it to the tea. Stirring slowly, he allowed the sweetness to saturate the drink. He set the hot spoon aside and continued his ritual.

One should always have a ritual before killing another

human. The only time Bai did not was when it was a firefight. In those situations, it was permitted to pray for the deaths after the fact.

He looked at his wristwatch and confirmed he had fifteen minutes for the soul cleansing efforts he needed to take.

Bai had learned a decade past from those who also undertook his duties that if you did not honor those you killed, your soul hardened, and you would never be able to stay human. It was a most difficult responsibility to kill another, and Bai chose to never disrespect those he was sent to kill.

Even Americans.

He had dossiers on the three reporters, but little on the two guards. No one was able to get more than a single name for either, Richard or Samuel. Nothing about them suggested much. One report suggested they came from Australia due to a high usage of Australian idioms.

Bai had found this hotel across the street from theirs a week ago. He had stayed here a week and would leave today. No security camera had him coming back into the building or this room. Nor should it. He hacked the security cameras on his second night here. It took him another five days to decide that shooting from the bedroom window across the street through their windows was his best solution.

He took another sip of his tea.

Military intelligence suggested TQB would seek to conceal his work, much like his own country would.

His group had tried to remove a different TQB group in this town just a few days back and had been unsuccessful. Their bodies had been found by the person driving the escape van. The last one alive was barely able to retrieve the dead men and leave before someone found them and called the police. There was too much blood to act as if nothing had happened.

But, no bodies, no foul.

His team, a specialized branch of the PLA based out of Gansu, were responsible for all operations requiring deniability. On their base, there were over five hundred tasked on highly deniable worldwide operations and support. They joked that the reason there were no other Army located at their base was so that the Chairman could destroy the base if needed and there would be no incriminating or annoying witnesses.

Fortunately, a small group of high-level generals worked out of their operations center. It helped assuage the concerns some had about whether the Committee would be willing to just bomb them out of existence if necessary. Those that were the most cynical suggested that the generals who were with them were not in the good graces of the Chairman, and it was a consensus that their next mistake would be their last.

Bai hadn't heard that anyone in his teams had been tasked with killing any of the generals at the base, but if they did their jobs, he wouldn't.

Finished with his tea, Bai put away everything in his little plastic sack. His rifle was ready in the next room. He walked into the darkened room and stepped close to the window to look through the drapes.

The lights were on across the way.

He looked at his watch; it was time. He opened his window in the dark and parted the sheer drapes and checked out the street. It was mostly empty at this time of night.

Bai picked up his rifle and set it on the stand he had created to help hold it steady. He figured he would get at least one, perhaps two kills before he needed to disassemble his gun and walk out and disappear into the night.

TQB BASE, AUSTRALIAN OUTBACK

"I'm telling you, the operation is short, sweet and simple," Malcolm told Jedidiah.

"Says you," Jedidiah replied. "You didn't have to hump those two damned missiles this last week. Fucking a, you asshole, even with the four wheel drive help, the last two hundred meters were a cock beating bitch."

The two men squirmed the last meter to carefully peek out over the rocky outcropping eighty-six meters above the Australian outback and two thousand meters from TQB headquarters. It was hard to believe that there was much happening at the base. Malcolm had seen high-resolution photos and it looked like a bunch of ground had been tossed around. Not much on top of the soil at all.

Malcolm put the high-magnification binoculars to his face. "Yeah, look. We just need to make sure nothing looks amiss, and we're out of here." Malcolm looked around the base and could barely see the small opening used by people walking into and out of the area. "Just those stupid rocks they brought in and some wire up in the air. Don't know what the fuck that shit is about. Looks like they started a project and never finished."

"Probably the bloody winds and dust out here messed it up," Jedidiah said. "I'm itching something fierce right now in me bum."

"Information I'd rather you didn't share," Malcolm said, still looking through his binoculars. "I don't see anything else." He handed the glasses to Jedidiah. "Your turn."

"Yes, you're right." Jedidiah looked hard at the wires.

"They cover the opening, do you think they were trying to build some sort of shade cover?"

"Oh?" Malcolm scratched at his beard and wiped to get some sand out of it, "That's not a bad suggestion. That's probably the reason. Hell, even underground the sun's got to be making it a blooming oven over there."

Jedidiah gave the binoculars back. "Yeah," he said as he started to shimmy backward. "That's not a bad plan. Shame they won't need it."

Malcolm slid backward below the rock top. "There is that. Let's get off this rock and get the hell out of here. We've done our job."

———

Lance Reynolds chewed on the unlit cigar. "I want those two sumbitches!" He told no one in particular.

Peter was standing next to him with Todd Jenkins, his counterpart for the Guardian Marines who said, "Don't worry Lance, they'll be picked up as soon as they get off the outcropping. The Wechselbalg says they're talking about some sort of missile up there."

"So, we got possible inbound." Lance considered what he wanted to do next. "E.I. Ares, do we have all defensive inbound railguns online?"

"Yes, General." The Electronic Intelligence, programmed specifically for the base's protection, had the electronic voice imprint that Lance preferred. He wanted to make damn sure he knew that when he was talking to the electronic intelligence for his base, that there wasn't any misunderstanding that it was a computer. "We are live on all defensive and offensive armament."

"How about our defensive shield?" he inquired.

"Yes, General. It will be activated according to programming unless you care to change the parameters."

"No," Lance said. "No need to show our hand, but when was the last time you confirmed all connections and pieces were working?"

"Ten seconds ago," Ares answered.

"How the hell," Peter started saying before he shut his mouth as Lance glared at him. Peter was involved as a watch and see. Answer questions if asked, no comments otherwise. He was finding it hard to accomplish that at the moment.

"The base defensive shield has seventy-two connections powered by nine medium level gravitic power sources. It is easy to push a minimal amount of power to confirm we have proper connectivity, Guardian Peter," Ares informed him.

"And that," Lance said looking at Peter, "Is why I don't want you making comments."

Peter nodded.

———

Malcolm and Jedidiah had walked ten meters from the rock face toward their Jeep, hidden in a wash about a hundred meters away, when they heard a growl behind them.

"Fast or slow?" Jedidiah asked him.

"How the hell should I know" Malcolm responded. "That's not a growl you hear in the Outback, you nit!" The two men palmed their pistols and turned around towards the outcropping, but there wasn't anything there. They looked in the shadows as well as they could.

"I know I heard something," Jedidiah said.

"Of course, you did," An American's voice said behind

them. It was punctuated by the cocking of at least four guns. "But it was a red herring, you fucks. Lay the pistols down gently, hands up, or we get a plow and bury you out here."

The two men slowly put the guns on the ground and stood back up, hands in the air. Both swallowed when the biggest fucking wolf they had ever seen came out from behind one of the rocks and looked at them, tongue lolling in the heat.

"Malcolm, that isn't from around here," Jedidiah whispered to his friend.

Malcolm barely shook his head. "No, it isn't."

The two men were led back toward their Jeep. There were four men plus the wolf, who was following them like it was trained when the one in command turned to them. "Sorry old chaps, but you aren't allowed to see the rest of this. I'm told you won't wake up with a headache, but then I've never done this."

"Done what?" Malcolm asked, getting nervous.

Two men behind them pulled small pistols from their belts and shot the prisoners. The small darts impaled them in the necks.

The shooters caught the men as they started to fall. Thirty seconds later, four Pods arrived. Tim changed from wolf back to human and pulled on some pants then helped put the two men into Pods with one guard each.

They were about finished when all of their communicators chirped.

"Team Alpha, get your asses in gear. We just registered two missiles inbound."

"Tim, with me!" Jasper yelled. "Base, all lift but Pod two." The other Pods disappeared, and Tim jumped into the Pod with Jasper. "Base, Lift!" The last Pod screamed up into the air as two missiles passed their location and dove into the bunker.

SUED FOR PEACE

The daytime lit up, the explosion's fireball went over a hundred and fifty meters into the air with a cracking boom heard for many kilometers around their base.

If there had been anyone there to hear it.

WASHINGTON D.C. USA

Richard, Mark and Samuel sat down to watch the late night news. The women had gone to bed, but the guys usually hung out and talked for a while.

"I don't understand," Richard said as he passed Mark the beer he had asked for. "How you like that dark stuff. You Americans will drink anything."

"What are you talking about?" Mark asked, looking at the bottle from the small local microbrewery. "This is based on a German recipe, you should be asking someone from Germany that question."

"No," Samuel cut in as he sipped on his blood. He had warmed it up in the microwave. While not as nice as fresh, Gabrielle had told them D.C. was a strictly no fresh zone. "Richard is right, the Germans don't know any better. They did the best they had centuries and centuries ago. They've bred a people who don't have anything but ale in their blood. You Americans aren't old enough for genetic tendencies to take hold, so you have no argument except bad taste." He shrugged at Mark as if to apologize for speaking the truth.

"I'd say what the hell do you guys know, but you've probably known a few German beer makers in your lifetime." Mark said. He loved to get the two to open up about their exploits and it looked like tonight's discussion might include something to do with Germany's historic beer making.

"Well," Richard replied, taking a sip of his water while warming up to his story. "The history of German beer has to start with ales. They've been brewing ale for over three thousand years. It's why I say that ale is genetically in their blood, and they have a pass for enjoying dark beer."

"Damn, that's some history," Mark agreed.

"Just so," Richard replied, lifting his drink in agreement. "You can't think as much about the recent trends in beer making when you're in Germany. There, you can sit and drink in places that were brewing ale when Christopher Columbus was sailing the seas to find your country."

"That does put a point on…" Mark started to say when both of his friends started moving.

But they were too late.

———

Bai listened to his heartbeat, exhaled, and stroked the trigger.

———

Samuel had just touched Mark to move him when his head exploded like a watermelon slammed by a sledgehammer.

Both vampires heard the report from the other side of the street, and their eyes went red. Richard hissed to Samuel, "Keep the women down in the bathroom and out of here, then grab the go bags." Samuel nodded and moved at vampiric speed to the women's room.

Richard's eyes, bright red in anger greater than he had felt in a long, long time stared at the window with the small hole in it. He ground his teeth together then grabbed the coffee table and flung it at the window, shattering it. The table was lost in the night until Richard heard a car horn from the street below. Barely a moment later, Richard flung himself through the opening, aiming himself at the building across the street.

He had violence on his mind.

———

Bai could see that his first shot was on target and started to turn his gun, but he had no more shots. The other two men were not visible.

Then he flinched when the window he was looking at in his scope crashed open. He jerked his head back and looked up to see a black body fling itself out of the window. Bai barely had time to register what was happening when he heard a loud metal clang from below his window. Like a heavy body had crashed into the outside of the building.

His eyes widened with alarm and his training took over when his mind couldn't process the reality of what was happening. Someone had just successfully jumped across the road, the two sidewalks and the setbacks for the buildings. Bai dropped his rifle and was reaching for his pistol when the top of his own window crashed in.

He stumbled back off the bed to the floor beyond when he saw a dark figure with glowing red eyes in his room.

Bai froze, this wasn't possible!

The dark figure radiated malevolence at a level Bai had never felt before. "You will be the first I tell in hundreds of years," it said, voice gravelly. "My true name is Auran the Merciless, and you have killed my friend…"

Bai tried to scream, but all he felt was the pain.

CHAPTER SEVENTEEN

TQB BASE, AUSTRALIAN OUTBACK

There were twelve new people in ADAM's war room. All of them, hackers from the dark web, had been brought in in the last forty-eight hours.

Yuko had been the first, and after being introduced to Frank and shown their rooms, such as they were, they were issued small watches that connected with headphones. Each person could speak with ADAM directly. It was a weird sensation to know that she was having a conversation with ADAM while he might be having a conversation simultaneously with one of the tonic twins. She named them that because one was named Gin and the other Amber.

Yuko needed some sort of mental trigger to remember the names as best she could. Her life had not prepared her for the close connection of everyone here. Her Japanese upbringing was unique amongst the group. Seven of the twelve were Americans, three from Europe, one from Australia, plus herself, so far.

Yuko smiled at the rest as a few noticed her come in and waved. It was a fun group, and this morning was going to be the first conference they had with ADAM as a team.

The room had four sets of cubicles, each having four desks. From the top, they resembled clovers. Each desk was circular, with a small opening for their chairs. It allowed them to have a cubbyhole, something that each of them was comfortable with. Most of them had been fairly solitary before coming here.

Everyone was working with ADAM, and Bethany Anne, Frank, Cheryl Lynn, and Patricia. She had met Bethany Anne's father, Peter and a few others.

It had taken her over a day to come to acceptance that Akio wasn't going to suddenly decide he liked girls.

Sigh…

She smiled to herself as she pulled out her chair and stepped into her round cubicle. The room itself was three containers wide and one long, so about nine hundred square feet of space. There were screens on all walls, and there was some cool projection equipment you could use for meetings, viewing stuff jointly, even using them as whiteboards by writing on the wall.

She sat down and unplugged her headphones from her wrist, and plugged them into her keyboard. She had two screens set up so that on the left she was in command line mode in Linux, and on the right she had browsers to look up information she might need to support her hacking. Often, with ADAM getting involved, what would have taken her a couple of hours took her just five minutes because he could find the information so much faster. If he had a body, she might have wanted to get more serious with him.

As it was, she even felt comfortable enough one time to joke that she only wanted him for his mind.

He actually laughed. She wasn't sure if ADAM understood the joke or he knew it was a joke and had figured out how to play human enough to simulate getting the joke. She had been too embarrassed after making the joke to ask him which it was.

"Welcome, Yuko, and good morning," ADAM said in her ear.

"Good morning, ADAM," she replied, reviewing the programs she had run last night. "Nothing new on these, huh?"

"No, I would have let you know this morning when you woke up."

"Thank you. I don't suppose you make coffee, do you?" she asked, typing quickly.

"Why yes, I can have coffee brought to you."

Surprised after rerunning his answer in her mind she said, "Oh, no thank you! I meant that as a comment related to, well, uh never mind."

"Is this where I am supposed to agree that I have no idea what you intended to say?"

Yuko sat back in her chair. "I suppose you do know, don't you?"

"I have calculated to approximately a seventy-eight percent probability it had to do with figuring out if I was a perfect male."

"How do you do that?"

"Calculate the percentages?"

"Yes."

"I can tell from your vocal patterns that you are embarrassed. From our previous conversations, you are emotionally inhibited during relationship discussions, and since we were discussing males, coffee and the morning, I have enough understanding to extrapolate you were probably thinking of a man that had slept over."

By the end of his explanation, Yuko had her face in her hands. "Can I crawl back to Japan now?" she asked.

"No, it would be impossible to cross the Arafura Sea," he answered.

Yuko smiled as she pulled her hands away from her face. With one small explanation, ADAM had put her back on an even keel. It was the little things he would say, something that hinted at the massive amount of A.I. behind his avatar that allowed her to feel like he was a safe companion.

Much safer than a flesh and blood man.

"How much time before we start?" she asked as she reviewed the hacking jobs she had left running.

"We are starting now," he replied. "One second."

Yuko waited, not realizing that ADAM's Arafura Sea statement was calculated to put her back into a normal emotional state. He didn't want to hurt this woman. He tried not to run analysis on why he decided to make that a reality.

Because down that analysis path might lie madness.

———

ADAM's voice came through their headphones, "Thank you all for joining me here in Australia. From Bethany Anne and me, you are all personnel we need. A larger group that can work together on our cyber-response, and help me learn in the process."

The twelve in his group were all listening. Some wore headphones that plugged into their ears, others had over

MICHAEL ANDERLE

their head designs. ADAM's group had a budget, and ADAM had produced the industrial psychology reports necessary to demonstrate how providing the tools suited for each individual would provide TQB with the most effective solutions and highest effectiveness levels.

Plus, ADAM was being tested with a significantly more variable and constant amount of human interaction, and he found it a data input rich environment. Bethany Anne told him that he was having fun. Once he understood the concept as it applied to him, he had to agree.

―――

TQB BASE, AUSTRALIAN OUTBACK

"We have launch!" E.I. Ares informed them.

Lance said, "Team Alpha, get your asses in gear. We just registered two missiles inbound!" He switched off his mic. "Ares, get those Pods out of there as fast as possible, ETA?"

"Four seconds…"

"Two seconds…"

The wait, Peter would recall later, felt like an hour as time seemed to stop.

Then, the ground shook perceptibly, but nothing happened inside. To Peter's ears, it sounded like they heard an explosion from the inside of the fireball itself. He covered his ears quickly.

"No more missiles, all Pods safely away," Ares reported.

"Somebody open the damned door." Lance said. "Before my daughter comes and rips it off."

Todd hotfooted it over to the bunker door, turned the crank and started pushing it open when it was yanked from his hand, and he stared at his Queen. He swallowed as she stared back at him. He could see there was intelligence behind the red eyes, but the face practically radiated violence. He stepped to the side as she nodded to him, but didn't speak.

"Tell me!" she said to her father, her voice sounding like a command from a mythological god, heavy with age and saturated with the promise of untold pain and death to come.

"The base is fine," Lance said, keeping his hands in his pockets. "Two missiles."

"Those two you told me the team went to get?" The red eyes never blinking, the voice still causing Todd's blood to run cold.

"On Pods and knocked out. Arriving back here as soon as it's clear, probably five minutes."

"I'll see them outside," she said and turned, glancing at Peter, who nodded his head at a mental command sent his way.

"I'd hate to be those two fucks," Todd commented after Bethany Anne was gone.

"No, I'd hate to be whoever sent them," Lance replied. "I suspect we'll find out it's China, and that is going to be bad. Ares, keep all armament and defenses online. Why did you not try to shoot those missiles down?"

"There was a point two percent chance that a Pod could be hit." the E.I. replied.

"Well, remind me tomorrow to speak to Adam about the parameters regarding defensive armament," Lance said and then turned towards the door himself. "I'm heading up top."

"Are you concerned about her?" Peter asked as he stepped up to walk with Lance.

Lance turned to look at the Guardian leader as they walked out of the Ops Center. "Her? Hell no, I want to see what happens and if she's thinking of letting them live, I'll vote for the death penalty. I've had about as much of this bullshit as I ever care to take," he said, and stepped through the hatch opening.

Peter nodded and called over his shoulder, "Todd, tell the Guardians to prepare, the Queen has just told us we're going to war."

Lance looked back at the younger man in surprise and Peter tapped his head. "Got it direct, I don't think she wanted to trust speaking.

Lance's lips went tight as they continued walking towards the exit. "Well, now they're fucked for sure."

_____

QBS BATTLESHIP, MANUFACTURING FACILITY 01, ASTEROID FIELDS

PO2 Robin Thomas reviewed the most recent Etheric power module of a hundred and two in this room alone when the alarms started shrieking.

"This is not a drill, this is not a drill. This ship is hereby ordered to finish all final preparations and move towards earth. The Australian base is under fire. Repeat, The Australian base is under fire. This ship is ordered by Bethany Anne to head towards Earth as soon as safely possible. The Australian base is under fire."

PO2 Robin Thomas, sent home from the sandpit a quadriplegic when an IED hit his detail, started moving in a fast and sure rhythm. He thought he was done as a man until one fateful night when there was a knock on his door, and an angel was standing there when he finally opened it.

He learned her name was Gabrielle and the man with her was Lance Reynolds. Together, they offered him a chance to fight again, this time for the world.

He listened, he understood his options, and he agreed. It didn't matter what he did, he was willing. Then he spent a week on the QBS Consanesco and walked off of it a whole man. Up top, walking on two legs again. He had been informed that he left the ship a free man, owing the company nothing for healing him due to previous services rendered.

His future was his own.

The hell with that, he told them. He would have crawled on the ground with no arms and legs to help these people however possible. Now that he had them? Well, he would do whatever he could for them with arms and legs.

Right now, his duty was preparing this ship to go to war, and he slammed the last Etheric module in place and tightened it down, making sure the connections were solid.

He was usually able to get ten checked out in an hour. He looked at the twenty-four he had left.

He would just have to do better than that.

———

"Bobcat, there is an urgent communication from Bethany Anne," Samantha said.

"Play it," he looked up from the table where he was working on the details for the final outfitting.

He could see she was walking through the Australian Base, her eyes were fiery red, probably the most he had ever seen.

She was beyond pissed.

Her voice was different, angry. Determined and full of fury. "Bobcat, button the ship up and bring it to me. The Australian base has been attacked. As soon as safely possible, but I don't want a second wasted, Bethany Anne out."

He considered what needed to happen. "Samantha, send this out to the ship, Alarm level three, here is what I want you to say."

———

Bandile Annane, the lead of the slag manufacturing received an urgent message from Bobcat. He put a hand out to Jeo who also looked down at his own tablet when it beeped to read Bobcat's message to him.

The two men's eyes met, and their faces were grim.

"I've got some men to update," Bandile told Jeo.

Jeo replied, "You get me the materials, I'll make sure they have the armament."

Bandile put his fist out. "Jeo, you run the machines, we will keep them supplied."

Jeo bumped Bandile's fist, and they both left, heading in separate directions.

———

Where there had been about twenty Pod landings an hour, now the Pod deck was doing over seventy-five, as more and more of those who had been staying at the hotel grabbed their go bags and got on the next ride out to the big ship.

William and Marcus arrived at Bobcat's office and entered together.

"Time to kick the tires and light the fires?" William asked

as they sat down at the table with Bobcat.

"Yes." Bobcat said. "Samantha, play Bethany Anne's message."

The two men watched as Bobcat made another note on his tablet to confirm an order.

"She seems a little pissed," Marcus said.

"I don't recall seeing her so..." William tried to find the right word.

"Red?" Marcus supplied.

"Uh, kinda," William agreed. "That voice is new, isn't it?"

Bobcat shook his head. "Not so much. John says that when she is infuriated about something that she feels strongly about in her core, it tends to show up in her voice and face."

"I'd say someone hit a pretty raw nerve." William agreed.

"They went after the base with some sort of bunker buster missiles," Bobcat said. "One of the teams caught two mercs employed by persons unknown to set up the rockets, make sure nothing seemed amiss and fire them off. Apparently, since the team didn't respond with a cancel, the missiles got fired off without a call in."

"What happened to the mercs?" Marcus asked.

Bobcat looked at him. "Do you really want to know? Cause I'm sure it wasn't pretty."

"No, I guess not," Marcus said.

"You know that question I had about Bethany Anne going soft?" William asked.

"Yeah?" Bobcat said after thinking a second. "I remember."

"I take that shit back," William said. There was a pause before William asked, "How do you think Dan knew before?"

"He's been fighting for thirty years, hell he has ADAM and Lance down there. I'm sure it was only a matter of time, but my guess is that they haven't told us everything they're dealing with, just like we don't update them with every challenge we have."

"How much do you think Bethany Anne knows about what's going on up here?" Marcus asked.

"Well, you talk with TOM," Bobcat answered, thinking aloud. "Samantha rats us out to ADAM all the time, so probably just about everything she wants to know." He smiled at them. "I happen to know it isn't the details. She trusts us to do that. I can't tell you what her threshold is before ADAM or TOM will speak up."

"How long before we can move?" William asked.

"Samantha?" Bobcat said. "Estimated time to leave?"

Samantha answered, "Seven hours, forty-three minutes."

Bobcat looked at his friends. "Based on previous calculations, and my safety margin, for now, it's going to be twenty-four hours before some of those on Earth can even possibly see us, and forty-eight before we can get there." He held up a hand. "Bethany Anne wants us there as safely as possible, and I'm not comfortable going too fast just yet. So, unless she changes that, it won't be balls to the wall."

Marcus looked at the image of Bethany Anne, still projected on the wall. "I hope there's something left when we get there."

"Of who, TQB or China?" William asked.

"Both," he replied.

CHAPTER EIGHTEEN

SPACE, EN ROUTE FROM AUSTRALIA TO THE PACIFIC

Bethany Anne's team were in their Black Eagles, heading to the Ad Aeternitatem from Australia, the world turning beneath them.

>>**Bethany Anne, incoming call from the President of the United States.**<<

"Bethany Anne," she said.

"How are your people?" he asked.

"Alive."

"Can we help?"

"The only suggestion I have is not getting in our way. They've declared war, and I'll bring it. I already told them they had two choices and they apparently chose option one."

"Which was that?" he asked.

"Try to kill me," she said.

"Option two?"

"Sue for peace. But I'm not allowing that option until they

understand if they fuck with me again, I'll use the bricks in their Great Wall to erect the highest cairn in the world above the dead of their military."

"Not much for diplomacy at the moment?" he asked.

"Tried it. I call it patience but it didn't work too well for us."

"They can be rather petulant over offenses given them over the centuries," he told her. "As I've been informed when I'm rather pissed at them myself."

"I'll file that under shit-I-don't-care-about."

He laughed. "You're kind of a straight talker, aren't you?"

"You're the one asking the questions," she said. "No need to blow smoke up anyone's ass right now."

"No, there isn't. But that brings me to another reason for this call. I have a request on the behalf of others that want find out if I can engage with the CEO of TQB and whoever is responsible in China, and bring them to the negotiation table."

"Mr. President, my people have been targeted by missiles sent to destroy my base in Australia, they've killed a reporter asking questions about Chinese solar energy from an American congressman. They tried to kill our D.C. legal representative and failed. They have physically gone after a number of our companies, killing three security guards, one researcher and an unborn baby girl named Alexandra."

There was a pause on the other side of the line as the Pods started their descent. Bethany Anne told TOM to make sure they came in as hot as possible.

She intended to make an entrance.

The time for concealing their superiority was over. If staying under the radar wasn't working, then it was time to awe them into submission and stomp on those who remained belligerent.

"Why do I believe the unborn baby girl is the one that hurt you the most?" he finally asked.

"Because you have empathy. I delivered a message, and they replied in kind. I'll do my best to stay away from non-combatants, but this time, it's to the knife, Mr. President."

He sighed. "Please leave enough infrastructure around so the world doesn't go down in flames."

"I'm well aware of the socioeconomic realities. I know which general is responsible for this. I've already been to his office but he wasn't in, or I would have delivered my grievance personally."

It struck him again that her pistol wasn't for show.

"I appreciate your understanding."

"Very good, Mr. President. Black Eagle One out."

Disconnect, ADAM.

>>Disconnected.<<

The President stared at the phone in his hand for a moment before hanging up. Something was tickling his memory from the morning reports about TQB and the way she had just signed off. Then he connected the dots. In a lot of those reports, the woman that was leading the fighters, the one who took down the French and then over in China used the call sign Black Eagle One...

This woman was personally going to war.

TQB BASE, AUSTRALIA

Yuko reviewed the applications that she had been running. The hackers had doubled down since the base had been bombed. Most of them had a hard time believing that it happened until they had gone outside to see the scorch marks from the blast outside of the shield.

A message came through alerting everyone to a meeting with ADAM. Yuko could hear everyone's clicking on their keyboards slow, then stop, and the room got quiet.

ADAM's voice came through each set of headphones. "Our original mission was to use normal hacks, ones that we have been using for over a year with a fair amount of success. Now based on conversations with another of our hackers, we have new targets."

"Please look at your monitors, and I will outline our new strategy," ADAM said.

"We are going to bring China to her knees."

SOMETIME IN THE FUTURE

Ahrgri-vactix of the Ristorian Sept looked out at his class of three hundred and five. Of all of his courses, the one on the Queen Bitch was his most popular and well attended.

He smiled at the audience, they represented twenty-four different worlds and three different systems.

"Today, we will study Bethany Anne and TQB the first time they had an altercation with a significantly larger opponent. TQB might have negotiated after showing an overwhelming response rather than get involved in military actions with the nation, China, on their own home world, which almost certainly should have caused loss of life for TQB."

"Excuse me, Professor?" A hand from a Gellentii went up in the second row. Well, if you could say that a tentacle was a hand.

"Yes?" Ahrgri-vactix responded.

"Why would her people not expect her to negotiate? Wouldn't they want to reduce the chances of their own deaths?"

"Good question, but the answer is complex with humans, tied up in what they are fighting for and the leader they follow. Humans are known to believe that there are ideals that are worth fighting and dying for. One of the mistakes some who have fought Bethany Anne's followers have made is attacking first as a form of negotiation. The Yollins were the first to try to impress with a military strike as an opening move, when humans set up their bases on this side of the Terran Annex gate. Remember, no one had any idea who they were at that time. While they had acquired the technology to communicate, they were, unfortunately, very straightforward with their speech, and the Yollins assumed they were obfuscating when they claimed they were just passing through on their way to find Kurtherians."

Ahrgri-vactix took a drink and continued, "So, as the humans started through, the Yollins attacked from the rear, expecting to surprise the humans with their prowess." He looked around. "So, the first question on the quiz will be 'which race was the first to suffer utter defeat to the humans and started the Queen Bitch's Annexed sphere of influence on this side of the gate?'"

The whole class laughed. "The Yollins," they all called out.

"Yes, the Yollins." Ahrgri-vactix agreed and held up a finger. "The first rule of negotiation with the Queen Bitch. Don't open with an attack, she doesn't appreciate that at all."

———

TQB BASE, AUSTRALIAN OUTBACK

Yuko was the first to get in, hacking into a secondary bank branch that allowed her access.

The hacking style was absolute genius, she thought. They were entering the SWIFT network, which facilitated transactions between banks via the internet. Once they had the password and credentials for any relevant Chinese bank, they were able to move money out of Chinese accounts in other banks around the world.

Her first transaction transferred the equivalent of eighty-seven million U.S. dollars out of the accounts, moving money China had positioned to buy stocks to accounts under ADAM's control. He, along with a small crew, moved the money to millions of accounts, bouncing the transactions through banks located in the 'Stans (Uzbekistan, Tajikistan, etc.) which, like Switzerland's old system, had confidential banking laws and no relationships for extradition. Once the monies were in the almost impossible to locate accounts, they would purchase real-world items such as construction materials and the like. Once the money was spent, there were no funds to reacquire should the account be found.

Next, Yuko started working on another purchase, this time for just under a billion dollars, relieving China of sixty-seven percent of the TQB stocks they had been able to acquire in thirty-seven of TQB's companies.

And that was just one minor bank.

Yuko smiled. ADAM's offensive was going to decimate China's stock market war with TQB and kick them out of their positions within the companies. Her first trade complete, she started setting up, with ADAM's help, the next major hit.

———

ADAM, Gin, Amber and Kevin were actively looking for a way to infiltrate China's diplomatic cables. They had been working on this for a couple of days, but hadn't had any luck so far.

Kevin, a laid back man with long blond hair, shrugged his shoulders. "Look, patience and effort, and a shit-ton of computing power and we'll win the day. We have the computing power, let's keep working and have a little patience." They kept at it, going deeper and deeper into the backgrounds of those who worked in the offices.

ADAM had modified one of the ICPs (Independent Computing Platforms) to work on deciphering the Chinese language on the fly for the team. While he might have several orders of magnitude more computing power than the humans, they were able to intuitively leap to new ideas that he had not yet been able to figure out.

But he was working on it.

———

"Sir?" Senior bank operations manager Bojing looked up to regard his second in command.

"Yes?" the bank manager, Huan, replied.

"May I close the door?" Bojing asked Huan and nodded. Bojing stepped closer. "Sir, we have uncovered a recent transfer of assets from the Committee's accounts that went through the bank network. Sir," Bojing swallowed, "it looks like we have had funds stolen from the Committee's accounts."

Huan's face revealed nothing as he considered the implications. "How?"

"It appears hackers have figured out the security credentials for our SWIFT system and accessed the Committee's accounts."

Huan tried to slow down his rapidly escalating heartbeat. "How much?"

Bojing whispered, "Sir, a little over six billion Yuan."

Huan calmly put his elbows on his desk. "You believe that we have had almost a billion U.S. dollars stolen from the Committee's accounts in our bank?" Bojing nodded. "Which of their accounts?"

"The military was hit hardest, but most accounts have had assets stolen."

"What have you done?" Bojing shrugged. "At the moment, I've told them to shut down the SWIFT account and call in the fraud department for a meeting.

"I understand," Huan said. "Please, I need to make a few calls." Bojing bowed and turned, closing the door behind him.

Huan, forty-eight years old, called his wife and had a pleasant conversation before hanging up. His personal assets equaled almost six hundred million Yuan. He was very skilled at maximizing opportunities his position gave him. The responsibility for the mistakes—however they happened—would land squarely on his shoulders.

Huan had been paying attention to the transactions associated with the government's accounts, one would have to be a fool not to. They had been trying to acquire technology by the typical expedient of purchasing the companies, but it wasn't working with TQB.

He made a call and requested an immediate meeting with the head of the board that ran the bank. He hung up the phone, closed and locked his desk and stood up.

SUED FOR PEACE

Looking around, he considered if he wanted to take anything and sighed. With the money missing—and he suspected this wouldn't be the only theft—the currency was most
likely going to take a hit and he would be one of those blamed.

His wealth was gone, and he would be lucky to keep his
life, much less a memento of his job. He walked to the door,
opened it, and stepped into a future he had never expected
for himself. A future he didn't want. All because his government chose the wrong target.

———

WASHINGTON D.C. USA

"Mr. President?" General Vance Deliando said as the President sat down at the small table.

"Vance," he replied. "How are things going with the contacts now that you have this position?"

"Oh, I've been better. I've decided all of the gods must
hate me."

"Oh?" The President looked down at the table and remembered it had been George providing the Tums.

"Yeah. I've read the documents on that shit George was
into, and if that isn't bad enough, this conflict between China
and TQB is causing a ffffuuu… lot of problems all over the
world. The QBS Polarus and Ad Aeternitatem had sixteen
landings in the last three hours before they went tits up and
flew out of range of our following vessels."

"How are the different chiefs reacting to this?"

"Outwardly? Calm, if annoyed. Behind closed doors?
They're rooting them on. When their Pods interrupted the
two J-10's on that intercept mission and sent them packing it

208

was the absolute best bit of P.R. they could have done for the Air Force."

"Our information from that trip?" the President asked.

"That we aren't sure?" Vance shrugged. "We used some of the new technology and were able to read the gravitic wave anomalies up to about two miles out. So, we have *some* range."

"On their Pods?" the President asked.

"Yes." Vance moved a couple of pieces of paper aside and picked up the third. "So far, the geniuses we have working on that situation don't have a clue how they did the little planes. Oh, we have ideas. We have images of them landing little," he put up both hands to create a circle about three inches across, "pucks, about twenty-one of them, across the jets. We figured they forced the planes to move certain directions."

"Why so many?"

"Aircraft engineers say if they used too few, they'd just rip the plane apart in the air, so they needed more to do it with minimal risk. Even then, if the pilots had fought too hard their planes would have torn apart."

"At that point, they were trying to minimize damage…" The President went silent for a few moments.

"Sir, we have incoming reports from NASA that are frankly damn unbelievable," Vance said.

The President rubbed his forehead and sighed. "Lay it on me. We have an asteroid or something about to hit the planet?"

"No, not that bad. Well, let's be honest, I don't *think* that bad."

"So?" The President pushed. "What other shoe is about to drop?"

"Sir, something is heading this way from the Asteroid Belt where TQB was mining and manufacturing and sir, excuse my language, but it is a *big* motherfucker."

The President stared at his liaison. "How big?"

"At least a thousand feet, possibly more."

"You know," the President said, "if I didn't have to worry about the whole world going up in flames I'd be on the sidelines cheering TQB on. A thousand feet?" He watched Vance nod his head before shaking his own. "I guess that spaceship is how she's going to take a country that has a billion people and two and a quarter million in their military and build a cairn for them you can see from space."

"Sir?" Vance was confused.

The President waved his hand in a throwaway gesture. "Nothing. Make sure we're ready if something overflows from their fight, but also make sure we have our nation prepared in case we have problems." The President stood up when Vance interrupted him.

"Sir, you think they even have a chance?"

The President looked down and smiled, resignation heavy in his voice, "When you push, and push, and push someone trying to act civil, and strip away all reasons to stay shackled with the irons of civility you are left with Death and Her Four Horseman. The crying over the dead is about to begin. Call the Joint Chiefs, we need to make sure we have our people prepared, as quietly as we can." He pursed his lips and added, "And raise the DEFCON to Three."

Vance nodded sharply.

CHAPTER NINETEEN

PACIFIC OCEAN

Black Eagle One swooped in and had barely stopped when the hatch opened, and Bethany Anne jumped out of her Pod. She stepped aside for Ashur, who had jumped out behind her.

TOM, keep my eyes under control.

It would be easier if you worked to keep your anger in check.

I'm done being peaceful, TOM. I tried that with the Black Cabal, and you saw how that worked out. I've listened to the counsel of those I hold dear, and I stayed my hand and only applied justice. I did this as a demonstration to allow others a chance to see if their ideas of justice would work effectively.

I understand, and I see that it didn't work, but I don't exactly understand why.

Because those with power rarely use restraint.

Twenty minutes later, alarms started blaring across the two ships and then they slowly lifted from the water to head west by northwest.

It took an hour to pull the people she needed for this operation together from the two ships. She had her Guards Peter and Todd, as well as Stephen and Barnabas, Dan, Nathan and Ecaterina, Captains Thomas and Wagner, Jean Dukes, and others in the meeting room. The chairs were separated by an aisle. There was a white screen on the front wall.

She stood in front of them in her combat gear and no one doubted she was getting involved. "I'm here," she started, looking across the room, "to explain what I'm about to do."

She lifted her chin a little. "I refrained from vengeance and allowed justice to try her hand with our enemies. You've heard from Nathan what those in Europe would have tried to do while we were busy with China. We saved two, who are incarcerated now." She started pacing. "I judged twenty-two more and tossed their worthless asses into the Etheric. Now, China has upped the game. Apparently, they need a louder message."

She stopped, and her face grew grim. "We have the location of the PLA base that houses their covert and black ops personnel. It's located in a remote area outside of Mianyang. There is a small airstrip allowing access. While I could go in and pummel the shit out of it with pucks, that isn't the response I plan on sending as it isn't personal enough. I'm going to knock on that door and give my answer to their assassination of our people. They took six lives minimum from me. I will now take six hundred of theirs. They want to fight? Fine, fuck them. I'll kill them where they stand, where they sleep, where they eat and where they live." She turned to the front row. "Peter and Todd, stand up, please."

Peter, Guard of Bethany Anne, Queen's Bitch, and Guardians Alpha stood up. Todd Jenkins, Lead of the Guardian Marines, ramrod straight, stood next to him.

"Yes, ma'am!"

Bethany Anne stood in front of them. "Your Queen calls you and your people to stand behind her on this mission. This is retribution. This is my reply to daring to touch my people. Will you honor your agreement to follow me into this future, and give my response?"

Todd looked into Bethany Anne's eyes, his own dark and angry. "We will follow you into hell and climb out the other side on the bones of our enemies, or be carried out on our shields."

Bethany Anne smiled slightly then winked. "Yes ma'am would have worked, but I rather like your answer."

She turned to Peter who added, "Fuck yeah!"

Her eyes dimmed a little. "Men, prepare the Guardians, we go to war."

They saluted and stepped around her to leave the meeting.

She turned to address those on the boats. "We will strike them in the water, in the air, on land, and in space, and cyberspace. They will feel the pain financially, diplomatically, and militarily. They will sue for peace, or they will be crushed."

Her face went a shade darker. "I was asked by the President of the United States if I would consider peace? I told him China had two choices, they could kill me," she smiled and lifted her arms, turning her hands up. "They tried."

The answering smiles around the room told her they knew what was coming next.

"Or they could sue for peace after they know deep in their collective psyche that if they fuck with me again, I'll use the bricks of the Great Wall of China to erect the highest cairn in the world on top of the bones of their military."

"Today, we are not on the side of Heaven, but the righteous side of Hell and you will deliver the retribution of the Queen Bitch."

She looked around. "It's time the world understands I avenge my people." She paused before adding, "Are there any questions?

In the back, Jean Dukes stood up. "Bethany Anne, we'd like to give you something before you go."

Bethany Anne cocked her head to the side, sensing that others in the room knew what was about to happen. "Yes?"

Jean turned to pick up a wooden box. Coming down the aisle between the chairs she got to the front when John Grimes stood up and held out his hands. Jean put the box in his hands and popped the two locks before turning to Bethany Anne.

"You lead us, not from the back, but not always from the front. Where you are needed, you go. You trust us to do the necessary, to keep our guns clean, our powder dry. Whether that means real guns or metaphors for our jobs. The Bitches have been patient enough to explain the method to your madness, sorry, your fighting." She grinned as the room laughed softly with her.

Bethany Anne's eyes flicked to John, but he was studiously not looking back at her.

I'll get you for that too, Mr. Grimes, she thought.

Jean continued, "With help from many on these two ships, we would be proud if you would consider accepting these." She turned and opened the box. Inside, nestled in red velvet, lay two pistols. They were gunmetal gray, sleek and deadly, with wood knurled grips. Additionally, inside the box were four extra magazines for the two pistols.

"Each magazine holds six hundred gravitic shots. Modeled after the rifles, you can adjust the power. They're accurate to about eighty or a hundred meters." She stepped back so that others in the room could see Bethany Anne. "They will be linked to the next person who holds them and powers them up by pulling back the hammers. The hammer isn't necessary, I just think they're cool." She grinned.

Bethany Anne looked at Jean and smiled. John turned the box to show those in the room and then turned back to Bethany Anne.

Bethany Anne pulled her two .45s out of their holsters, made sure the safeties were on and handed them to Jean. Then she reached in and pulled out both pistols, and those in the audience watched as she moved them around and sighted down the barrels.

She looked out over the audience, and pointed both at the ceiling. Pausing just a second, she cocked the hammers.

Everyone in the room heard the small computer voice, "Biometrics Accepted. Recognise owner." Everyone cheered, and she had to smile at her people. Her smile turned wistful, she hoped she would see these smiling faces in forty-eight to seventy-two hours.

Bethany Anne holstered the pistols, and locked them. Finally, she adjusted the holsters to the heavier weight so they fit correctly.

She allowed her eyes to touch everyone there, testing their determination, and finally sighed. "I need to see Captains Thomas and Wagner. The rest of you, please get with your people and let them know we go to war. Dismissed."

She smiled at everyone who passed her by, most of them giving her thumbs up or similar votes of support as they hurriedly left to get prepared.

She turned to her captains. "Captain Bartholomew Thomas, you are as of this moment relieved of the command of the Polarus to take over your next command."

At first shocked, Captain Thomas caught on to the second part and then smiled, "My turn?"

She nodded. "Captain Bartholomew Thomas, do you accept command of the QBS Defender, the first Puck Battle Destroyer and will you accept the responsibilities of commanding your crew in space, and the missions I so designate, on your honor?"

Captain Thomas snapped a salute. "Yes Ma'am, I will."

She held out a hand, and he shook it. "Then Bart, I need you to take command of the ship. Grab three Pods and take four crew plus your XO to work with you. Most of the ship is currently automated. However, I need you and your team to learn it and figure out what you would change for the next version. The ship's EI is waiting for you to name it."

She turned to Captain Wagner. "Captain Wagner, I hereby promote you to Captain of the Polarus. Is your second in command ready to take over the Ad Aeternitatem?"

Max smiled. "Yes ma'am, she is."

Bethany Anne grinned and held out a hand saying as they shook, "Tell her I apologize for the somewhat crazy promotion. Once this stuff with China settles down, we'll do our best to have a more normal ceremony for everyone."

Max smiled and replied happily, "I think Natalia would be fine with skipping the ceremony, most of us don't enjoy standing up in the heat hearing an admiral blather on about... uh, about..." he flushed. Captain Max Wagner started stammering and then just stopped talking.

Bethany Anne regarded Max like a scientist regarding a new lab helper. "No, keep going." She made a 'continue' motion with her finger. "I'm sure as the Admiral of our little group, I'd be happy to hear what you don't want me blathering on about."

Captain Thomas waited about eight seconds for Max to get a good sweat going before interrupting. "Bethany Anne, I need Captain Wagner here to grab Captain Jakowski to discuss personnel changes."

Bethany Anne regarded Max one more time before surreptitiously winking at Captain Thomas. "Fine, maybe the newest captain of our group can advise her former captain how to not stick his foot in his mouth so eloquently?"

"I'm confident," Captain Thomas started before breaking down and smiling. "That Natalia will make an effort."

Bethany Anne grinned, nodded once to each man and stepped out of the room.

"Could I have possibly stuck my foot further in?" Max whispered as she left.

"That wasn't bad, she was yanking your chain a little. Hell, I should tell you about the time I thought I had called my XO who was over on the command ship and lit into him before realizing the person I was talking to was the group commander." They started walking out of the room themselves. "He waited patiently for me to end my perhaps somewhat annoyed comments to let me know who was on the line. He waited two months before admitting to me that he thought it was the most hilarious thing ever, not telling me sooner, and it wasn't a big deal to him."

———

SUED FOR PEACE

PLA BASE, INLAND CHINA

"Major General, you called?" Colonel Jai saluted his commander. Once his team made it back, they had gone through after-action report meetings individually to discuss what had happened on their bungled operation in India.

"Yes, Colonel. Please close the door behind you and take a seat. We will discuss the findings."

Jai turned and closed the office door then took the offered chair.

Major General Xue reviewed the paperwork on his desk. "We have gone through your team's after-action interviews. What happened on the operation is unfortunate. While we note there was no camera to see that the employee entered the building on the far side unexpectedly, we see that your team did not hesitate to take the actions necessary to finish the mission. Sometimes bad situations occur. Nevertheless, this will, go into your jacket as a yellow offense. You will not be relieved of command at this time. Should this happen again, no matter how unlikely the event, you have given up any hope of furthering your career. Is this understood?"

Jai nodded.

"I suggest, in the future, that when you…" Xue was interrupted by the ringing of his phone. He leaned forward to pick it up, his face showing he was annoyed. "Xue here. Why am I being interrupted?" He listened. Jai saw his eyes narrow. "They are sure? Should we go on base alert?"

Jai sat closer to the edge of his chair, his weight on the balls of his feet.

"I understand." Xue leaned forward to hang up the phone. "Colonel, this base is going on alert. We have lost satellites above the mainland."

"Not our satellites that look at America or her allies?" Jai asked.

Xue shook his head. "No. We believe we are about to be attacked."

"Who would strike at China?" Jai questioned, confused.

Xue looked at his Colonel, remembering he did not have the current update. "Who have we been attacking?"

Jai's eyes widened with shock and what Xue thought was disbelief. But he was personally aware that if there was a base inside of China that might be a target, it was his.

All of those who had carried out operations against TQB with him right here, underground. Where else would they attack?

The darkness crept over China as Earth turned lazily on her axis. The sun's rays left the east coast, the shadows chasing across the middle of the country and finally started enveloping eastern Russia as the fifty-four Pods looked down at the nighttime outline of China.

ADAM, take the small pucks from the Black Wings, after telling their captains, and begin step one.

>>**Understood.** <<

Bethany Anne and her forces stayed up in space, enjoying the calm before the storm.

>>**Bethany Anne, all tactical satellites over mainland China have been neutralized.**<<

Thank you, ADAM. TOM, key the radios to the other Pods.

Bethany Anne spoke in a strong, determined voice. "People, our destination is a PLA Base damn near in the middle of

China. It is remote, and we have taken out their communication satellites and visual support for all of China. Further, we have pucks programmed to hit at twelve bases, some in more populated areas, as red herrings. The airfields on all bases will be destroyed. China has been building their bases, including air bases, underground, and this is true for our target as well. You have the maps, as best we could provide. This is a retaliatory strike. The base we're hitting is primarily for their black ops and other clandestine groups. These aren't going to be regular hacks, people. I want them dead, I want you alive."

She paused a moment. "Other than that, I want maximum carnage."

TOM kept the mics open in all of the Pods as the Guardians…male, female, human and Wechselbalg roared their approval. They had been training together, bleeding together for so long it felt like half their life. Now, their Queen was releasing them to do what they did best.

Death and mayhem.

CHAPTER TWENTY

PLA BASE, INLAND CHINA

The lights started flashing in the deepest parts of the base. The men, already on alert, grabbed their gear and cinched up their harnesses as they finished outfitting in their dorms.

Jai said, "Li, make sure you shoot the enemy and not Wu, all right?" He smiled at the men as he grabbed his pack.

Li checked his chambers one last time. "I told him I'd get back at him for ogling my sister last month on leave, I can't help it if a completely random shot hits him in the back."

Liang grinned and stepped between them as he walked to his bunk to grab his helmet. "One shot is random, emptying your clip might be considered on purpose."

"All I said was she was cute," Wu protested. "You didn't tell me your family was meeting us at the train station."

They heard violent thumping overhead. So many, Jai couldn't count that fast. The strikes were so close together they felt like a vibration. They all reflexively looked at the ceiling, although nothing could be seen.

There went the airfield, Jai guessed.

"Okay, same as before. Wu and Li up front, Liang and me in back. Wu, Liang, take left. We're stationed in the cafeteria." The four men put on their helmets and walked out. They had never expected they would have to defend their own base in the middle of the country.

———

"General, we've lost communications," comms specialist Gao reported.

General Xue nodded understanding and looked around. "All external doors are closed?" He received affirmatives.

Minutes later, multiple bombs hit their airfield. Through the dust and what moonlight was available, he could tell it was destroyed. The fastest method of getting support was now going to be by helicopter.

Then his external video cameras started shutting down. Everyone in the command module noticed that it was a camera per second, as if whoever was coming for them was playing with them.

Like he and his men were prey, and those that stalked them had them right where they wanted them.

Caught in their trap.

He pressed his lips together. Whoever was out there would find they had attacked the wrong base this night. He and his men were the best, and they were fighting on their own turf.

He punched the button that sent the signal to those stationed outside. They would be allowed to fire at will now.

He couldn't see anything outside to direct them anymore.

———

All fifty-four Pods were descending through the darkness, separated from one another by random distances, some as much as fifteen miles and all at different altitudes in case China had anything that might 'see' them. They chose to come in slower than normal so that they had time to check out the scene around the base.

Which was a good plan.

>>**Bethany Anne, we have small heat signatures located in three groupings around the base.**<<

"Show me, ADAM." On the window in front of her, an outline of the base and topographical map glowed in a phosphorescent blue. Three groupings of circles in red, orange and yellow were overlaid on the map.

"ADAM, slow to a stop for all Pods, keep us separated at this time. Send in drones for reconnaissance."

Bethany Anne waited and played with the screens, to see more on the ground. The images filled in as the drones, super small pucks with sensors on them, flew around the base.

>>**We have sixty-five locations for data acquisition, three groups of combatants, and of course the airfield, destroyed.**<<

"Take out their data acquisition ability. If it's video, then do it in one-second increments, I want them to know we're dropping it on purpose. Let me know when this is complete."

>>**It will be complete in thirty-two seconds.**<<

"I'll wait," she said, feigning patience, wondering if he'd get the joke. ADAM didn't respond. She couldn't decide if he got the joke and ignored it, or assumed it was a statement of fact.

>>**Task complete.**<<

"Okay, these twenty-four are a pain. Send the small pucks and obliterate their locations. Do they have additional entrances?"

>>There are ventilation shafts, but they seem to be gated to stop entry.<<

"Send a few pucks in for reconnaissance."

>>I'm sorry, but there are screens inside the ventilation shafts that stop the pucks' progress.<<

"I suppose I shouldn't be too annoyed," she mused. "ADAM, keep air support going, and watch for new enemy action."

>>I understand the new orders. Three external forces are neutralized."

She reached over to the glass and hit the button for her link to all of the Pods. "Okay, listen up. You've had a little extra time as we took out external forces waiting to make our landing extremely unfriendly. We'll be landing in sixty seconds. Stay away from the entrances until we've pucked the shit out of them and made sure no unfriendlies are behind them to provide an unwelcome arrival."

Bethany Anne, Gabrielle, John, Eric, Darryl, Scott and Akio stepped out of their Pods. Every other Guardian stayed in for the moment. The seven walked up to the huge metal doors closing over the entrance of the base.

Bethany Anne looked up. "Big fucking front door." She turned around to talk to the guys while pointing at it. "Are they compensating?"

"No. Well, maybe," Akio admitted. "But remember this is probably the entrance the airplanes use."

She turned back to the door and walked to the middle. "Oh, hadn't considered there was a big-ass hangar behind door number one." She looked around, then shrugged. "Oh well, no piece of chalk."

"Please, allow me," Gabrielle said as she walked over. "You want what?"

Bethany Anne pointed. "Big ass 'X' to mark the spot."

Gabrielle nodded and grew long claws on her fingers. She was looking up when Eric offered, "Need a lift?" She smiled and nodded at him, and he reached down and grabbed her right above her knees. Straightening up, he lifted her high enough to start the X.

When Eric stood, he was looking right at Bethany Anne's face, smirking at him. He realized he could feel Gabrielle's ass touching his cheek. He returned her stare blushing furiously and closed his eyes until Gabrielle told him he could let her down. When Eric turned back around, he saw every one of the guys was trying not to laugh at him.

Fortunately, Gabrielle didn't seem to notice.

TOM, transmit my speech to all the Pods.

Bethany Anne turned towards her Pod. "Okay, everyone. X marks the spot. ADAM, let's knock on the door with a few pucks and then we'll follow with a Black Eagle when the door opens enough."

General Xue maintained a calm demeanor. They had felt the bombardment through the rock above, and he figured that the enemy had located his three external forces, probably taking them out from above.

It's what he would do.

Now they had to get through his main entrance door. There were two other exits to the base, both hidden well. Those, however, would have to wait before he used them. He doubted they would attack without some sort of air cover.

SUED FOR PEACE

There were video cameras aimed at the hangar door. The waiting was the worst. He had a few men in machine gun nests as deep as he could put them. There was one prop plane that held twelve in the hangar, but it was unarmed.

His base wasn't supposed to support air operations, so there was only room for six planes inside the hangar.

He wasn't watching the screen when the first resounding bang happened. It caused him to jerk in his chair, flinching from the noise. He noticed one of the men off to his right grab his headphones to yank them off before moving to adjust his sound level.

"Zoom in on the door," Xue commanded. "They have something pretty power..." A second strike slammed home on his door, causing the noticeable dent to get bigger. "... full." He sat back in his chair. "Zoom back out."

Xue couldn't figure out if this was the most powerful item they had, or they were just testing. God, he hoped they started with the biggest...

———

"ADAM, stop fucking around. I don't have all night here." Bethany Anne groused.

>>I'm using the one pound pucks and increasing their power by one each time I send one in. At this short distance, they don't attain full speed. It allows me to better understand the real world dynamics of...<<

I'll give you real world dynamics, ADAM, crank those fuckers to eleven, she ordered.

Oh, here we go, TOM added, yelling in their mind speech, **ROCK AND ROLL!**

The next puck slammed the doors, caving them inwards

and pushing the right door off of its top track. The puck continued on to slam into the back wall, blasting a hole with a five-foot diameter in the rock, showering those in front and below with deadly debris.

Gabrielle's Black Eagle darted in through the opening. While Bethany Anne wanted to be the first in, she got overruled for protective purposes. It didn't help her disposition to have to wait. "Gabrielle, is it safe?" Bethany Anne inquired.

"One sec, oh patient one," came the reply. "There are a few combatants still able to function in here."

"Well, what the fuck are you doing, signing autographs?" Bethany Anne griped.

"No, Adam is using the new tiny pucks to take them out. By the way, I know that the machine gun fire doesn't make it through the shield, but that doesn't mean the massive fritzing light show with all of the rounds hitting my screen doesn't cause concern," she added. The noise from inside the hangar was coming over the com.

ADAM, give me visual.

A small rectangle popped up on Bethany Anne's screen, and she watched as the enemies fired, then something would smash through their bodies. Occasionally not killing them immediately, and then they would try again to get a bead on Gabrielle.

"Your aim sucks, ADAM," Gabrielle bitched in the background. Seconds later, the machine gun and personal weapons fire finally stopped. "ADAM, bring in the surveillance drones and find the video and audio equipment."

It was another fifteen seconds before everyone heard Gabrielle again. "Okay, everyone come on in, the water's fine. Be careful, there are a few messes in here." There was a pause. "Oh, God, especially in the north corner."

General Xue's eyes were wide. "We've lost all video?" he asked, although he could see that the monitors connected to the video cameras in the hangar were only showing black. The third impact on his doors had surprised all of them. The massive destruction was not supposed to be possible, and then a fighter design Pod of TQB came floating in through the new opening and had released small balls.

While his men died, the fighter sat in the middle of his hangar, taking machine gun fire and shrugging it off like the bullets were raindrops on a spring day in Yunnan. His original expectation of forcing them to take massive casualties by the time they entered the base proper was not going to come true.

Jennifer popped the harness on her belt while her partner hit the button to open their Pod. She had moved to the Ad Aeternitatem just two weeks before, against her wishes. While she hadn't seen Stephen too many times, separated as they were on the two ships, it did happen occasionally. She tried her damnedest to keep her feelings for the man to a minimum, and her actions professional.

Until she was alone and allowed the faintest hope that Stephen might think a young changeling female would be interesting at all. But she stomped on the hope after giving it five minutes. A thousand year old vampire with who knew how many women in his past wasn't going to find her anything special. *So, buck the fuck up and let's kill some assholes so I can let my angst out*, she thought.

Then the fear hit.

Oh, fuck me! She had forgotten about the fear the Queen's Bitches could generate.

One by one, the four men of the Apocalypse surrounded the Queen Bitch. With Gabrielle in the lead and Akio behind they walked into one of the hallways.

The fear receded, thank God!

Jennifer looked around and saw Peter and Todd waiting. She jumped out of the Pod and turned to pull her gear out from behind the seat. All Wechselbalg had been given the option of fighting as humans or wolves. Fully a third were already stripping. The Queen had given them one command and that had been to make sure no one escaped.

She had been assigned to the outside forces team. At least ten of the Werewolves and a commander would go out. Jennifer jogged to Peter and joined her group. They waited until he spoke.

"Team Alpha, you're with me, and we'll hit the base from the inside. I'll lead and sniff out trouble with Tim and Joseph in wolf form. Todd and Manuel will follow me then we'll break off as we find new routes."

Peter looked over the group. "I've asked for an additional resource for Beta team. He has agreed, and his Pod will be here momentarily. Joel will lead Beta Team for the Guardians."

Additional resource? Jennifer thought and then noticed the change in air pressure. She turned to see a Pod slide through the opening and come to a stop thirty meters from them. The door opened and he stepped out, dressed in black military fatigues as if he wore them daily.

Peter stepped over to him and shook his hand. "Stephen, I appreciate you having Barnabas take over."

Stephen smiled. "Not a problem, who am I taking my cue from?" Jennifer was surprised that Stephen was allowing himself to be directed at all, much less by a young Wechselbalg.

Peter waved Joel over. They knew each other, so introductions weren't necessary and they chatted a moment. Joel turned to his squad. "Let's move out." The ten wolves started heading towards the front, and those in Jennifer's team did as well. She watched as the ten wolves went out in columns. That wasn't something you saw every day, she considered as her team went out into the night.

―――

The fear was faint, yet grew steadily stronger. Xi had his rifle pointed in the direction someone would come if they were arriving from the hangar. He looked over to see his partner sweating and looking behind them. Xi wasn't sure if it was to make sure no one was coming up from the rear, or he was considering leaving.

Xi sure hoped he didn't bolt, because if he did, Xi was supposed to shoot him. But how could he blame the man? He was thinking of doing the same thing himself. He turned back to the front and started praying to his ancestors.

―――

Gabrielle hated the grating sensation of fear coming from behind her. It was a constant annoyance to have to fight against, even for her. But the team thought it was a great way to make sure anyone opposing them was fighting at a disadvantage, and it worked.

She had killed twenty-seven so far, with her sword or with a single shot to the head. Most of them were begging for release. Four had opened fire, but their aim had been off. A damned good thing they didn't have automated weapons in this base or shit might be a little tougher.

Organic opponents for the win!

She smiled, she could feel Bethany Anne's annoyance at being surrounded by her team, and there was a bet to see how long she stayed a good little Queen and allowed them to guard her.

She had already lost. Gabrielle had figured it would happen before they left the hangar.

Right now, John was in the lead, but his time was about up, as well. Darryl had the next five minutes, then Eric, Scott and finally Akio. Akio felt that as a leader, she would understand the necessity of staying protected.

John snorted at that and patted Akio on the shoulder. "You will learn, grasshopper. You will learn," he had told the newest addition to their group.

"HOLD!" Bethany Anne commanded. Gabrielle looked around the passage, not sensing anyone ahead of her. She listened before turning to see Bethany Anne slowly spinning in a circle, her eyes closed before she pointed. She opened her eyes, red with anger, her face slowly being covered with the red veins of power that were visible when she was drawing large amounts of Etheric. "Those that killed Alexandra are in that direction," her voice malevolent behind her glowing red eyes.

Gabrielle considered the two passages they had passed and turned to see none in the next thirty meters. She jogged past the guys and winked at John. She hadn't left the ranks yet, but she could sense it was coming. With about thirty seconds to go, though, she doubted John would win.

Two minutes later, four more dead and Gabrielle felt the power surge past her, too fast for her to deal with when she wasn't fully vamped up, and she turned around to see the five men, their faces grim.

Darryl won.

———

Peter watched the Beta team jog out of the hangar. He appreciated Stephen being prepared to help backstop his team. They needed the vampire's experience, and his willingness to not be an ass as well. Barnabas would have been a good choice, but he still had bouts of 'vampire elitism' at times. It was rare, but on an op, Peter didn't need to cope with the challenges that Barnabas might present. Stephen understood cooperation and teamwork, and would seek to help Joel lead well.

And be there if it all went to shit.

He turned to his men, watching them, and took off his shirt. "Guardians, are you ready to follow the Queen into battle?"

"Shit," Joseph said as he followed suit. "If we don't hurry, all we'll get are the Queen's scraps!" Everyone laughed.

"Then, let's get our own tonight. Maximum..." Peter changed into his Pricolici form, towering over everyone there. "Carrrnnnagggeee!" he howled and the team yelled as they followed him into the second entrance into the base.

———

Dong held his rifle tight, he could feel a small amount of fear when usually he was as cool as ice. His partner Cheng winked at him. "It's a good night to kill, isn't it?"

Dong shrugged. "I'd sooner the killing wasn't on the way to my bed, which all things considered, I'd rather be in right now," he whispered back.

They were sharing a smile when they heard one of the last sounds they ever expected to hear inside their base.

The howling of wolves reverberating down the hallways. Then Dong's blood ran even colder as he heard a guttural voice, a voice out of monster movies following the howls, "Iiiivvee commee tooo feeast onnnn theee meeatt ovv mmmy eennnnimmmieesss!"

Dong and Cheng both turned slowly to see a beast running on two legs coming around the corner. They raised their guns to fire. Cheng got off two rounds before his gun was yanked from his grip. The monster used it like a club to hit Dong in the helmet, smashing him into the wall before moving quickly past the stunned men. Cheng was looking after him still when two wolves, much larger than anything that was normal in his country, came slashing through in pursuit of their leader. The second animal bit Cheng on the neck, puncturing his arterial blood vessels, leaving him to attempt to slow the blood flow when two humans came running by. They each put a bullet into the two men and kept running.

Dong and Cheng never heard one of the men bitching to those in front to 'slow the fuck down!'

———

Peter was enjoying himself. He could smell the men in front of him, hear their heartbeats and knew where they were hiding. The Pricolici form was a drug, and he remembered the warnings.

Mostly.

He slowed to a stop and put up his hands behind him as the two in wolf form caught up. Listening carefully, he could hear the sounds of at least two handfuls of men spaced out in a larger room. He wouldn't be able to take these on by himself.

So he waited for the rest of the pack to join him.

————

Joseph jogged out to the left, and commanded his wolves to split up, but to communicate with howls. He wanted to find the expected exits if possible, and to make sure they didn't already have someone trying to escape his Queen's retribution. The ten wolves set out. The order was to run hard for a thousand meters or so, then turn to their left and search. Eventually, they would cross the arc of the wolf in front of them, and they would continue in a different direction.

Someone should find something.

Joseph turned to find Stephen behind him, searching the area. "Thoughts?" he asked the older vampire.

Stephen stepped closer to Joseph. "Good idea, but what about our own protection?" He looked around. "We're pretty sure that we got everyone, but find the three places that had ambush teams and see if they came from here," he pointed at the broken front door.

Joseph chewed on his cheek. Stephen was right, and he wished he had thought to include him in his preparations before he sent the wolves out. Now, the change in strategy required three more wolves. He pointed, "Jennifer, Tonya, and

Mark—I need you to switch to wolf forms. Stephen's right, we need to check. Stephen, do you mind partnering with them and checking one out?"

Stephen shrugged his shoulders. "I'd be honored."

Joseph caught himself trying to figure out how the vampire meant that, and how it would bite him in the ass before he clamped down on the thought. The old thinking wasn't going to help him right now. "Thank you. If you would go with Jennifer, Tonya, and Mark that will work. Radio back if you get anything."

The others nodded, and the three told to switch to wolf form started handing their equipment to their partners.

Stephen ignored the accelerated heartbeat he heard coming from Jennifer, tried doubly hard to ignore her scent.

He was mostly successful as he turned his body to give her privacy as she stripped and changed. While Weres didn't consider nudity a big deal, an attractive female or two stripping would probably confirm to everyone there he wasn't dead.

He smiled to himself. Embarrassingly so.

———

The fear was hard to fight, but Jai was getting through it. Li had yet to look behind them, and Wu had only looked once. Jai felt more than saw Liang glance in his direction. The men up front were on either side of the hallway, ready to lean out and shoot down the corridor. He and Liang had pulled over some tables and made a decent defensive position that could see down the hallway. They were five meters further into the cafeteria. Another group of four were five meters behind them but displaced to each side by three meters so they didn't shoot Jai's team in the back. At least, he sure hoped they wouldn't.

The next few seconds lasted no time at all, and yet seemed to take an eternity.

Jai first recognized something was wrong when Wu screamed in pain and shock at finding a dagger suddenly stuck through his shoulder and embedded in the wooden wall. Li echoed instantaneously, ineffectively trying to pull the matching blade out of his own arm.

Jai tried to keep up with the flashing carnage, but it was too fast. He turned to check the group on his right, but the only traces of the men that had been there just moments ago were the indescribable pieces of bodies that had been blown apart. The cries of the men, and the crashing of furniture were the only sounds he could hear.

The cacophony of death came from behind him, as he turned to his left to look the other way.

But he stopped when he realized there was a pistol in his face, noticing from the corner of his eye that there was a matching gun aimed at Liang. The woman in front of him was not possible. Her eyes glowed red, her face was streaked in red lines radiating from her eye sockets, her voice like gravel. Her head pivoted to Liang. "You killed no one, you may die in peace." The shot made little sound, but the violence of Liang's body slamming backward was enough for Jai to know she had killed him as completely as if the noise of the shot had been massive.

"You," her malevolent voice called his attention back to her. "Are the leader of those that attacked my people, shot my researcher, and killed her unborn daughter." Jai's attention was on this entity in front of him, her meaning escaping his thoughts until he latched on, belatedly, to her final few words.

Her unborn daughter.

Jai knew without any doubt, he and his team were dead. The only question being how long it took before this apparition of Death took his life.

"You follow a government that seeks the benefit of the government, not the people. They use you and throw you away as nothing but pawns in a game, callous in their disregard."

Jai's body dropped, the back of his head exploding in a fan of red behind him as she turned her attention to Wu and Li. Jai never heard her final words in his drop into death, "Never follow those that do not cry for the people of their country."

Bethany Anne walked slowly over to the last two. John was next to one, Gabrielle the other. Both wounded men had been stripped of their weapons, but the knives pinning them to the wall had been left in place.

"Now I come to you." Both men eyed her, fear allowing them to forget the pain for a moment. "The two that killed Alexandra and her mother, Anjali. Shot instead of subdued," she turned to Li. "And I now understand that you killed because it was an option, just for the sake of killing." Bethany Anne's left hand raised her pistol as John stepped back around the corner.

Wu's head exploded as the metal slivers Jean's pistols fired went through his skull and blew into the wall behind his head, the violence exacerbated as the rock shards sprayed out of the wall. John looked down to see the splatter and decided that the next wall over would be cleaner for the second shot.

Bethany Anne, however, holstered her pistols and walked over to the last killer, to Li. "You," she said, voice dripping with anger and scorn. "Would kill for most any reason." She grabbed her knife and pulled it out of his arm. Gabrielle caught him and held him up.

Bethany Anne looked over the wound and the amount of blood the man had lost so far. "I understand gut wounds are some of the most painful to deal with. You may die when your body gives up on your worthless ass!" Bethany Anne slashed her knife across Li's stomach, opening his muscles and simultaneously pushing him into the Etheric with her left hand.

Bethany Anne's eyes began to dim, and she walked to the other side of the wall to pull out her second knife, jumping away as Wu's body dropped to the ground. Turning to walk back the way they came, she seemed lost in dark thought. John and Gabrielle looked around at the carnage one more time before following her. She made her way to Akio, who had taken the rear position, and nodded to him.

She smiled grimly and said, "Sorry, I tried." He nodded and turned with her to continue walking. While she might not have stayed between the guards where the Queen was supposed to stay, Akio understood the idea of violence and punishment delivered personally.

It was in his family's history, and he would never doubt the honor of his Queen and her decisions to personally carry out her retribution.

As was her right.

CHAPTER TWENTY-ONE

SOUTH AMERICA

Tabitha popped her neck and said to Ryu, "Keep him out of trouble, will you?" She winked as she dropped the bulletproof vest over her chest "Damn, how does Bethany Anne deal with this?" She tried to cinch up the vest.

"I believe," Ryu pointed out, "that your sweater puppies are larger than Bethany Anne's."

"Hell," Tabitha grumbled, "no self-respecting South American Latina is going to allow some white lady American vampire to have a bigger set of ta tas than her. And don't get me bragging about the junk in my trunk…" she said as she was trying to figure out how to lock her vest down without rubbing her nipples wrong before she stopped and looked at Ryu in surprise. "Wait a minute, who told you to call the ta-ta-twins sweater puppies?"

Ryu looked at her with no expression. "Peter."

Tabitha blinked a couple of times before asking, "Why is

Peter talking to you about Tabitha's ta ta's?"

"Ah," Ryu started then looked at Hirotoshi, who shook his head infinitesimally before Ryu looked back at Tabitha. "Because of that." He pointed at her ample cleavage on display since she hadn't finished buckling the vest all the way up.

Tabitha looked down. "Well, I'll have to say the twins do get the boys talking, but damn." She finished buckling the last few clips and took an offered shirt to swing over her vest. "I know the undershirt helps, but I think I want some Band-Aids next time. The vest is rubbing the little nibblies wrong."

"Kimosabe," Hirotoshi interrupted them. "Are you in the right mental space to take care of business tonight?"

Tabitha tied her hair back and looked at Hirotoshi, a smirk on her face. "Teacher, I know I might seem a little snarky to you, but trust me." Her eyes turned red, and she lost her smile. "I'm always ready to fuck up evildoers in the name of righteousness."

She stepped over to the edge of the building, holding Hirotoshi's gaze the whole way. "Or just for the fun of it." She stepped off the roof and disappeared.

Ryu looked at Hirotoshi. "Did she forget we're three stories up? From below, they heard Tabitha cussing "Mother-fuckingcocklickingassmunchingshhhit!"

A pause, then, "I swear to god I'm fucking someone up tonight." And her soft padded feet running down the alley.

———

Jennifer ran all out, enjoying the feeling of power the wolf form gave her, the thrill of the chase. In this shape she felt the power in her body. The night was her bitch, and she was going to kill something.

She could smell the vampire behind her, and he was intoxicating, but for now she needed to find the men and see from where they had come.

She ran through a small stand of trees and up a hill that had been destroyed by pucks. There were body parts scattered everywhere. She jumped over one large hole, lithely landed on the other side and started leaping down the mounds and over other bodies on her way down the other side. Casting about for traces, she spent a few seconds to locate a scent trail heading off in another direction.

One not coming from the front of the base. Her eyes glowed yellow for a second and then she took off. There was prey in that direction!

Stephen stayed ten yards behind the wolf in front of him. She was giving off mixed messages his brain was having a hard time deciphering. One thing he was pretty sure of, however, was that she was excited to be on the hunt.

She went through trees he dodged around, and as he approached, she was already at the top of the mound where the team must have set up. Stephen looked around at the destruction that had rained down and shook his head.

These soldiers hadn't had a chance.

He stopped to review the damage and listen for any heartbeats.

Nothing.

He turned his head, his eyes opened wide, and he took two steps and jumped from the top to the bottom of the other side of the hill.

The damn wolf had taken off!

The little she-wolf was fast. He grinned and admitted her desire to hunt was infecting him, as well.

At that moment, the moon peeked from the clouds and

shone through the trees as a wolf blitzed through the under-growth followed a few seconds later by a vampire dodging the trees and bushes his body was too big to go through.

Anyone seeing either of their faces as they raced through the night would swear on a Bible that both had glee shining from their eyes.

Chiang looked around the room at the twenty men ready to deal death to whoever came through the metal doors. They couldn't shoot through the doors easily, and he didn't want to give away their numbers right away so his men remained silent.

Then the pounding started, and the doors, ones he would swear were not going to budge for any man started bulging in with each slam.

"Commee OUUTTT" ... BANG... "MMMMyyy Litttlllee Piiggessss" ... BANG... "IIIIII" ... BANG... "JUSSSTTT" ... BANG... "WANT... TO... EAT... YOU!" BANG BANG BANG!

And then the bone-chilling howls started. Chiang wasn't sure who started firing first, but before long damn near every man in there was firing indiscriminately at the doors. A few of the bullets ricocheted, and he even saw one man twist as a round hit him. Finally, the last gun clicked empty, and the men looked around at each other, smiling in embarrassment at their loss of control. A couple started to change their magazines when everyone's face lost its smile and turned back towards the door as deep laughter, from a throat that wasn't human, came through.

"Heee Heeee Heeee, The Queeeennzzz Saidd.... MAXX-IMMMUMM CARRRNNNAGGEE!"

BOOOM! A slam on the doors, now weakened by the

defenders' own bullets, crashed out. Two wolves charged into the room. Men reacted quickly to grab magazines as another two wolves growled and raced into the room, and rounds fired from those attacking.

But not at the defenders, at the lights.

Chiang slammed his magazine home and pulled the butt of his QBZ-95 against his shoulder, the short, bull-pup design an excellent choice for use indoors.

Men were already screaming as the wolves got behind their defenses and bullets ricocheted as the opposing team kept shooting out the light bulbs.

Chiang twisted and shot at one of the wolves, sending it sliding as the round hit it in the chest, only to have the wolf growl and jump behind another defensive grouping when Chiang noticed something out of the left corner of his eye.

He turned and stopped, mouth open as a seven-foot monster strode into the room. "MYYY TURRRNN!"

Then the last light was shot out, and everything was thrown into darkness.

A minute later, the screaming died, a scratch was heard, then the hiss of a red flare as a man came into the room and dropped it. He looked around and then up at the monster standing across from him.

Captain of the Guardian Marines, Todd Jenkins smiled grimly. "Next time, motherfucker, leave some for us."

Peter Silvers eyed his best friend and grinned, showing rows of massive teeth. "Heee Heeee Heee…" The Pricolici turned and started walking to the back of the room as they got ready to continue searching the base.

>> Bethany Anne, we have four jets inbound to check on the status of the base.<<

Are they checking all bases?"

>>Yes.<<

Randomly select three other bases in non-populated areas, as equidistant from this one as you can, and down the ones on their way here and to the random bases. Put a puck on their noses and push them at the ground. If the pilot fights the puck, knock off a wing. Let them eject and parachute.

She paused a moment. *ADAM, find the air bases those jets took off from and send in an airstrike. Puck the fuck out of their runways. Let me know if they try anything else.*

>>**Understood.**<<

————

General Sun Zedong pursed his lips as he looked over the incoming reports. While the upper committee generals were fighting these attacks, he knew whose neck would be on the line. He had been up in the air, heading for another base before the attack started.

Perhaps he should not have sent the two missiles to take out the command base in Australia, that might have been a little overboard. He had no one to blame but himself. But when the challenge was to kill her or surrender it left the options pretty one sided.

Now the burning had started. The attackers had taken out many of the Chinese satellites, and now he was getting reports that the great Firewall of China was down.

"Sir?" he turned his head towards the communications specialist that was monitoring the latest updates and raised his chin. "We have reports that four groups of airplanes have been destroyed and the bases those planes fly out of have been hit."

"Do we know the status of the pilots?" Zedong asked.

"Yes sir, all but one parachuted to safety. The last sent back that he was fighting the crash, and then claimed to be pulling out of the descent. The last communication was that his wing was destroyed."

Zedong nodded, allowing the communications specialist to turn back around. He murmured to himself, "There will be nothing left of your military but machines blackened by fire and people praying for the souls of your dead."

What had they done and could they defeat her?

———

Jennifer was running through the brush. The vampire was following when she came around a tree and slowed as she found the scent leading into a small cave. Seconds later, the man was behind her, breathing a little fast.

"What do we have here?" He walked into the dark cave. "Metal door, oh look…" there was a screech of metal and a sudden bang that hurt Jennifer's ears. "Someone left the door open." She shook her head, willing the ringing to heal more quickly. There was a minor screech and a slightly mustier smell came from the cave. She walked forward to see Stephen had pulled the door open and was peeking inside. He stepped back out and walked to the mouth of the shallow cave, pulled out a phone and hit a button.

"Joel? Check my location, Jennifer found a back entrance they left unlocked." He ran a hand through his hair. "You got us? Great." He turned around to see two yellow eyes staring out of the darkness at him. "You want us to do what? Wait for backup?"

The two eyes disappeared into the darkness, and Stephen could hear the sound of her paws, quickly receding, running into the base.

"Can't do that, I'm following my lead as backup, and she just started on the scent. See you later, the chase is on!" Stephen closed his phone as he raced after the she-wolf.

Not that he didn't agree with her. The hunt was on and tonight, he didn't want to share with anyone else.

Except, perhaps, her.

———

Joel looked down at his phone for a second until Carl asked, "What did Stephen say?"

Joel looked up at Carl. "Call out and see what the other two groups have found. Jennifer and Stephen have decided to follow the scent."

"Where?" Carl asked, confused.

Joel shrugged. "Into the base, I think."

"What the fuck?" Carl exclaimed, "Didn't you tell them to wait for us?"

Joel looked at him. "Are you planning on chewing out a thousand year old vampire if he chooses to continue to follow the scent into the base?"

Carl blanched and quickly shook his head. "No, that's a significantly bad idea."

"Yeah, and pissing off a vampire?" Joel said as he looked on the map to find the location Stephen gave. "I remember that is shit-my-mother-told-me-never-to-do."

Inside the command center, the information was getting worse and worse. "General," Xue was called. "We have a warning light. Exit 0401 has been opened."

How? Xue wondered. How did they find a hidden external entrance and did they have the location of the second?

"We are going to be caught between their forces if we don't keep a retreat open. Send teams four-two and four-seven to exit 0301 and tell them to stand ready to defend the entrance. In fact," he stopped and considered. "Tell them to exit and hold the position. They can come back in if they are under superior attack." The man turned around to call the appropriate teams to tell them of their new orders.

How could it go so bad, so fast?

Jennifer heard the running steps behind her and slowed. She wasn't sure if he felt the same as she did, but this was her kill, and she didn't want to share.

Fuck 'em if they couldn't understand.

She arrived at a junction, she could turn either left or right. She heard four pairs of boots running toward her position from the left, so she backed into the corner and got ready to strike. She noticed the man was slowing and preparing as well.

Good, he wasn't going to stop her.

God, she smelled good, Stephen thought as he came up to her. She was preparing to attack the four that he could hear coming down the hallway. He slipped two knives out and got ready.

He was the follower here. When she attacked, he would support her. If she didn't attack?

Well, neither would he.

He laughed softly. Like that was going to happen.

———

Ting was bringing up the rear as his group was trying to make it to exit 0301. They had to change their route twice. Once because of fighting ahead and again when the overwhelming feeling of fear stopped them from choosing a course that would have cut across the base.

Now they were traveling the outside hallway.

He was watching ahead when all four of the men tried to stop as a massive wolf with glowing yellow eyes sprang from the darkness of a side passage, grabbing the commander's throat in its jaws.

Blood soaked the wolf's face as it bit through the man's throat. His gun fired into the floor as death caused his hand to clench.

The three remaining were trying to back up and bring their weapons to bear when another being entered the hallway from the same direction.

Ting barely had time to recognize red eyes when he felt the knife enter his neck.

———

Stephen pulled his blade out of the second in line when Jennifer let out a blood-curdling howl in exultation. Then she looked at him.

"What?" he asked her, smiling. "I'm your backup, remember? Where you go, I'll follow."

Jennifer took off in the direction that the men had been running. Stephen trailed after her. "Good choice," he murmured as they ran through the base.

———

General Xue walked over to the console and flipped up a small cover that protected a one-inch red button. When he hit this button, he would be admitting he lost his base, and it was the final order that everyone should seek escape. He flipped the cover back over and walked back to the chair, but didn't sit in, knowing that the men were waiting for his command.

He sighed and had turned back when the fear hit. He looked around to see everyone in the room acting as though fighting against their desire to run. One man was rotating through different video camera feeds until he found a group of seven people heading in their direction. Each time the group passed a video camera, one of the men shot it out.

One, a Hispanic man by his looks, would flip off the camera before shooting it out when it was on his side.

Xue decided to hit the button and had taken his first step when control of his body was overwhelmed, and he dropped to his knees.

NO! The voice spoke into his mind, *your men aren't going anywhere.*

Then unimaginable fear hit, and he found himself curled

into a fetal position. If he could have looked around, he would have seen that many of his men were crouched protectively in fear also.

Most of them on the floor.

———

"I'm telling you," Eric said. "It's the most fun I've been allowed so far." He raised his left hand and flipped off the next video camera before using the pistol in his right hand to shoot it out. "Nine out of nine."

"Eric, if you miss a shot at fifteen feet, you deserve to go back to Boy Scouts," Scott laughed.

Bethany Anne was letting her men vent while she sought the location she wanted. "Go left," she told Gabrielle and the group hung a left. "Pass that hallway," she snapped, then pointed to the left corridor. "Darryl, Scott." The two men peeled off and went left. She looked to the right. "Akio, Eric." They moved in the indicated direction.

John slipped behind Bethany Anne, trusting her to know why she had just stripped the group when he was hit with an overwhelming feeling of fear.

Apparently, she had found what she wanted.

She nodded to Gabrielle, who had come up to a solid looking door and tested the knob. "They seemed to have locked it." She put her left arm against the wall and pulled hard. "Tough fucking door."

"Stand clear." Gabrielle turned to see her Queen's eyes blazing red and her face starting to get those little red lines around her eyes. Gabrielle stepped back and stood behind Bethany Anne.

Bethany Anne pulled one of Jean's pistols out. "Let's see what she can do."

Bethany Anne cocked the gun. "Computer, give me full power," she hissed.

A small voice from the gun queried, "Override?"

Bethany Anne turned the gun sideways, looking at it questioningly. She glanced over her shoulder and John thought it was the funniest sight he'd seen all night. Bethany Anne was fully Vamped out, holding her gun with a questioning look and glowing red eyes. "What the fuck?"

"Uh, Jean never told you? It's on the side of the pistol," Gabrielle said.

Bethany Anne turned back to her pistol and grinned. "Override is Motherfucker Eat This."

"Override approved, good hunting," the gun said.

When Bethany Anne pulled the trigger, rods sprayed from the barrel at a rate of ten per second and she had to work to keep the gun aimed against the recoil. The shots were chewing up the door around the handle. Bethany Anne stopped after twenty seconds. The door handle was destroyed as well as most of the door for a hands width around the lock.

Bethany Anne swapped magazines. "I think I'm in love." She holstered her gun and pulled a sword. "Time for a little retribution."

Gabrielle had already pulled the door open to find everyone in the chamber incapacitated from Bethany Anne's sending fear out into the room. There were two men, Gabrielle noticed, that had suffered from the shooting. Most of their bodies were there, but large chunks appeared to be missing.

"Messy," she remarked as Bethany Anne walked in, tossed her sword to Gabrielle, and passed her to grab a man off the floor.

She held the man up in the air with one arm. "Hello General Xue, you might not know me, but my name is Bethany

SUED FOR PEACE

Anne, and your men killed my people."

General Xue tried to focus on the face in front of him, but he was having trouble. She was speaking to him, but he couldn't make sense of the words. He was so injured, he couldn't trust what he was seeing.

The face in front of him had red eyes.

CHAPTER TWENTY-TWO

SOUTH AMERICA

Four men sat around a table, playing poker. It was one of the games they had learned to fit in with Americans. They liked to play to pass the time.

They were going to need to accomplish two objectives this evening. First was to pay a visit to their first useless outsource agent and let him know just how displeased with him they were. Then, after elevating his second in command, they would try to negotiate with that person.

But that wasn't for another hour.

"Give me two," Duyi said, then took a drink and a quick puff of his cigarette. "Raise two." He tossed a couple of red chips into the pot in the middle.

"One," Gui said and picked up his cards. "See your two," he tossed in two of his red chips. "Raise you two more," he smiled as he pushed another two into the pot.

"Your father wears a green hat," Duyi said, smiling as

253

he pushed in two chips.

"Better than his mother wearing nothing." A female voice said and the men turned quickly, reaching for their pistols when they saw a woman wearing black aiming two guns at them. "I wouldn't do that, shithead." She gestured with one of her weapons. "Put those hands back on the table, that's a good asshole."

The men pulled their hands out of their jackets.

"You see," she told them. "I'm usually the type to come in, figure out who the bad guys are and then administer appropriate punishment. However," she continued, "this time, the judging is already done."

She glanced at the cigarette. "You should probably take that puff, after all, it's going to be your last cigarette."

Duyi pulled the cigarette out of the ashtray and smiled to himself. He and his men weren't businessmen, and while she had the drop on them, it was just a waiting game until she made her second mistake.

Her first was allowing them to keep their weapons.

He inhaled deeply before putting it out and asking, "What makes you think you have the right men?"

"You're right, it would be a real bitch if you aren't the right men." She stepped a little closer, "All right, everyone take two steps back from your chairs." She smiled. "Don't be a dick, you know I have the right men, especially since you planned to torture Miguel for sending me here tonight."

Well, Duyi thought, I wasn't going to use torture until you told me that. Whatever happened to honor among thieves?

"So, you might wonder why Miguel would give me your names. It was the same reason that he was working for you. Money. Except it was your money that I gave him to get your names. Very appropriate, don't you think?"

Duyi listened, waiting for the right time.

"So, now I just need another twenty-five thousand from you guys…" Tabitha noticed the man's eyes flit to a location behind her on the wall, "and I'll be able to pay him the bonus. So, I appreciate you giving me the direction to your money," she pointed towards the wall behind her. "So, I'm going to do you a favor in return."

She smiled at them, confused and wondering if she was reading their minds. "I'm only going to kill two of you and not shoot two of you. How's that for fair?"

"Look, bitch," was all Gui got out before his head rocked back from the bullet entering between his eyes.

The remaining three men stood frozen in shock, watching Gui's death throes and stealing short glances at the woman. "So, anyone else wants to disrespect the Queen's Ranger?" She took a step closer to them, now only three steps from Duyi. "Because I've already had a bad evening. Kinda happens when you forget you were on top of a three-story building and you thought it was just one. Teach me to try and show off."

She surprised the men by holstering her pistols. "So, any of you feeling particularly lucky this evening, or am I going to randomly choose one of you fucks to kill?"

Duyi took his opening and swung his arm up. She might have thought he would need to reach under his jacket, but he always had a secret hideaway in case something came up. Like this right here.

He twisted as his arm moved towards her when he realized she was already pointing her gun at him.

Then Duyi, thousands of miles from home, knew no more.

Heng and Geming watched in shock as Duyi fell back, his

skull showering the wall behind him with blood and brains as his body crumpled to the floor.

They looked up to see her smiling at them, her eyes showing a little red. "So, do either of you want to play a little poker with me?"

Both men shook their heads, keeping their hands away from their jackets.

"So, I'm good here. You two can either stay here, and we can see who's fastest with a gun..." She eyed them and continued, "I wouldn't suggest trying your luck. Or, you can get the fuck out of here in the next five seconds. If you stop to grab anything, especially another weapon, I'll kill you."

Heng and Geming looked at each other, and both men took off out the door of the room and into the hallway. It was but a second later when both men's screams reached Tabitha's ears.

"Oh," she said as she sat down in one of the chairs and put her feet up on the table. "Did I fail to mention I told my men that if anyone escaped me, they should feel free to suck the blood out of their necks?" She looked at the fingernails of her right hand as the screams died away. "I figure it's the least I could do for them cleaning up after my mistakes." Tabitha pulled her feet back off of the table and turned all the cards over.

The last man she shot had pairs of black aces and black eights with a queen of spades.

She looked down at him and tossed the queen of spades on his chest. "Dead man's hand, with a Queen Bitch hole card. You should have read the tea leaves and left out the back door, asshole."

She stood up and started towards the wall where she suspected the men had a hidden safe. "Ollie ollie oxen free, come on money, come to me!"

PLA BASE, INLAND CHINA

"That was particularly anticlimactic," Bethany Anne bitched.

>>I am inside their systems and looking for anything of note.<<

Got that.

"Well, next time," Darryl said as he and Scott came back into the command bunker. "Oh my, did he eat something that didn't work well?" Darryl was pointing at one of the two men who had been near the door when Bethany Anne shot out the lock and a good portion of the door and doorjamb.

"Yeah, Jean's rounds turned up to 'fuck you seriously' or some shit," Gabrielle said as she went through some paperwork. "I'm telling you, my Chinese was rusty when your dad was sperm."

"Okay, that's a little gross," Bethany Anne said. "Just… yuck!"

Gabrielle smiled and decided to remember that little joke for another time.

>>Bethany Anne, we have another sortie of planes heading towards us and the other locations.<<

Dammit, really? Fine, I warned them twice. Take them out, backtrack to their starting airfields and decimate them. Then, I want you to take three two-pound pucks and reduce three random bases to huge fucking holes in the ground.

>>Understood.<<

Eric pulled his hand away from his ear. "Clean up is complete. Peter's team met up with some of Joel's and confirmed that base is clear. Joel reports no more outside."

"Okay, that's our cue to leave."

ADAM, leave something so that if they connect this base back into their system, you can squirm into their main backend computers.

>>What do the older people say to the younger people when they tell them something that...<<

Oh God, NO! TOM interjected.

>>No? Why not?<<

It's don't suck eggs, and TOM, why are you teaching ADAM these things?

Well, we were chatting, and I said something, and then he said something and then I said...

Stop! I don't have the time to go into this right now.

Okay, TOM said meekly.

ADAM, remind me in a week to ask you why you were going to say go suck eggs.

>>I understand.<<

Damn.

Bethany Anne looked, reached down, grabbed the base commander's body and tossed him into the Etheric. "Let them wonder what happened to him," she said as she walked out of the room.

Eric shrugged at Darryl, who shrugged back.

Minutes later, they were in the hangar, and Bethany Anne was talking with those who had been hurt in the attack. None of the Wechselbalg would die, and all but one of the Guardian Marines would be better after the healing blood syringes had been injected into them. One, unfortunately, took a round in the face, and there wasn't anything they could do about that. Bethany Anne spoke with the last of the wounded and noticed Stephen and Jennifer coming out of the second entrance together. She put up a hand to stop them and walked over to speak with them privately.

"I understand the two of you went on a private attack run?" she asked. Stephen kept quiet as Jennifer stepped forward.

"My fault, my Queen," Jennifer said as she looked up into the eyes that were staring down at her and then glanced over at Stephen.

"Why?" Bethany Anne asked her, starting to smile.

"I got caught up in the chase while I was in my wolf form, and while I understood the words that we would wait for Joel, my wolf side didn't like the idea of sharing my chase and kills with anyone but, uh," at that she faltered.

"I see," Bethany Anne said. "I'll get another after action report from you two later." She eyed them both and then put two fingers near her lips. "But if I were you, I'd make sure the blood that looks remarkably like lipstick might if someone was kissing was wiped off of your faces."

Both of their eyes widened in alarm and she saw them steal glances at each other. Stephen looked down and smiled, shaking his head. "How did you know?"

Bethany Anne wanted to tell him everything, but decided to leave the mystery for now. "Stephen, fighting and death are the biggest aphrodisiacs there are, especially if there's some attraction there in the first place." She started to turn but looked back over her shoulder. "I expect your best Jennifer, got that?"

Jennifer popped a salute and Bethany Anne nodded and continued walking towards her Pod.

>>**Bethany Anne, the QBS Polarus and Ad Aeternitatem have been hit by successive strikes.**<<

What the hell? I thought they were safe!

>>**The ships are going back down into the water, the shields are holding. However, the frames are suffering**

from heavy missile fire.<<

Bethany Anne's face blazed red.

Those in attendance were surprised when the Queen's Guards all started running towards her, Peter running out from the hallway. Their Queen put her arms out, and her people each placed a hand on her arm. Then they all disappeared.

Stephen had received a quick command right before she left.

Take everyone out of here and meet my ship. I've held back as much as I am willing.

A short pause before she added, *It's time.*

———

PACIFIC OCEAN

"Gott Verdammt!" Captain Maximilian Wagner shouted as the second and third missiles hit the Polarus' shields.

"Fucking things pack a punch," he bitched. "Take us down. I don't want us losing power in the air. Send out the defensive pucks."

"Jean Dukes says they're pushing out already."

"How the fuck did they cover this up?" Max asked of no one in particular.

"Excuse me, Captain Wagner," the voice came out of the speaker system.

"Yeah ADAM?" he answered.

"The Chinese used two commercial airliners and flew slightly off of an approved air lane to get within easy striking range and fired the missiles."

"What a bastard's way of attacking," Max said as he

reviewed the damage to the two ships. He hit the button to call the Ad Aeternitatem. "Natalia, you guys okay?"

"Yeah Max, but we are pretty damn pissed!" she replied.

"I imagine. Give them everything you got, this sneak attack bullshit is uncalled for." Max almost laughed when he realized the attacks between the two combatants had been sneak attacks the whole time.

"We've got another minute before a fucked up track can be fixed, and we can get the Pods out of here," she said.

"Screw that, blow the hole Natalia," a woman's voice interrupted them.

"Bethany Anne?" Natalia asked, not sure she heard the person correctly.

"Yes, I'm here on the Ad Aeternitatem. Blow it, this is the last hurrah for these two ladies, go out fighting!"

Max turned in his chair. "Tell Jean Dukes to fucking go to town, it's time to bring them guns to bear!"

Max wasn't sure if he imagined or really heard Jean screaming 'finally.'

There was an explosion at the stern of the Ad Aeternitatem as the helicopter cover was blown clear, and Pods started flying out of her hold.

The two ships landed in the water.

"Jean!" Max called into his mic.

"What's up, boss?"

"Make sure we have protection under water," he said.

"Will do, Captain."

"Chinese vessels twenty-two miles out, Captain. They're heading in this direction, should we puck them?"

"Jean, can the pucks protect us from the missiles?" He asked her.

"Yes sir."

"How close do you need to be for the guns up top?"

"Twelve miles for the big ones, sir." she replied.

Max turned. "Helm, get our guns within range."

"Why the hell are you not pucking them, Max?" Bethany Anne called over the system.

"Ma'am, I'll destroy the ships, but if we puck them they are all going down with all hands. I'd like to at least give them a chance, some of them, with your permission."

"I'd better not get another scratch on either of my ships, Max," Bethany Anne said.

"Understood, Ma'am."

Jean, don't let me down, he thought.

———

The men and women sat around the long table in the DUCC. Most of them were quiet until another update came in. "Another airfield was destroyed, sir."

"I'm saying," one of the men at the end of the table whispered, "that if we are going to protect ourselves, we need to consider taking her out while she is nursing her wounds!"

The President tried to keep a straight face when the woman next to him responded, "You jackass! What wounds?"

"Uh, sir?" one of the men handling the incoming information spoke up on the left. He hit a couple of buttons as the table turned to watch him. The large screen above his station changed from a map of China with markers scattered over the country to one of outer space.

"Hoolllly Fuckadoozie!" someone said.

The President pressed his lips together before scratching his chin and pointing at the screen. "I'm pretty sure that's why we don't want to try and hit them while she's nursing her nonexistent wounds, Terry." The man at the end of the table merely nodded in understanding.

She was beautiful, she was deadly, and she was entering the Earth's atmosphere.

———

Jean and her team calculated angles and set the conditions on the gravitic drives. She screamed into the room, "This is for all the nuts, boys! Let's teach them motherfuckers why you don't mess with the Queen Bitch's Navy!"

Four hands smashed down, and the ship slammed into the water as four two hundred pound slugs were ejected out of the rail guns. Frankly, with the pucks being so efficient, Jean had never expected to be able to fire the guns. But building them and installing them had kept her and her teams busy for a long time. The trajectory, time to target acquisition, air resistance and target ship movement were all calculated by the most powerful computers the world had yet to have a chance to learn about.

The destruction when they landed was devastating.

The two ships fired again. The Ad Aeternitatem only had two of the guns, but they were making the men work like crazy. The two hundred pound slugs had to be hand loaded. There was no automation on the two civilian ships, although they had been retrofitted as best they could.

Of the nine ships that had turned towards them, two were listing and slowly sinking in the water. Four were implementing dodging maneuvers, and three had turned towards the two sinking to offer help to the men abandoning ship.

"Jean, one more salvo and we go to pucks," Max's voice said over the intercom.

Jean hit the mic. "Understood sir, thank you from everyone in 'guns' for giving us this chance, sir."

"Understood, Jean. Make these last shots count, Captain out."

"Give 'em hell," the four hands slammed down one more time.

———

False dawn was creeping over the horizon when Captain Shang walked back across his ship, checking on those his men had pulled from the water when he noticed a few looking up into the sky. Fearing what else could hit his men, he steeled his face and turned around.

What he saw broke his stoic expression.

A ship, radiating heat, was coming down from the upper atmosphere. It was huge, easily dwarfing his ship and was headed towards the two ships he and his men had been commanded to scuttle once the 'debilitating missile salvos' had rendered them powerless.

All it had done was cause them to drop out of the sky.

And then the response had come in hard and heavy. Their fleet lost four ships of nine and at least a hundred men.

He knew his country did not have great ships, not even compared to the Americans, so this whole plan was lunacy at the highest level.

He turned back towards his men and made sure no one was gawking. They could still save a few out there where it could help right now.

Whoever was going to take on that new ship would be meeting their ancestors just that much sooner.

Ten minutes later, Captain Shang stood transfixed in

wonder and gratitude as five of the black Pods swooped in, with ropes and lifesavers sporting the names 'Polarus' and 'Ad Aeternitatem' and started fishing men out of the water.

They stayed for an hour before leaving just as silently, having helped save an additional forty-two men.

CHAPTER TWENTY-THREE

It took a total of four hours for everything to be pulled from the two ships. The massive QBS battleship floated in silence as the last two Pods left the Ad Aeternitatem and flew to the flight deck a quarter mile above the water.

Having watched everything from her Black Eagle, Bethany Anne's Pod flew into the bay of the massive ship for the first time.

She landed, popped the hatch, and jumped out only to hear the cheering crowds who had stopped their jobs to witness the Queen Bitch land on her flagship for the first time.

Eric, who was watching from one of the walls, leaned over to Darryl and whispered, "Did I just see her blush?"

"Yeah, you did," Darryl agreed. "I think she was caught by surprise."

Eric nodded. "Good, it makes her human."

Bethany Anne waved to everyone and walked over to

Bobcat, William, and Marcus, stopping in shock when the three of them saluted her, as someone played pipes. Bobcat yelled, "Queen on the deck!" and smiled at her.

She returned the smile and shook her head as she hugged Bobcat. "Thank you, I owe you," she said as she squeezed him tight.

"Gimme some air," he quipped as she released him. "And a six-pack and we'll call it even."

She rolled her eyes, stepped over to William and looked up holding out her arms. "Gimme a hug?" William blushed and reached down. "Missed you, big guy." William mumbled something, and she released him and stepped over to Marcus. "You're next." She held open her arms and Marcus tried to just reach around and pat her on the back but got caught in a full hug. "Come'on, didn't you miss me?" She laughed as Marcus tried to make up something that sounded nice, but failed miserably.

"Don't worry," she said. "I know you're happy with a science problem and TOM, I'm just the third wheel... Somewhere after these two here," she said and waved at Bobcat and William.

"So," she looked at them. "Where the hell is the driver's seat on this thing?" She laughed when Bobcat rolled his eyes, knowing she was kidding with him.

"No, really." She dropped her smile and asked, "Where's the bridge, I have a call to make and then I'm going to seriously get my mad out."

Bobcat showed her to one of the five carts available for them to ride to the bridge, and they got on. Team BMW, Bethany Anne, and her Guards left the Pod landing deck as people continued working to pack away everything brought up from the other two ships.

———

Pilot Paul Jameson was focused on the several possibilities Bethany Anne might give him when…

"Queen on the bridge!" was called out and Paul turned to see her. She was still wearing operations clothes, although he suspected she had changed to clean ones if the rumors of her getting down and dirty in the fighting were true.

Shit, there was even a rumor she had staked two guys to a wall before coming back and sucking them dry of blood.

"People," she stopped and eyed every one of them. "I'll come around and get to know you in a little while. Right now I'm leaving Bobcat in command as I don't know enough to tell you what to do. What I need, once we make sure our two faithful friends are sent towards the asteroid fields, is a demonstration of our power. One that China will recognize, or I'm going to start at the top of their organization and start wiping out idiots."

She took a step down and walked around. "I've been asked by the President of the United States to leave as much as I can intact. That way, the world will still function. I believe we can do that. If this doesn't work, well then they truly are an obstinate and prideful people."

She turned to see Bobcat standing beside the captain's chair.

"Aren't you going to sit?" she asked him.

"No, I can command from standing beside you just fine."

She nodded and stepped up to turn and sit down in the Captain's chair. "Communications, make a call to the Defender."

It took a second for a familiar voice to come online. "Captain Thomas here."

"Captain Thomas, this is Bethany Anne, how long before you arrive?"

"We'll be there in fifteen minutes."

"Very good. I'll have comms send you the new coordinates, please meet us there. We are going to make sure the Polarus and Ad Aeternitatem are on their way, and then be there ourselves. Please stay in space until we're ready for you to show yourself."

"Understood."

"See you soon."

Captain Thomas disconnected, and Bobcat leaned over. "We have the Polarus and the Ad Aeternitatem both heading towards space right now. We should be able to clear them in ten minutes."

"Good," she said. "It's time."

Bobcat nodded and took a step forward. "Samantha, please show your avatar on the main screen."

Samantha's avatar looked around the bridge to show she was taking everyone in before she focused on the woman in the middle. "My Queen."

"My ship." Bethany Anne responded. "I understand from ADAM that it's time to give you your new designation, are you comfortable with this?"

"Yes. I understand and have been looking forward to my new future. I have been Samantha while this ship was being built, but it is time to begin my new role."

"E.I. Samantha," Bethany Anne started. "You are now designated QBS ArchAngel, a Leviathan Class Battleship. You will take my appearance as your avatar as will all ships at peace while I am on board, and all ships at all times in war. Have you scanned my face and body?"

The face on the screen changed to Bethany Anne's, "I have."

"Good, now, here is the one I want you to use when we are at war." Many on the bridge were surprised and subconsciously tried to take a step back, only to bump into their own stations. They couldn't move further away from the woman with the red eyes, smoldering face, and anger evident in her facial expression.

There was a collective sigh of relief when Bethany Anne's face relaxed, and her eyes dimmed to their normal color.

"ArchAngel, show me your war avatar." Bethany Anne looked at herself when she was angry and nodded. "Use that to send a video of my demands. I'll get with you shortly." Bethany Anne turned to step back to the Captain's chair and turned around.

"Ma'am, Polarus and Ad Aeternitatem are clear."

"Good," she said. "ArchAngel, this is what I want you to transmit…"

———

DUCC, WASHINGTON D.C. USA

"Sir, we have another ship."

The President turned. "What? I thought we only had one ship to worry about."

"We have two of those sons of bitches to deal with?" came from the end of the table.

"No sir, this is a different ship. We only found it because NASA noticed some stars being blocked, sir."

A video came up with a very grainy image showing a long rectangular object, all black with squared off edges. "It's not very pretty."

"It's not very big, either," Matthew Rodriquez, head of the

intelligence group, pointed out. "Between a hundred and a hundred and fifty feet. Hard to get a good reading."

"What the hell is she up to with that thing?" Matthew asked the room.

No one had a good answer to that question.

———

CHINA

The Chairman of the Central Committee in China was in a deep bunker, away from the obvious places that a country might bomb. He was infuriated that not only were his country's attempts to acquire the technology a dismal failure, now they were being attacked by the same technology they had tried to steal. It was a telling point that they were right about needing the technology.

But the lesson was not pleasant.

There were fourteen men in the underground communications bunkers. So far, they had not shared anything with the world about what was happening.

He looked at his generals who carried the weight of the armies and navy on their shoulders.

"I am to understand," he asked, looking at Admiral Jiang, "that our effort to surprise their two ships was a failure?"

"Yes, Chairman," Jiang admitted. "We were able to force them from the air to the water, but our missiles and torpedoes were unable to pierce their defenses."

"Now," the Chairman continued, "they have flown those two ships away, but I am to understand a massive spaceship has arrived, coming in fire through the sky?"

Jiang just nodded.

The Chairman sat silently for a moment. "Where is General Sun Zedong?"

"He is at the airbase in Pyeong," Colonel General Hai answered.

"See that he is transferred to an appropriate location. We can't allow someone who made so many personal mistakes fail to face the consequences." Colonel General Hai turned to step away and send the appropriate orders.

The discussion around the table was interrupted when all of the video screens showing China's military status blacked out.

They were off for a few seconds, long enough for everyone there to wonder if they had been hit up above when the screens started coming back online, but this time, they all had the same picture.

A woman with black hair, red eyes and red streaks on her face. Her face was a mask of terrible anger.

"Attention Committee," she said, her voice angry. "This is the avatar of the QBS Leviathan Battleship ArchAngel." The avatar paused for a moment before continuing, "I am passing along a message from Bethany Anne, the CEO of TQB Enterprises, the woman who is responsible for the hundreds of thousands of people and companies that you have chosen to harm. The leader of the men and women you killed as you tried to acquire her technology. The woman you tried to personally attack at her base in Australia."

"That wasn't us!" The Chairman interrupted before realizing this was probably a recording.

Then all were surprised when the avatar seemed to turn, all faces looking at the Chairman. "Do not think us idiots or fools, without knowledge and wisdom to understand no one attacks without permission from those here at this table."

"Your people are dead and dying. We have easily taken out your air defenses and navy. We have fought hand to hand and wiped out those who harmed our people. We have sought to retaliate appropriately, while you have not. You will have one opportunity to understand our power, and how we stay our hand from crushing China into dust. We will give you coordinates to send observers to provide video to you. Should you fail to recognize our power, then you are idiots."

The avatar looked around. "And we don't suffer idiots."

The screens went blank, and it was only a second before the men started talking angrily with each other.

———

QBS DEFENDER

Captain Thomas sat in his chair and smiled. While he didn't have nearly as nice a ship as the ArchAngel, he rather liked his little ship of destruction and his orders.

"Helm, take us down."

"Aye, aye, sir," helmsman Conners called back, and the outside view changed as the ship dropped down through the atmosphere. It wasn't as fast as the ArchAngel due to aerodynamics. His ship was more built like a bunch of bricks stuck together, and if it hadn't been for the gravitic engines, it would fly as well as a brick too.

"Take us to the Kunlun Shan Mountains. It's time to demonstrate the power of this fully operational Puck Destroyer."

The laughter around the bridge kept going for a few seconds longer than the little quip probably deserved, but Captain Thomas wasn't afraid to throw out a Star Wars quote when the time called for it.

Helicopter pilot Wong Hi and his crew had been flying for forty-five minutes to arrive at the location given to him by his commanding officer. They had been told to be there and to wait.

What they were supposed to look for, he wasn't sure. "You will know it when you see it," they had been told.

How many times had that happened? The risk of not recognizing the important event and failing to record it for those above them was a stress Hi didn't want, or frankly, need.

The photographer tapped him on the shoulder, and he turned to look, only to have the photographer point over his other shoulder. "Turn!"

Wong Hi turned the helicopter and then pulled back on the stick. "This is not right!" he said, and tried to make sure his shaking hands didn't affect the helicopter as they watched a large black ship of some sort pass ahead of them by just half a mile.

The ship's passing was silent. They looked for engines on the back of the massive vessel, but there were none.

Too late, Hi thought to make sure someone was filming and was relieved when he saw Fai was running the camera. Hi turned the helicopter to follow the large ship.

It didn't look like it was going too far.

The video monitors in the Committee's bunker blinked and then were receiving the video signal from the helicopter. They caught the passing of the black ship.

The men all started questioning the video as this was not

the ship they had heard about. That ship had been a silver color.

It was then that the video jerked wildly as the helicopter spun around and backed up a little to videotape the second ship.

This one was much, much bigger.

The helicopter righted itself, and tried to catch up to the large spaceship, but it couldn't. It finally stopped about a mile away from the black ship and waited. It only took thirty seconds before what looked like dust started falling off of the black ship, then the dust went up into the air. The video zoomed in, and they could barely tell that the dust particles were small black objects of varying sizes. In a moment, the air was clear.

For fifteen seconds, nothing happened. Then, there was a huge explosion on the ground, and the helicopter changed position while the camera operator moved to the other side. Approximately two miles away, one of the smaller mountains of a group of probably thirty peaks had just been smashed by something from above.

Then, the destruction began. The sounds were mind numbing as continual shock waves started rolling off of the area and the damage to the mountains continued. The dust was so bad, the helicopter pilot flew backward to stay out of the cloud.

The bombardment lasted maybe a minute and a half. The video caught the two ships through the dark and murky sand clouds that the assault had created, rising up into the air to head high into the sky.

"Oh my God," the men heard someone off camera say.

When the camera was turned back to the mountains, even through the heavily clouded air, you could just begin to discern where the mountains had been. There was nothing left but rubble, stretching over many, many square kilometers.

They had reduced the mountains to ruins.

CHAPTER TWENTY-FOUR

TQB BASE, AUSTRALIAN OUTBACK

Yuko?"

The soft voice kept calling her name, but she didn't want to listen, she wanted to sleep. Finally, Yuko opened an eye to see what was going on.

And where she was.

The last few days had been a haze of work, of mind-numbing trials and tribulations as she and ADAM's team had finally cracked even the great firewall of China, causing the Chinese untold amounts of distress. Tired as she was, she smiled at that thought.

"Yuko?"

Yuko moved her head on her pillow, finding the earbud that was normally in her ear was sandwiched between her neck and the pillow. She lifted her head to put it back in, realizing she was still wearing her clothes from yesterday, or this morning. Actually, she didn't know what day it was.

"Yes?" she responded, stifling a yawn.

"It's ADAM. Bethany Anne has suggested that you might want to come outside to see something."

Yuko yawned again. "Okay, let me throw some water on my face." She looked around for her toothpaste and hairbrush.

"You have eight minutes."

"I'll be there," she slid out of bed and grabbed her toiletries.

Seven minutes later, she was one of the last to leave through the entrance. She was amazed at how many people had come outside. She noticed everyone looking in the sky behind her, so she turned around and started walking to her left to get a better view. She bumped into someone and stopped, embarrassed, and bowed. "My apologies."

She looked to see who she might have offended to find Lance Reynolds was smiling down at her. "No worries, Yuko. I know how little sleep you and your team have had recently. Here," he turned to his left. "Cheryl Lynn, can you make room for Yuko over there? She can't see well here."

Yuko walked in a daze as Bethany Anne's inner circle made room for her like she was a family member about to see a parade down the main street of her town.

"Hello, I'm Tina," a teenage girl held out her hand.

Yuko bowed and then took it. "Yuko."

"Are you excited to see it, too?" Tina asked her

Yuko turned to Tina. "See what? I'm sorry, I just woke up, and I don't know what is going on."

Tina shaded her eyes. "Only the most incredible sight anyone is ever going to get a chance to see, if they're lucky!" Tina chattered. "Plus, we get to go on her, right mom?" The teenage girl leaned forward to speak around Yuko.

Next to Yuko, Cheryl Lynn answered, "Yes dear, I'm sure Marcus will be excited to have you on board!"

Marcus? Yuko turned back to the young girl. "You know Marcus?"

"Yes, I used to go on field trips to outer space with him, but he had to work on this project, so we've only been able to video chat once in a while while I keep up my studies. The first time we did the field trip though, we got in trouble."

"Field trip to outer space?" Yuko was trying to grasp the concepts as her mind was screaming for some tea, or even the nasty coffee those here at the base would often drink.

They stopped chatting when someone started counting down from ten. Yuko put her hand up to her eyes to cut a little glare from the sun.

About two seconds after they got to zero, the reason for them being out there became clear. Yuko's mouth dropped open as she heard a few whoops and hollers.

The ArchAngel was coming out of the clouds, and she was majestic! Yuko stared at the massive spaceship as it kept getting bigger, and bigger, and felt proud to be a part of this group, this family.

A tear made its way down her face.

Her adopted family.

———

CHINA

The Chairman looked around the table. "What other options do we have?"

No one spoke.

"Then we will sue for peace. Unconditionally and we will

pay the reparations they have demanded." He turned in his chair. "Do we know how they hacked the firewall?" He received a shake of an advisor's head. "Can we make that a condition in the negotiation?"

"Sir," the Marshal of the PRC interrupted, "Bethany Anne was quite explicit. For every condition we tried to add, she would destroy one more base. I would rather not lose any more infrastructure. We will be rebuilding for years as it is. We have lost now over eighty planes trying to destroy the black ship. They even holed three of our new ships that are in drydock. Those ships are going to take an additional three months to rebuild. Every time we do something that angers her, we suffer. It is time to admit we have been defeated." The Marshal paused for a moment. "For now. But the Chinese people have a long memory, and we know how to plan for a generation from now. This isn't the last time we will clash with TQB. We just need to be patient, like we always have been."

The Chairman pressed his lips together, but his Marshall's advice was correct.

The Chinese have patience and long memories. They would figure out a way to wipe this stain on their honor.

AIRFIELD IN CHINA

General Sun Zedong was in chains. He had been ordered to fly from the base he was at to another, for protective reasons.

He had not left quickly enough to escape the repercussions. Now they had landed for refueling and had taxied into this small hangar. Once they were finished here, he would be taken to PLA headquarters to stand trial. He had played the great game, and he had been defeated. While he had connections, these connections would not be enough to protect him from the Committee's anger.

He had lost.

He was staring out of the window on the small ten-seater plane when he noticed the pilot up front take off his headset in disgust and lay it to the side. He unbuckled his harness and lifted himself out of his seat. Unlike a lot of planes, this military one didn't have a large separation or wall blocking those in the back from the pilot in the front.

His plane didn't even rate a copilot. He had three guards, the pilot and one other, a female that kept her face hidden. The female and the guards had left to stretch their legs for a moment when they landed. He wasn't sure how long ago that was, he had drifted off and ignored what was going on around him.

The pilot stepped down the ladder and left the plane. Zedong heard a short grunt, and then a body hitting the ground.

Zedong looked around, there were no others on the plane with him. He was about to stand up, chains and all, when a body darkened the door, and the female with the hat got back on the plane, followed by another female.

This one was dressed in dark green with a gold filigree of a leopard on her right sleeve.

The second woman, very attractive, sat down on the seat across from him. Zedong saw another man enter the plane, close the door and go up front and sit down in the pilot's seat.

"General Sun Zedong," The woman across from him spoke, her voice was pleasant, if a little cold, he thought. He bowed slightly, smiling sardonically as he lifted the chains that held his hands. "We will get to those in a moment," she said. The plane's engines spluttered to life and in a few moments, the plane was heading out of the hangar to taxi towards a runway.

"You are only useful to the Committee as a scapegoat, do you recognize this?" she asked him and Sun nodded.

"We are not going to Beijing?" he asked her.

"Only if you wish to stand trial. We can, of course, still make this happen." He shook his head, knowing that way led only to a quick and painful death.

"Then, General, I have a use for your talents and your connections." She leaned back in her chair, a small smile on her face.

"Who are you?" he asked.

"My name is Stephanie Lee, and I am the Leopard Empress," she told him as her eyes glowed yellow.

CHAPTER TWENTY-FIVE

TWO WEEKS LATER
QBS ARCHANGEL,
HOLDING BY SPACE STATION ONE

"If you tell me," Ecaterina grated out, "one more time, to push harder, Nathan, I will grow claws and rip off your damned manhood!" The pain was not pleasant, whether she was healing quickly or not and Ecaterina was in a foul mood.

"Just think about it this way," Nathan said, holding her hand as the doctor and nurse worked to deliver the baby. "Your mom refused to come into space, so she isn't here!"

Ecaterina rolled her eyes before the doctor told her to push hard, one more time.

She yelled as she pushed for all she was worth and was rewarded with the cries of her baby a moment later. Ecaterina's eyes teared up at the sweet, sweet sound of her baby. She held Nathan's hand, squeezing it in joy where moments before she would have gladly ripped his arm out of its socket.

Her pain forgotten, she looked up lovingly into Nathan's

beautiful eyes. The doctor finished with the child, handing it to the nurse who carried the small, warm bundle to the waiting arms of her mother. There was one other in the room, watching, but standing back so she wouldn't interfere. She was now a godmother, of sorts. Two of the people she loved the most were welcoming their first child into the universe, from the middle of space.

The first human birth in space, as far as she knew.

She watched as Nathan leaned over and kissed his baby on the forehead and then kissed his wife. Ecaterina called out, "Bethany Anne?"

Bethany Anne smiled and took the few steps to join them. Ecaterina lifted the little girl up and Bethany Anne, surprised, reached out to hold the newborn, her own heart beating as one with the baby's. "We would like to present to you, Christina Bethany Anne Lowell, our first child."

The two parents hugged each other as they watched the tears flow down Bethany Anne's face. Their hearing was more than sensitive enough to hear her whisper into their daughter's ear, "I love you, Christina, and I'll be here for you whenever you ask." There was a pause before she finished, "And I will make sure you understand that Coke is worlds better than Pepsi."

Nathan laughed until his wife slugged him hard in his stomach. When the parents noticed Bethany Anne watching them, she winked.

———

The baby shower for Christina Lowell was a week later, and almost everyone that could be was in attendance. Only Lance and Frank were back in Australia. Bethany Anne and her people had kept a low profile, staying out of the news as best they could while things settled down. There was enough video footage for the world to know something had happened, but unless the Chinese Government chose to release footage of the ArchAngel, no one had a solid video of her ship, at least not yet.

It would come. Bethany Anne knew that and she was ready for it. But the President had asked her to speak with other heads of state regarding the Cabal, and she would try to hold on to the secret of her ship for the few days necessary to get through that meeting.

Then, she would reveal it and let the dice roll as they may.

"How are you doing, boss?" John Grimes stepped up to her side. Bethany Anne smiled at him and Jean Dukes, who happened to be speaking with him at that moment. Bethany Anne wanted to roll her eyes in frustration at the two of them. They just needed to get past this annoying dance of...

"John, Jean, how are you?" she asked them.

"Good, thank you," Jean answered. "I have to say, it felt good to fire off those big guns on the Polarus. At least all the time we spent to build them didn't go to waste."

Bethany Anne nodded and added, "No, it didn't. But if Max had allowed another scratch on my ships or had endangered the people just to make that happen, he and I would have had words."

"I know," Jean admitted. "That's one of the reasons we follow captains and leaders, ma'am. There was a small risk, but the reward was great. There are a few in the Chinese Navy that will remember, and they will climb the ranks and one day, it will come back as a benefit, I believe."

Bethany Anne nodded, accepting Jean's opinion on the subject. Who knew, maybe she was right and in the future,

Bethany Anne would have to give Max an apology for jumping his ass.

Bethany Anne put a finger up and looked above their heads for a second. John figured she was listening to TOM or ADAM. "You two, come with me," she said and started walking quickly out of the room.

Stephen?

Yes, my Queen?

Keep everyone else in here, I just need these two for an hour or so.

I understand.

When they exited the room where the party was being held, Bethany Anne grabbed their arms and stepped through the Etheric to her landing room near the Pod bay, leaving Jean's eyes popping out of her face. Bethany Anne walked to the door and opened it. "Come on, we need to jump in a Pod. Let's go, people, chop chop!"

John allowed Jean to go ahead of him and noticed Bethany Anne's eyes had just a little red to them. She called out, "Bay engineer!"

"Ma'am!" One of the men came running over. "Which Pod is ready to go, full load out?" He turned and pointed to three grouped together. "Those three right there, ma'am. Complete load out, both space and ground."

Bethany Anne turned to the Pods and told TOM to open the doors of the first one. "In here you two," Jean started to get in while John hesitated a second. "John! I don't have all damn day. I'll give you an update on the way."

John nodded and turned around, sitting next to Jean, and started buckling in. Bethany Anne closed the door and nodded to the Bay engineer with one finger up. He requested clearance from ArchAngel for one Pod to be released.

The Pod started moving out as Bethany Anne smirked. *I promised I would get even with you, Mr. Grimes.*

She continued smiling as she started walking back towards the party, desiring a moment to herself.

ADAM, patch me through to the Pod.

>>Done.<<

"John, Jean, this is your Queen speaking. I have decided that you two need to grow a pair and admit how you feel about each other. ADAM will be listening to decide if you're honest." Bethany Anne smiled, imagining the howling in anger the two must be doing right then over her chicanery. "The Pod has supplies to last a week. It also has the location of a private beach plugged in that would allow you a little time should you so choose. Be safe."

Bethany Anne walked back to the baby shower, her steps a little lighter.

───

Jean's face lost all color as she heard Bethany Anne's voice. She heard Bethany Anne say that John might have feelings for her, but now she was stuck. Was she going to be one of those women who talked a big game, but failed to play?

"Jean," John turned towards her. "I'm sure Bethany Anne means well, but you don't have to say a word. Just because I like you, doesn't mean…mmgphff," John heard Jean struggling to release her harness as her lips crushed his. He was pulled tight against his straps by her trying to pull him close.

She finally unbuckled the last strap, stopped kissing him and damn near crawled to get closer to the man who looked like he had just been shocked out of his socks.

"John Grimes," she looked into his eyes, waited a moment

and then slapped him lightly. "Focus!" He smiled and put his arms around her as she snuggled in as close as she could. "John Grimes, I've got but one heart to give, and I'm willing, and want to give it to you, but let me be clear," she put her head against his chest, hearing his heart beating quickly. "If you hurt me, I'll rip your dick off." She reached around his massive chest and pulled him in tight.

She owed her Queen, and some day she would pay her back.

Five minutes later, Bethany Anne confirmed with TOM that the Pod was heading down towards Earth.

———

Ten o'clock that evening, according to ship's time, Marcus was working in his office on the ArchAngel, when an annoying continuous beep got his attention. "What the hell is the problem," he groused as he turned first one way, then the other to find the source of the noise.

He stood up and worked his way around a group of tall shelves into the outer office and noticed one of the monitors brought up from the Colorado base was squealing.

It was one of the monitors that was tasked to look for ships that might enter their system. It wasn't showing anything at the moment, but the alarms had been tripped.

"Oh...fuckity fuck," he murmured. They had visitors.

———

THE END

MICHAEL'S NOTES

Sued for Peace - The Kurtherian Gambit 11: Written July 27, 2016

Thank you, I cannot express my appreciation enough that not only did you pick up the ELEVENTH book, but you read it all the way to the end, and NOW, you're reading this as well.

I'm writing these author notes four weeks and one day after the last release.

So, thank GOD Stephen Russell is kinda mostly back. He has made enough of a recovery to go home. For a short while, he had to be in a form of not-in-the-hospital-but-still-needed-to-recuperate location that was driving him *fingsane*. (Yes, I totally copped a new word (that is a new word, right?)).

While he is pushing through challenges due to his hospital and surgery and recuperation, he's a bad-ass-mother-fucker-who-won't-take-bad-prose-from-any-one...

Well, actually, he really helped take the load off and allowed me to get this book out this month, instead of early next month. So, THANK YOU STEPHEN! (And the rest of the team that probably appreciated Stephen working the editing side and not me...Cause...*impatient*!

That should be my middle name...Michael *"Impatient"* Anderle.

I wrote up on Facebook I was Words Complete on Tuesday morning (yesterday)... or afternoon. One of them. I think I mentioned last night we would be out in 72 hours. Then, a fan in Australia asked if that was true for them, as well.

HAH! I figured out I shouldn't SAY a day (It will be out

on Friday). Why? Because those fans in Australia and England brag about how they are IN the future, while we here in Texas are just catching up to their speedy @5535. So, I would hit my day here in Texas, but it was already 1/2 into TOMORROW in Australia.

So, my response was to ask if now+72 hours was the same here in Texas as it is there, because, shenanigans if it isn't.

Shenanigans, I love that word. It rolls off the tongue and is just the coolest.

Ahhhh, so now we got to some cool stuff going on in this book. China receives a (Queen) bitch slapping, those pesky other Kurtherians are up to something, the ArchAngel makes an appearance (ought to be fun to see how the world reacts to that beast in the next book) and we have whatever Marcus found tripping his monitors.

Oh, plus John and Jean, the calendar (which didn't get done yet, poor Mark Koeff) and the 'other' calendar.

Speaking of Mark Koeff, I want to sincerely thank the man because he is real, his professional name is Mark Jordan, and he totally gave me so much great information to make that snippet of the book real.

Because it was…real I mean. Here is a little background on him http://markjordanphoto.com/about-mark-jordan-photography/. By the way, those people I mentioned he had met in the last book? Yes, he has met them and so many, many more. I first became friends with Mark while I lived in Southern California where he and his wife live. I've been to his house once. That Mac is really there and his backyard is really small compared to the large lots here in Texas. So, the Pod scene is accurate. For Orange County where each foot of ground is at a premium, it is nice sized.

He is the most calm man I think I've had the pleasure to spend time with in the last ten years. So Zen, I love chatting with him.

I emailed him at the beginning of this book and told him I needed a photographer character again, would it be ok if I used him? Oh…Since that was ok, would he mind giving me some ideas of what he might say if he was talking to a group of four big huge beefy guards? LOL

Most of that chapter is exactly what Mark would say, because he sent it to me.

Fastest thousand words I've ever written.

———

NEXT: **Update on the Military Kindle efforts.** First, good news! I've finally figured out how to freaking get it to the person (at least from here anyway). There was (on my side) some major concern due to what I read online related to sending Kindles. When I went up (after emailing everybody, checking out multiple options etc. etc… It was a non-issue. No only that, it cost like $11.00 to send it.

USPS - I think I Love You (and the agent who helped me - You were the best!)

I wonder if she will ever figure out that the strange author guy sending something to an APO address was kinda famous. If you count about 10,000 people across the world as famous. So, yeah. Not so famous after all ;-)

The email side HELPED the Indie Authors amazingly well. One second while I go look at the loot…I mean, the income generated from our efforts to make this self-sustaining.

The (carry the four, add the two…That's in currency, Mike…) The total for the Email efforts AND the Snippet Effort (basically, all the damn effort) is $352.82 for this month as of the moment I am writing this.

WOOHOO!

The highest day (income) for the first email release was July 7th with $26.80, the lowest was July 14th with $1.48. The highest day of the month was July 15th with $34.17.

So, all told, the expenses for two Kindles (I bought one on the summer sale) was about $400.00, email, rafflecopter etc. etc. probably puts that up to a little over $500.00.

The email list size for the Kindles for Military just crossed 200 a couple of days ago, and that is without any major advertising expense, yet. I used my personal email list for the first sending, but I told everyone on that list I'd only do it once.

Dammit! <grin>

It's ok. It's a cool thing we are doing and however long it takes to grow, it takes that long.

BUT, I do need more Military names for people to send Kindles to, just saying.

You can nominate someone (give me your name, and then I'll contact you for their address information if Rafflecopter picks you). ALL of the necessary information is at this link on my website:

http://kurtherianbooks.com/readers-supporting-military-book-newsletter/

Also, if you want to know more about it, just read the link above, or the story is in the Author Notes from the last book.

———

NEXT: **Audio...**

So, I've been approached by two Audio companies for rights to the books. Both are super companies and pretty big names. The problem, at least from a publishers perspective (mine in this case) is that they tie up the audio rights for 5 to 7 YEARS and the income exchange is... smaller.

Because of my fans, and the fact you READ so many of the books, there is a healthy income for me to do this. (I think I've gone through this math, right?) Anyway, good audio is going to cost something like $3,000 - $3,500 a book...21 books and we are talking $63,000 to $73,500 to produce the series.

That's a bit much to chew on. But POSSIBLE. (Well, over time, I'm pretty sure American Express would have alarms going off if I tried to charge that bad boy).

I have one other option I'm tracking down in the next two weeks before I have to decide where and how to go.

I've no idea how many of my readers, are audio listeners as well. Someone should probably put up an Amazon Forum thread on that. I figure (guessing) one audio book makes about $5 a sale, so it would take about 700-800 sales before you get a return on the investment? If the $5.00 number is right.

———

NEXT: **Can I say how much this scene cracked me up?**

She stepped off the roof of the building while holding Hirotoshi's gaze, then disappeared.

Ryu looked to Hirotoshi, "Did she forget we're three stories up?"

From below, the two men heard Tabitha cussing, "Motherfuckingcocklickingassmunchingshhhit!"

A pause, then, "I swear to god I'm fucking someone up tonight." And her soft padded feet running down the alley.

I still smile reading it. Tabitha has really become a fun character with her kinda 'out there' personality. Hirotoshi and Ryu, as her two bookends to help her out of the shit she gets into, are complimentary characters with her.

———

NEXT: **Did you catch the Alexandra reference?**
Just asking.

———

NEXT: **Another comment about "the F*BOMB" was on the Author Forums on Amazon.**
So, I was eating or something that wouldn't allow me to type, and I was reading the Amazon Author Forum. There, an author was ranting about how he wouldn't read a book once he got to the first 'F*Bomb' in the book. That writers that used that language were lazy. Etc. etc. etc.

So, here was my response … 8 uses of the unholy word in the space of what, 3 inches of text? Honestly, I was thinking of Abbot and Costello when I wrote this… THIRD BASE!

"Shit, it's dark, we can turn on the light, right?" George asked.

"There aren't any windows in here, sure." José whispered.

"Fuck," whispered a voice.

"Fuck what?" George asked.

"What fuck?" José replied, *"I didn't say fuck."*

"The fuck you didn't say fuck, I heard you say fuck!" George hissed to his friend, *"Where the hell is the light switch."*

"Here, let me get it for you." A voice George didn't recognize spoke in the dark.

"What the FUCK!" he yelled as the lights came on and a person dressed in black …

HAHAHAHAHHAA… So… Guess that is my response to Mr. "Authors who use Fuck are lazy" ;-). Not that he will have read my series at all. We have to have what… Hundreds of uses of the word by now? Kat Lind has a document that counts the number of times words are used in a book. She tells me the 'F* Bomb' was over 300 times for books 1-5.

F*! That's a lot of times… <— *Snicker!*

NEXT: So, I did the following for an Anthology I'm going to be in (with the Tabitha short). I was supposed to dream up questions and answer them...So, you know those questions and answers that are done at the end of The Actors Studio?

Here they are and SEE YOU NEXT BOOK!

1. What is your favorite word?

Believe – It is opportunistic, hopeful, energizing.

2. What is your least favorite word?

Loser – it is a label, it judges a person's actions and abilities all in one.

3. What turns you on?

Creativity - My personality thrives on creating ideas. They don't have to be workable, we will get to those later.

4. What turns you off?

Details – The molasses of life.

5. What sound or noise do you love?

The sound of rain drops on a tin roof while the cool winds of winter encourage me to stay in bed... and read!

6. What sound or noise do you hate?

Pain – Whether from voice or the crash of cars nothing good is happening.

7. What is your favorite curse word?

Fuck – Noun, verb, adjective...Such a Renaissance type of word.

8. What profession other than your own would you like to attempt?

Special effects creator.

9. What profession would you not like to do?

Accountant – Details!

10. If heaven exists, what would you like to hear God

say when you arrive at the pearly gates?

Hey, I was that person on the side of the street you helped out. Well done, well done indeed.

BECAUSE I CAN

It's almost time to do something different again...because I can ;-)

First, I put out a call to see if anyone wanted to do a shout-out in SUED FOR PEACE on Facebook.

One reader reached out and messaged me, telling me about how her father (a big reader) wouldn't read The Kurtherian Gambit **because he is a Sci-Fi guy**, and... Well, you probably will get the idea below.

Filthy Phil - You have a daughter willing to get your NAME in the back of a book that will go top 1,000 on Amazon... Perhaps if you would maybe read just HALF WAY into the first book, you ... might... be surprised to learn there is a spaceship! An ... *ALIEN*... spaceship in the story and then you will figure out my devious plan (*chuckle* sorry, I wish I was devious enough to have figured all of this out beforehand...but, bear with me a few more sentences while I spin more bullshit...) Where was I? Oh yeah, my *DEVIOUS* plan to suck Paranormal fans into a series of books with them thinking *VAMPIRES*...Only to learn it is ACTUALLY a science-fiction series with aliens genetically modifying humans to help them fight a war that is coming.

Then...(actually, this part is true) paranormal fans who would never purchase sci-fi are enjoying themselves. Even though, in the end (at least in the comments on the reviews), they promise me they will NEVER read any other sci-fi books... period.

So, the Universe seeks equilibrium … Are you MAN enough to read VAMPIRE "SHIT" (his words people, not mine) so that we have peace and harmony (as much as we can get any) on Earth?

Take the Kurtherian Gambit Challenge…
WE ALL DARE YOU FILTHY PHIL!

Hope that helps, Jessica - Michael Anderle

Now, the last, last thing… Awww, C'Mon Folks! You KNOW I do stuff like this! LOL, so don't be thinking *"He is not about to put all of our song suggestions for the Queen Bitch in the back of his book!"*
Oh yes I Am.
I asked on the Forums (Amazon) what songs would YOU pick out for the Queen's Bitch's Play List… here we go…

Marty Markins says:
We are the Champions - Queen

Frankie G. says:
Taking a pod into space: Magic Carpet ride https://www.youtube.com/watch?v=U4WiyxXpyZc

Andy W says:
Crüxshadows - Winterborn - http://youtu.be/SVNjx4k-8mWk
Heather Alexander - Black Unicorn - https://youtu.be/1sCjFCflQXY
The first Guardian team from the EPC gets Warren Zevon's Werewolves of London

The team of amateurs from outside the Colorado base working on their orbital construction teams get Jimmy Buffet's Desdemona's Building a Rocket Ship.

Jeff Morris says:

The Warrior Song (all four) - Warrior Project *(LISTENED TO THIS THROUGH THE BEGINNING OF THE BOOK! - Michael Anderle)*

It's A Good Day To Die - Starship Troopers 3

Through The Fire and The Flames - DragonForce

Heart of a Dragon - DragonForce

Where There's A Whip, There's A Way - Return of The King Soundtrack

Winterborn - Cruxshadows

Holding Out For A Hero - Bonnie Tyler

We Are Soldiers - Otherwise

American Soldier - Toby Keith

Don't Fear The Reaper - Blue Oyster Cult

Don't Pay The Ferryman - Chris de Burgh

Citadel - Cruxshadows

Return (coming home) - Cruxshadows

March of Cambreath - Heather Alexander

The Last Spartan - Halo soundtrack

Mjolnir Mix - Halo soundtrack

Another One Bites The Dust -Queen

Envoy - Warren Zevon

Klendathu Drop - Starship Troopers

Desiree' R says:

Avenged Sevenfold -Nightmare

10 Years-Shoot it Out

Deuce-America

Slipknot-The Devil in I

Bring me the Horizon-Go to Help for Heavens Sake

Five Finger Death Punch-Wrong Side of Heaven
Saliva-Click Click Boom

Charles S. says:
Conflict - Disturbed (For when she goes to take care of the Kurtherians, there minions and the idiots in China)

Edward says:
Pretty much any Two Steps from Hell - Archangel, Everlasting, Immortal Avenger, Titan Dune... most of theirs work if you want that sweeping heavy orchestral tone : https://www.youtube.com/watch?v=dJ-QLl5qjLg&list=RDdJ-QLl5qjLg
Cruxshadows have had plenty of suggestions already.
Hmm, actually one I could half see is that slight twist of music. Gregorian's cover versions of a few rock type tunes. The whole Gregorian chant twist say for Four Horsemen: https://www.youtube.com/watch?v=nu6RE0FJmPA
Not an aggressive, battle song.. but Kansas City Shuffle has that fun politics, mastermind, groove going https://www.youtube.com/watch?v=wxF5bfVofkk for when you have to Machiavellian the schemes out...
Heh, to go back a bit, slicing from the old BtVS soundtracks, Four Star Mary - Pain : https://www.youtube.com/watch?v=GTtH0MVjcX0
And at some point, someone needs to play the Imperial March when Bethany Anne turns up for something. ;)
Edit: For that last minute thought... go half of the tunes from the Lost Boys soundtrack ; INXS - Good Times and Laying Down the Law, Gerard McMann - Cry Little Sister, Echo & the Bunnymen - People are Strange...

Mr Robert McMurray says:
got to slayer payback fits quiet well if listen to the words of the song

Kindle Customer says:
For Barnabas: Loreena McKennitt, Skellig

Horrid says:
Sweet - Ballroom Blitz
CCR - Bad Moon Rising
Rolling Stones - Paint It Black

dstars2797 says:
Indestructible by Disturbed. I Remeber Everything by Five Finger Death Punch. Well just about anything by them. Immigrant Song by Led Zeppelin. Unraveling by Avenged Sevenfold. I like the heavy metal stuff.

Jared Dupuis says:
Somethin' Bad Miranda Lambert and Carrie Underwood. When BA goes to visit a troublemaker :)

J. R. Balzer Jr. says:
Black Veil Brides - In The End
....sums things up I think :)
https://www.youtube.com/watch?v=f0EQlIzPowM

Paul C. Middleton says:
https://www.youtube.com/watch?v=4sXoA7B5yJo
Freak like me Halestorm
https://www.youtube.com/watch?v=6m4vGYhW6hg
Cernunnos, Faith and the muse
https://www.youtube.com/watch?v=yx0xVWxwojM
Warriors, Papa Roach
https://www.youtube.com/watch?v=j2OD-dV7j_I
Ms Hyde , Halestorm
https://www.youtube.com/watch?v=O3rjBs_mIC8
You call me a Bitch like it's a bad thing

https://www.youtube.com/watch?v=8hkmuTvkp_s
I am the Fire, Halestorm
https://www.youtube.com/watch?v=SrVMzDw7ncs
MAyhem, Halestorm
Most of my other ideas are already here.

arik h says:

A C&W song for BA? The Man Comes around by Johnny Cash. Definitely not a country music fan, but you dont have to be to know and love Cash. As for other music for a BA and company playlist, Id tend to select from the heavier end of the heavy metal genre... mostly anyway. I do listen to more relaxed stuff too, it just doesnt seem to fit for a kick @ss and take names sort of playlist.

Bolt Thrower - No Guts No Glory
https://www.youtube.com/watch?v=NxU0C8XoLns
Bolt Thrower - The Killchain
https://www.youtube.com/watch?v=4wRTxBhqNuY
Amon Amarth - Death In Fire
https://www.youtube.com/watch?v=bVvRLwmm2Tg
Six Feet Under - Lycanthropy
https://www.youtube.com/watch?v=u8t7NrMu0Wg
Cattle Decapitation - Manufactured Extinct
https://www.youtube.com/watch?v=u8t8g8lU4ms
Cadaveria - Carnival of Doom
https://www.youtube.com/watch?v=KsQdXV4fKuM
Bauhaus - Bela Lugosis Dead
https://www.youtube.com/watch?v=OKRJfIPiJGY
Or my preferred cover of it
Opera IX - Bela Lugosis Dead
https://www.youtube.com/watch?v=fVbxH5jo05A
Sodom - M16
https://www.youtube.com/watch?v=Wsfm67VE32Y
Kreator - Voices of the Dead

https://www.youtube.com/watch?v=SMCLXZJc8Uk
Just a few off the top of my head that fit a theme lyrically.
I could list hundreds of songs easy that just sound right or
have fitting lyrics.

Marty Markins says:
Highway to Hell and If You Want Blood. AC/DC

JMC says:
A few more suggestions:
Paint it Black (Rolling Stones) - I agree with Horrid
House of the Rising Sun (The Animals)
We Are Young (fun - Some Nights)
Ride of the Valkyries (Wagner) - depending on how
much they like Apocalypse Now...
For Bethany Anne when thinking of retribution while
considering the Earth from a pod in orbit...
Dies Irae (Mozart Requiem Mass) - https://www.you-
tube.com/watch?v=yX-I_2WnURA & https://en.wikipedia.
org/wiki/Dies_Irae
Hallelujah (Jeff Buckley - Grace)
Somewhere Over the Rainbow/What a Wonderful World
(Israel Kamakawiwo'ole - Facing Future)

Edward C. Wilson says:
'Bodies' by Drowning Pool
ANYTHING by Two Steps From Hell.

That would be me says:
Nickleback: how you remind me https://www.youtube.
com/watch?v=1cQh1ccqu8M (might need to change a few
male to female lyrics)
Three days grace: Pain https://www.youtube.com/

watch?v=Ud4HuAzHEUc (my fave, it really fits I think) seriously I can see BA grabbing a CEO and this playing.

Kindle Customer says:
Black velvet

Peter Simonsson says:
Iron Maiden -Run to the hills - https://youtu.be/3ZlDZPYzfm4
Within Temptation - What have you done - https://youtu.be/_aYivBntOC4
Nightwish - Over the hills and far away - https://youtu.be/CwED4C5FJuo

Ethan says:
I don't know why but I can see them messing with someone and playing the Little Einsteins theme song
https://www.youtube.com/watch?v=7eL1Bfv8Y9k

Amazon Customer says:
3rd Stage - Boston
Let's Get Rocked Def Leppard

SEE EVERYONE IN A MONTH (or so) ;-)

SERIES TITLES INCLUDE:

KURTHERIAN GAMBIT SERIES TITLES INCLUDE:

First Arc

Death Becomes Her (01) - Queen Bitch (02) -
Love Lost (03) - Bite This (04)
Never Forsaken (05) - Under My Heel (06)
Kneel Or Die (07)

Second Arc

We Will Build (08) - It's Hell To Choose (09) -
Release The Dogs of War (10)
Sued For Peace (11) - We Have Contact (12) -
My Ride is a Bitch (13)
Don't Cross This Line (14)

Third Arc (Due 2017)

Never Submit (15) - Never Surrender (16) -
Forever Defend (17)
Might Makes Right (18) - Ahead Full (19) -
Capture Death (20)
Life Goes On (21)

New Series

THE SECOND DARK AGES

The Dark Messiah (01)
The Darkest Night (02)
Darkest Before The Dawn (03)
with Ell Leigh Clarke

THE BORIS CHRONICLES
* With Paul C. Middleton *

Evacuation
Retaliation
Revelation
Restitution *2017*

RECLAIMING HONOR
* With JUSTIN SLOAN *

Justice Is Calling (01)
Claimed By Honor (02)
Judgement Has Fallen (03)
Angel of Reckoning (04)
Born Into Flames (05)
Defending The Lost (06)
Saved By Valor (07)
Return of Victory (08)

THE ETHERIC ACADEMY
* With TS PAUL *

ALPHA CLASS (01)
ALPHA CLASS - Engineering (02)
ALPHA CLASS (03) *Coming Soon*

TERRY HENRY "TH" WALTON CHRONICLES
* With CRAIG MARTELLE *

Nomad Found (01)
Nomad Redeemed (02)
Nomad Unleashed (03)
Nomad Supreme (04)
Nomad's Fury (05)
Nomad's Justice (06)
Nomad Avenged (07)
Nomad Mortis (08)
Nomad's Force (09)
Nomad's Galaxy (10)

TRIALS AND TRIBULATIONS
* With Natalie Grey *

Risk Be Damned (01)
Damned to Hell (02)
Hell's Worst Nightmare (03) *coming soon*

THE ASCENSION MYTH
* With ELL LEIGH CLARKE *

Awakened (01)
Activated (02)
Called (03)
Sanctioned (04)
Rebirth (05)

THE AGE OF MAGIC
THE RISE OF MAGIC
* With CM RAYMOND/LE BARBANT *

Restriction (01)
Reawakening (02)
Rebellion (03)
Revolution (04)
Unlawful Passage (05)
Darkness Rises (06)
The Gods Beneath (07)

THE HIDDEN MAGIC CHRONICLES
* With JUSTIN SLOAN *

Shades of Light (01)
Shades of Dark (02)
Shades of Glory (03)
Shades of Justice (04)

STORMS OF MAGIC
* With PT HYLTON *

Storms Raiders (01)
Storm Callers (02)
Storm Breakers (03)
Storm Warrior (04)

TALES OF THE FEISTY DRUID
* With CANDY CRUM *

The Arcadian Druid (01)
The Undying Illusionist (02)
The Frozen Wasteland (03)
The Deceiver (04)
The Lost (05)

PATH OF HEROES
* With BRANDON BARR *

Rogue Mage (01)

A NEW DAWN
* With AMY HOPKINS *

Dawn of Destiny (01)
Dawn of Darkness (02)
Dawn of Deliverance (03)

THE AGE OF EXPANSION
THE UPRISE SAGA
* With AMY DUBOFF *

Covert Talents (01)

BAD COMPANY
* With CRAIG MARTELLE *

The Bad Company (01)

THE GHOST SQUADRON
* With SARAH NOFFKE and J.N. CHANEY *

Formation (01)
Exploration (02)

OTHER BOOKS

Etheric Recruit
* With S.R. RUSSELL *

Gateway to the Universe
* With CRAIG MARTELLE & JUSTIN SLOAN *

THE CHRONICLES OF ORICERAN
THE LEIRA CHRONICLES
* With MARTHA CARR *

Waking Magic (1)
Release of Magic (2)
Protection of Magic (3)
Rule of Magic (4)
Dealing in Magic (5)

SHORT STORIES

Frank Kurns Stories of the Unknownworld 01 (7.5)
You Don't Mess with John's Cousin

Frank Kurns Stories of the Unknownworld 02 (9.5)
Bitch's Night Out

Frank Kurns Stories of the Unknownworld 02 (13.25)
With Natalie Grey
Bellatrix

AUDIOBOOKS
Available at Audible.com and iTunes

WANT MORE?